INCARNATE LOVE

Incarnate Love:
ESSAYS IN ORTHODOX ETHICS

Vigen Guroian

UNIVERSITY OF NOTRE DAME PRESS
NOTRE DAME, INDIANA

The author and publisher are grateful for permission to reprint the following, some
retitled or in revised form:
"Notes Toward an Eastern Orthodox Ethic," *Journal of Religious Ethics* 9 (no. 2 Fall
1981): 228–44; "Love in Orthodox Ethics: Trinitarian and Christological Reflections,"
Cross Currents 33 (no. 2 Summer 1983): 181–97; "Seeing Worship as Ethics: An
Orthodox Perspective," *Journal of Religious Ethics* 13 (no. 2 Fall 1985): 332–59;
"The Problem of an Orthodox Social Ethic: Diaspora Reflections," *Journal of Ecu-
menical Studies* 21 (no. 4 Fall 1984): 709–29; "The Americanization of Orthodoxy:
Crisis and Challenge," *Greek Orthodox Theological Review* 29 (no. 3 Winter 1984):
255–67.

Library of Congress Cataloging in Publication Data

Guroian, Vigen.
    Incarnate love.

    Includes index.
    1. Christian ethics—Oriental Orthodox authors.
I. Title.
BJ1250.5.G87   1987   241'.0419   86-40591
ISBN 0-268-01162-1

TO JUNE, RAFAEL, AND VICTORIA

Contents

Acknowledgments

I AM ADVANCING INTO that stage of life, early middle age, when one sure measurement of an academic person's wisdom or foolishness is whether or not he recognizes the extent to which his colleagues and students, family and friends are contributors to the work he calls his own. I am deeply grateful to many people who have assisted in small as well as large ways toward the completion and publication of this book. There are also institutions, foundations, and persons to be named which have provided grants without which several summers might not have been left free for writing. I make these acknowledgments with great joy, for this is an opportunity to recount my good fortune and remember friends.

Will Herberg probably never suspected I would write a book such as this. However, immediately upon coming under his tutelage at the graduate school of Drew University, he encouraged me (and indeed embarrassed me with my own ignorance) to learn more about my Orthodox roots. Thus began a mostly extracurricular inquiry of Orthodox theology—for this reading did not figure much into my formal course of graduate study. Also, at this time, I began to worship regularly in my church, the Armenian Apostolic Orthodox Church. The first Orthodox work I picked up for reading during graduate school was Fr. Alexander Schmemann's *For the Life of the World: Sacraments and Orthodoxy*. As I mention in the Introduction, Schmemann's analysis of the status of Orthodoxy in the West and the challenges it faces, together with Herberg's thesis about ethnicity, religion, and the American Way, has influenced me greatly.

The thinking and preparation for the first two essays in this volume began at the University of Virginia (1978–81), where I taught in the Department of Religious Studies. Having arrived at the University with a freshly prepared dissertation on Reinhold Niebuhr and Edmund

Burke, the last thing one might have imagined is that I would begin teaching courses on Orthodox theology and social thought. But I think David B. Harned, chairman of the Department of Religious Studies at the time, recognized the possibilities my Orthodox background held for future contributions to the discipline. He negotiated for my attachment with the Center for Russian and East European Studies. This relationship allowed for the preparation of an introductory course on Orthodox theology and one on Russian social and religious thought. It further enabled me to bring my ongoing inquiry into Orthodoxy out of the "closet" and to blend that study with my interests in theological and social ethics.

During the academic year 1980–81, I prepared an essay, "Notes Toward an Eastern Orthodox Ethic," eventually published in the *Journal of Religious Ethics*. That essay, retitled and in somewhat revised form, stands as the first chapter of the book. In the process of writing "Notes" I also conceived the plan for this book. James F. Childress strongly encouraged me in this aim. It was he who first impressed upon me the potential significance of such an Orthodox contribution to the field of religious ethics. Over the years he has remained a steadfast friend and source of guidance and encouragement.

The same needs to be said of Nathan A. Scott Jr., also at the University of Virginia. He has read a number of the essays in this volume and has from the beginning insisted that my background and training were especially suited to bring into such constructive work Western sources, particularly contemporary Protestant and Roman Catholic theologians and ethicists. He has understood the need for this in order to make the project accessible to non-Orthodox readers. He has encouraged my efforts to draw out the prophetic strains in the Orthodox liturgies and rites and to advance those elements in a critique of the culture.

In 1981, I accepted a post at Loyola College in Maryland. To Loyola College I owe thanks for two summer research grants. In addition, I received substantial grants for 1985–86 from the philanthropist Edward Mardigian and from the Marguerete Eyer Wilbur Foundation. These generous contributions enabled me to devote three full summers to the book.

At Loyola I have been blessed with colleagues who all in varying degrees have contributed thoughts and ideas for the book. Over the past four or five years much of the book has been read by my Loyola colleagues and discussed by them at meetings of our monthly department colloquium. Special thanks are due to James J. Buckley and William McFetridge Wilson who far surpassed collegial obligations in their reading, study, and discussion of my writing.

I have to mention two other persons who have contributed in a special way to this book. Fr. Stanley S. Harakas stands as the lone pioneer of Orthodox ethics in America. When I began thinking about writing on ethics out of the Orthodox tradition, it was to his work that I immediately turned for example and guidance. Fr. Harakas has supported me throughout this project and has been a key respondent and commentator on my work in the Society of Christian Ethics, in which, as of this writing, we unfortunately remain the only two Orthodox members. In several places I take issue with Fr. Harakas's writing. Our uses of the tradition do differ. And he has been less inclined than I to draw non-Orthodox sources into his constructive endeavors. The differences stand, but should not be mistaken for fundamental theological disagreements. It was almost inevitable, since Fr. Harakas has been virtually the sole interpreter of Orthodox ethics in America, that he would become a principal conversation as well as sparring partner.

Stanley Hauerwas has read every bit of this book. And for the past four or five years we have corresponded regularly — more often than not about some part of this book. He is a friend for whose time spent reading drafts of chapters and commenting on their strengths and weaknesses I am profoundly grateful. Undeniably, his own writing has influenced the manner in which I have searched out my own tradition for resources with which to speak ethically and to address Orthodoxy's role in the American culture.

There are other colleagues in the field of religious ethics and friends who have been conversation partners at various stages of my writing. These include Paul Ramsey, Russell Kirk, William J. Everett, Dennis McCann, Clark Brittain, Gilbert Meilaender, Timothy F. Sedgwick, David Little, Anton J. Ugolnik, Fr. Alexander F.C. Webster, Lisa S. Cahill, and Fr. Thomas Hopko.

During these years I also have come under the influence, both spiritual and intellectual, of Archbishop Tiran Nersoyan, the grand elder churchman and theologian of the Armenian Church in America. He has read my work, commented on it at length through the mail, and shared long and happy hours with me in his New York apartment discussing how my academic study might serve the greater well-

being of our church. I have been honored and humbled by the interest and love he has bestowed upon me.

Every author is indebted to at least one person who has helped
with typing and editing. At Loyola it has been my good fortune these
past two crucial years of having nearby a former student of mine at
Loyola and the present Theology Department secretary, Lisa M.
Flaherty. Her natural affinity for theology and exceptional efficiency
has made the whole matter of preparing the manuscript for publication much less toilsome. Further credit goes to the ladies at the Loyola
Communications Center who have had most of the chapters of this
book pass through their hands and into the word processor.

I must mention my parents Grace and Armen Guroian in this
first book and thank them for having raised me right and having
placed so much love and confidence in me for nearly forty years.

Our children Rafi and Victoria have grown from infancy to
childhood during the book's composition. They have inspired words
written in it for which neither I nor they could fully account. Indeed
they have taken turns being in my office during more than a few hours
of their father's labor, coloring or reading at a small table behind my
desk.

My wife June, who fortunately married me for reasons exceeding
any promise I might have as a theologian, has endured with patience
and levity my sullen moods on days of fruitless tapping at the keyboard;
has often wisely sent me out to the vegetable garden when the hours
at the desk got too long; and has always helped me keep a healthy
perspective on time spent at this labor and that given to my young
family. Her love for me and our children belongs to the very substance
of this book.

Introduction

THE DIFFICULTY OF ORTHODOX ETHICS

THE GOAL OF THIS BOOK is to do ethics out of the Orthodox tradition within a North American context. Indeed, Orthodoxy has contributed very little to the distinct enterprise of religious ethics. Stanley S. Harakas's systematic treatment of Orthodox ethics, *Toward Transfigured Life: The Theoria of Eastern Orthodox Ethics* (1983), stands as the sole book of its kind written in North America by an Orthodox theologian. Other books and articles by Orthodox authors about historic Christian moral concerns and contemporary ethical issues are notably few.[1] Their existence, however, ought not to be overlooked, and the prospect is that within a generation Orthodox will become full partners in the North American conversation.

There are several ready explanations for the present want of Orthodox ethics. The first is historical and sociological. It has to do with the fact that the Orthodox Church is the last great Christian confession to send large numbers of its own to America. The great dispersion of Orthodoxy over the past century uprooted the Orthodox ethnic and national churches from their historical cultures of Eastern Europe, Russia, and the Middle East, casting them largely unprepared into the Protestant and Roman Catholic West. Only in the past few decades, since Orthodoxy has been drawn out into ecumenical dialogue and also has felt the pressure of the society impinging increasingly upon its inner ethnic and spiritual life, have Orthodox theologians begun to address the pressing moral and political issues raised by such cultural forces as religious pluralism, nationalism, technology, and an advancing secularism.

A second factor contributing to the dearth of Orthodox ethics is theological. Historically, Orthodoxy has not made the formal distinction, oftentimes near separation, between theology and ethics which is taken for granted in much of the contemporary literature. Harakas raises this matter almost immediately in *Toward Transfigured Life*. He writes: "For Orthodox Christianity, doctrine and ethics may be distinguished but they may never be separated. It is only the 'division of labor' in which some theologians of the Church turn their attention to the things, which in the words of St. Athanasios 'make known the word concerning Christ, and the mystery regarding him,' on the one hand, while other theologians concern themselves primarily with the Christian teaching, again in the words of St. Athanasios, whose intention it is 'to point to the correction of habits.' " Harakas concludes: "It would thus appear that the distinction between the discipline of ethics and the discipline of dogmatics . . . is rooted in the tradition of the Church. The mistake, for Orthodox theology, would be to separate them."[2] Yet this distinction between dogmatics and ethics rarely has been drawn out by Orthodox theologians. Thus, even Harakas's book is out of the ordinary. It is a book explicitly in ethics which endeavors to address a whole agenda of queries and problems which have not received explicit attention within the Orthodox tradition, the exceptions being a handful of twentieth-century Greek theologians influenced by European philosophical and theological trends. Indeed, Harakas has written his book cognizant that there is a significant initial disadvantage to being Orthodox and gaining entry into the world of North American religious ethics.

In contrast, Roman Catholicism came to America with a distinct moral theology, based in the natural moral law, specified under the practice of the sacrament of penance, developed by the canon lawyers, and applied in a juridical fashion consistent with that church's definition of itself as priestly authority. Even this well-developed discipline of moral reasoning conflicted initially with Protestant biblicism and the exhortative and subjectivistic quality of much of Protestant ethics. Nevertheless, once the initial historic antagonisms and suspicions between these two great confessions of Christianity abated, Roman Catholic moral theologians found it possible to converse with Protestant ethicists. In its Reformation sources, Protestant ethics, whether Calvinist or Lutheran, was hardly distinguishable from the rest of Protestant theology. But Protestant ethics, particularly under the later influence of Kantianism, has moved increasingly toward an autonomy from worship and doctrine as a separate discipline. Protestant ethics has thus gained a rigor and integrity even if at the expense of severance from theological, liturgical, and ecclesiological loci. This discipline has helped Protestants to address the hard-put moral questionings and tough-minded casuistry of Roman Catholic moral theology.[3]

Beneath the long-held differences between Roman Catholicism and Protestantism is their actual historical and cultural proximity to one another which has served as the background and context for dialogue. It is impossible to understand fully why Protestant ethicists reason the way they do and take the positions they do without serious study of Protestantism's historic relationship to Roman Catholicism and vice versa. But no such method of reference to Western theology is applicable to Orthodox ethics. For as is well known the theological cross-currents between Eastern and Western Christianity are not so easily traced, especially after the late Middle Ages. And even well before that time Eastern and Western Christianity had grown far apart in theological style and substance. The positions staked out by East and West on even the most important of doctrinal and ecclesiological matters were not achieved with much understanding of or, as time went on, interest in what the other thought or did.

In spite of such difficulties and obstacles, Orthodox ethics is possible. While Orthodoxy is never likely to grant ethics the autonomy which it has attained historically in Roman Catholic theology and more recently in Protestantism, there is room within Orthodoxy for a more direct and developed approach to ethics than it has taken in the past. That is, certainly, the conviction out of which this book was written.

THE THEOLOGICAL METHOD OF THE BOOK

Theological method is a term which refers to "an array of decisions every Christian theologian must make in the course of doing theology.[4] While writing these essays, I have kept in mind several key points of decision which help to determine what the theologian envisions the theological task to be and how best it might be accomplished. These are the contemporary cultural context, subject matter (e.g., doctrine, religious symbols, and narratives), audience, and goal or purpose.

Historical-Cultural Context

A primary concern of these essays is the new historical-cultural context in which Orthodox theology and ethics are being done subsequent to what Alexander Schmemann described as the "tragically spectacular collapse" of most of the "Orthodox worlds" over the past century and the diaspora of the several ethnic and national Orthodox churches to societies of Western Europe and North and South America.[5] This new historical-cultural situation of so much of Orthodox Christianity is this book's background, the attempt being to "tease" out of the tradition an Orthodox ethic suitable to and consistent with the Church's historic understanding of its mission in the world. Stated somewhat differently, out of the great dispersion of Orthodoxy to the West has arisen a crisis in the Church's ecclesiology and missiology along with a challenge to articulate a new social ethic in North America. Not accidentally, these essays move progressively in the direction of social ethics. From first to last they also are increasingly less descriptive and more critical-normative.

Subject Matter of Orthodox Belief

The first two chapters of this volume, however, do not explicitly reflect a decision about the historical-cultural context. These essays mainly describe the subject matter of Orthodox belief. They explain the content and meaningfulness for ethics of Orthodox beliefs about the divine-human relationship. Such description, I have thought, is appropriate especially for the sake of non-Orthodox audiences which otherwise might have little knowledge of the doctrines, liturgies, spirituality, and historic ecclesial forms of Orthodoxy.

Audience and Goals

My first purpose regarding audience is to awaken Orthodox to the social ethical problems facing their church in North America and to the possibilities for the church's American future. Telling, however, of the other important audiences and goals that have figured in my writing is the fact that of the collection's five previously published essays (all revised) only one has appeared in an Orthodox journal, the *Greek Orthodox Theological Review*. Two were published in the *Journal of Religious Ethics*, one in the *Journal of Ecumenical Studies*, and another in the interdisciplinary journal *Cross Currents*. An audience nearly as prominent in my mind as the Orthodox is colleagues and students of religious ethics. I have sought to make the essays in this book fully accessible and useful to such people in their scholarly work as well as for classroom instruction. A strategy for achieving this purpose was to press in these essays toward a critique and normative stance on a common ground of relationship, interaction, and concern among all the Christian churches in America—namely, the American culture and polity itself. It has not been easy to keep these several audiences and purposes in tune. Indeed, no single essay succeeds in that goal. I think the book as a whole fares better.

STRUCTURE AND CONTENT

This book was not written as a traditional systematic, in the hope that it thereby could avoid becoming just another book on ethics or even just another book on Orthodox theology. The newness of Orthodoxy to this culture advises against such an ambitious project. Attempts to write such systematics risk erring in one of two directions: either to borrow uncritically the apparatus and agenda of Roman Catholic and Protestant theology or to transport the whole Byzantine theological structure into the new environment without the slightest attention to the unreality it exhibits in such a radically different context. Nevertheless, this is not to say that the essays together are without theological logic. The book begins with a description of the faith which gives rise to the worship and action of the Church upon the world.

Thus Part I, "Theanthropic Ethics," is, as I have said, largely descriptive, exhibiting the theological and spiritual resources (e.g., trinitarianism, Christology, anthropology, and soteriology) of the tradition for exploring the divine-human relationship. The essay "The Shape of Orthodox Ethics" sets forth some preliminary reflections about the structure and content of Orthodox ethics. This essay reflects the inner dynamic of Orthodox theology, a movement in its more experiential and practical expressions from a concern with virtue to a reflection on love, and from love to the theme of mystical union with God. This, however, is not a detached or otherworldly mysticism. It is, as I attempt to show in a later section of the essay, one grounded in the social vision of the Kingdom of God.

"Love in Orthodox Ethics: Trinitarian and Christological Reflections" expands upon the themes of Christian love and virtue introduced in the first essay. Two central arguments in the essay flow out of the

Orthodox doctrines of the Trinity and the Incarnation. The first is that the highest love *is* reciprocal and mutual love. We learn this from a reflection on the Trinity. The second is that in Orthodox spirituality and ethics *agape* and *eros* are envisioned as united. This is a christological claim. In both these essays I am displaying an Orthodox theological anthropology which insists that the mysteries of the Trinity and Incarnation lead to a distinctively Christian understanding of human personhood and community. These first two essays should not only set the stage for those to follow but also offer at least some minimal statement about how an Orthodox ethic handles some fundamental and long-standing queries in Christian theological ethics. Most notable among these are the subjects of Christian love (e.g., the relation of divine love and human love) and the role of the virtues in the formation of Christian character and community.

In these two essays I have referred relatively infrequently to familiar historical and contemporary Protestant and Roman Catholic theologians and ethicists. The descriptive goals of these essays dictated against such a procedure. I simply wanted to display some of the doctrinal and theological moorings of Orthodox ethics early in the book where there was the best opportunity to do so, even if at the expense of more critical or constructive possibilities. I hope my readers will agree that this was a justifiable choice, recalling that Protestant and Roman Catholic ethicists hardly have endeavored to draw St. Gregory of Nyssa, St. Maximus the Confessor, Vladimir Lossky, or Alexander Schmemann into their orbit of discourse, especially in matters peculiarly Protestant or Roman Catholic. There are some good and bad reasons why they have not done so. And there are some good, as well as some not so good, reasons why in these early essays, at least, I have not advanced the dialogue very far. Nevertheless, these essays do invite comparison and contrast with such Protestant writers as Anders Nygren, Paul Tillich, and Reinhold Niebuhr, or Roman Catholics such as Gérard Gilleman, Josef Fuchs, and M. C. D'Arcy who have written on the subject of Christian love.

In Parts II and III Roman Catholic and Protestant ethicists as well as secular sources *are* brought into a vital conversation with Orthodox theology, especially at the level of a critique of the culture. This tack of cultural critique was taken for several reasons touched upon already. First, there is an immediate need for the Orthodox Church in America to make ecclesiological sense of its dispersion and relocation in America and to redefine its mission in the context of a culture which is historically not Orthodox and growing increasingly secular. A ritual rehearsal both of what Orthodox believe and of the glory of some real or mythical Orthodox past in which they behaved consistently with what they believed will not answer this need, though this tactic has been tried for all too long. Rather, Orthodoxy needs to put its vast spiritual, liturgical, and ethical resources to work toward a theological critique of this culture in order to gain the critical, empirical footing necessary for the Church to bear witness to the catholic faith—not only to the many nominally Orthodox who in the process of having been culturally dislocated were also displaced from the life of the Church, but also to the American society as a whole.

Yet Orthodox are not in the habit of criticizing cultures. They are in the habit of sacralizing them. This observation supports my second reason for doing what I have done. It is often said that religious rites and liturgies are about legitimation. Certainly there is considerable truth in this description. This is something of which no Christian believer need automatically be embarrassed and in which, in some settings, the Christian can take cautious comfort. It is my conviction, however, that in addition to their primary action of gathering together, forming, shaping, and nurturing the people of God the Orthodox liturgies bring to this particular secular society a profound judgment and critique of its ways. Thus the essays in Part II, "Liturgical Ethics," move well beyond the descriptive and explicatory. While allowing the liturgies, prayers, narratives, symbols, and creeds to speak for themselves, I have sought to demonstrate not only the power of such worship to cultivate Christian virtue and form Christian community but its ability as well to expose the sinful deviations and idolatries of the society at large.

An Orthodox critique of the culture was very much my concern in writing "Seeing Worship as Ethics." This is probably no less true of "An Ethic of Marriage and Family." This essay seeks to set forth some alternative ways of thinking about marriage and family in their relationship to the culture, but also, more importantly, in their relationship to the Church. For my central argument in the essay is that if marriage, even Christian marriage, is in trouble today, this—while it might be a problem for society which sociologists would wish to explore in functionalist terms—must be viewed by the Christian theologian as a problem for the Church and a failure of Christian mission.

The full social and ethical meaning of Christian marriage is grasped and its efficacy as a vocation of Christian witness made possible only when considered in its relation of service to the Church, whose own significance for the world is not instrumental but sacramental and eschatological.

In sum, I would like to think that both the essays in this section make a genuine contribution to American religious ethics by showing the integrality of worship and liturgy to Christian ethics. Liturgy does not belong just to the professional liturgists, nor does its significance have solely to do with symbolic forms and actions. Ethics is not a property of ethicists alone, nor are its sources restricted to those contained in the often-recited litany of primarily systematic works in Western theology.

The essays in Part III, "Social Ethics," open wide into a critique of the culture based in a review and restatement of Orthodox ecclesiology. This, however, is not a critique just for the sake of critique. As I state in "Orthodoxy and the American Order: *Symphonia*, Civil Religion, or What?" the purpose is to redirect Christian social ethics back to its missiological moorings and vision. The critique must serve the purpose of revisioning ecclesiology and not vice versa. Upon the basis of this ecclesiology an Orthodox ethic can be built which is fit for the task of renewing in an American key the mission of the Orthodox Church.

A critique of American culture is inevitably a critique of American religion since the story of such religion tells of an accommodation and ultimately a vitiating compromise by the larger body of American churches with modern liberalism and nationalism. In "The Problem of a Social Ethic: Diaspora Reflections" and in "Orthodoxy and the American Order: *Symphonia*, Civil Religion, or What?" I have juxtaposed salient chapters of this story of religion in America with those of the Orthodox past in order to indicate the shape of an Orthodox ecclesiology capable of handling the special challenges and temptations of this American secular, pluralistic, democratic order. I have explained why because of its past history and relationships with historic cultures the Orthodox Church will be strongly tempted to take up the offer from such a society to assume a respectable place among the mainline denominations of American religion under the aegis of the so-called doctrine of separation of church and state. My prescription is that the Orthodox Church reject such an offer and concentrate on a missiological social ethic which would be far more consistent with its soteriological faith than the denominationalist subservience to civil religion to which so much of American Christianity has succumbed. I do not pretend that this prescription reflects a dominant point of view among Orthodox. Presently Orthodox are rather confused about just how to relate to this culture. The essays in Part III thus issue a challenge to Orthodox to think hard about what kind of a church they wish to be in America.

The first two essays of Part III seek Orthodox entry into the historic and contemporary American discussion held among and between Protestants and Roman Catholics over Christian social ethics. The relevance of these essays to the present debate over church-state relations and the role of religion in society also should be obvious. If I have succeeded in my analysis and constructive arguments, then it will be seen that the Orthodox history and tradition enable Orthodoxy to articulate a social ethic which is at crucial points (e.g., church-state relation different from the main varieties of Protestant and Roman Cathc social ethics. The key to this is the distinctive Orthodox ecclesiolc The challenge issued to Protestant and Roman Catholic ethicists attend more conscientiously to their respective ecclesiologies.

The less formal style of the final essay, "The Americaniza Orthodoxy: Crisis and Challenge," indicates a shift in audier essay was the only one of the five previously published essays c from presentations delivered before Armenian and other Or diences and published finally in an Orthodox journal. Its volume is in its inductive method and specification of arguments developed in the preceding two essays. Mor where else in the book, this essay provides the reader of the author on his home turf, in his own church, the very real problems of acculturation and seculariz front that church.

THE NEED FOR ORTHODOX ETHIC

Three reasons have prevailed above all others fc was written. In one fashion or another I have mentione But in order especially to emphasize their personal bi ground, I wish to review these three reasons as a wa this introduction.

First, this book grew out of the need of a second or third generation Orthodox (depending on how one counts generations) to make
some sense of the Orthodox presence in America. The significance of
this problem was stressed by my graduate training, received at a Protestant institution with a course of study which focused on American
religion and culture under the tutelage of Will Herberg. The Orthodox
dispersion affects not only the Orthodox Church as institution. It affects the life of every individual Orthodox who wishes to live rightly
by the Orthodox faith and yet also to engage fully the culture and
participate in this society conscientiously.

Second, the essays in this volume were written in response to a
theological and ecclesiological need within the Orthodox Church itself
to define its purpose and mission in North America. Far too often Orthodox theologians have attempted to define this purpose and mission without attention to the empirical context. They have avoided
the hard test put to Orthodox theology and the Orthodox ethos by
American pluralism, pragmatism, and secularism, despite the brave
and prophetic voice of the late Alexander Schmemann, whose influence
can be detected on virtually every page which follows.

Last, having spent my roughly eight years of teaching outside of
Orthodox settings, first in a secular university and later in a Roman
Catholic college, colleagues in the fields of theology and religious ethics
have invited me to lend an Orthodox voice to the conversation. These
invitations have not gone unheard. It is time for such a book as this
written by an ethnic (in this case Armenian) Orthodox Christian who
considers himself also thoroughly American. With the large presence
of Orthodox Christians now in America it will no longer do to speak
of Protestant and Roman Catholic ethics as if they represent the whole
reality of Christian ethics in North America. Such a short book could
not possibly cover the full range of subjects and concerns in Christian
ethics. Indeed, it has not been my intention to do so. But I hope that
even with all its limitations this book might still demonstrate that the
Orthodox tradition and presence bring liberating challenges and new
points of departure to Christian ethics in North America for the future.

PART I

Theanthropic Ethics

1

The Shape of Orthodox Ethics

THERE HAS BEEN MUCH written of late about virtue ethics. Some of it has been overly anxious to designate this or that ethic as a virtue ethic in contrast with others which are natural law ethics or love ethics. The degree to which virtue language shapes Orthodox theology and spirituality is impressive. And it would be convenient simply to classify Orthodox ethics as one example of a virtue ethic. Yet I doubt seriously that any Christian ethic is so simple as to be described adequately by a single handy rubric such as *virtue ethic*. This observation certainly applies to Orthodox ethics. A discussion of virtue and love in Orthodox ethics is, however, helpful in introducing the content and contours of an Orthodox ethic. This and the following chapter do just that.

VIRTUE AND THEOSIS

An Eastern Orthodox ethic values virtue highly, but not rationalistically so. The virtuous person is not Aristotle's *spoudaios*, in whom right reason alone reigns supreme. Such a person is, rather, the new Adam, the theanthropic being in whom divine love is incarnated and creature is reunited with Creator. "In love," wrote the fourteenth-century Byzantine theologian Nicholas Cabasilas, "the brightness of all virtue consists, and, as far as human effort is concerned, it constitutes the life in Christ."[1] Right reason, argued Cabasilas, is not sufficient for human beings to achieve the full theanthropic potentiality of their nature. Indeed, "right reason shows that it is impossible" for persons "to become perfectly virtuous" without the transfiguring power of love. "Perfect virtue is possible only for those who have been set free from all envy and malice, and who display genuine and perfect

love towards their fellow men."[2] Right reason identifies the good and
understands that the good must be sought for its own sake. But only
love for the good and God who is the source of all goodness frees the
human being to go "beyond his nature and [become] like God."[3]

Theosis is the theological concept through which Orthodox
theology has explained the progress of the person toward divine similitude. Theanthropic life is the vocation which was given to Adam at
Creation and denied at the Fall, but it was followed to perfection by
Jesus Christ. In the words of Cabasilas:

> The Savior first and alone showed to us the true man, who
> is perfect on account of both character and life and in all other
> respects as well.
>
> Since incorruptible life is truly the end of man, God formed
> him with a view to this goal. . . . But while the former [Adam]
> fell greatly short of perfection, the latter [Christ, the second or
> new Adam] was perfect in all respects and imparted perfection
> to men and adapted the whole race to Himself. . . .
>
> So then . . . man strives for Christ by nature, by his will,
> by his thoughts, not only because of His Godhead which is the
> goal of all things, but because of His nature as well. He is the
> resting place of human desires; He is the food of our thoughts.
> To love anything besides Him or to meditate on it is a manifest
> aberration from duty and a turning aside from the first principles
> of our nature.[4]

Jesus Christ, the express Image of the Father, is also the God-man and
forerunner of a redeemed and sanctified humanity. The Second Person of the Trinity became human, even as he remained fully God,
thereby deifying his human nature. This does not mean that human
beings are able to become God in his essence. But it does mean that
they can become "gods" by grace, even as they remain creatures of
a human nature.

This soteriological meaning of *theosis* is succinctly stated by St.
Maximus the Confessor:

> A firm and trustworthy basis for hope of the deification of
> human nature is God's Incarnation, which makes of man a god
> in the same measure as God Himself became man. For it is clear
> that He who became man without sin can also deify nature,

without transforming it into the Deity, raising it to Himself in the measure that He humbled Himself for man's sake.[5]

The Incarnation also presents the theanthropic vocation as a new moral imperative, that human beings strive to imitate this Jesus Christ who is both archetype and perfect example of a deified humanity. Clement of Alexandria undoubtedly had this in mind when he wrote in the *Propteptikos*, "The Word of God became man that you also may learn from a man how man becomes God."[6]

Thus, Orthodoxy speaks of an *imitatio Christi* but does not accept or express in this a Pelagian rationalism. The old Adam is not capable on his own power to imitate Christ perfectly and fashion himself into a new Adam. Orthodoxy regards seriously the psychology of the old Adam which St. Paul summarized when he confessed, "I do not do the good I want, but the evil I do not want is what I do" (Rom. 7:19 RSV). *Theosis* is made a possible potentiality for an otherwise fallen humanity by the power of God's grace in Jesus Christ. *Theosis* is a possibility only because Jesus Christ already has liberated the old Adam from sin and restored within his own person the distorted image of God in human beings. The redemption of our humanity in Jesus Christ enables us to cooperate with God ascetically and mystically toward deification. "We are God's fellow workers [*synergoi*]," writes St. Paul (1 Cor. 3:9 NEB).

IMAGE AND LIKENESS

Morality has to do, finally, with the restoration of the image of God in humankind. Conscience is the spring of the moral life. It discerns what is good (and the proper end) for the human being and impels the human being toward it.[7] But conscience is no mere faculty of mind, nor is it limited to practical reason alone. Rather, it is an intellectual, volitional, and affective movement of the whole person toward perfection. As such, a lively conscience builds up character through the attainment and use of virtues natural and theological. Character adds new definition to the diminished image of God in the person. Corresponding to its relation to virtues natural and theological, character is the product of a cooperation of human and divine energies. It is the unique impress, yet in conformity to the character of Christ, left upon the person in his or her body-soul unity as a result of the right use of freedom and the action of divine grace.

Traditionally, Orthodox theology has approached this subject through the complementary yet distinct meanings given to the two terms *image*[8] and *likeness* as they appear in the biblical account of the creation of humanity. "Then God said, 'Let us make man in our image, after our likeness' " (Gen. 1:26 RSV). John of Damascus summarized the Orthodox interpretation of the text, "For the phrase 'after His image' clearly refers to the side of [human] nature which consists of mind and free will, whereas 'after His likeness' means likeness in virtue so far as that is possible."[9] *Image* connotes that each individual human being is an integral personality having reason, free will, and moral responsibility. Each person is by God's own creative act a subject free to affirm and fulfill humanity. *Likeness* connotes vocation, exercise, virtue, and growth. *Theosis* is not achieved in a moment of conversion. Rather it is accomplished through a lifetime of constant striving and maturing.

ETHICS AND SOTERIOLOGY

The moral life in all its conscientious attention to and striving for the good is finally taken up into the spiritual life. For the good is not simply the norm of life; it is the divine life itself. Christ is the archetypal ethical human being but as such he is also the God-man. With this knowledge comes the imperative not only to do good acts but to participate in the divine life.

> Grace and peace be multiplied to you in the knowledge of God and of Jesus our Lord; seeing that his divine power has granted to us everything pertaining to life and godliness, through the true knowledge of him who called us by his own glory and excellence. For by these he has granted to us his precious and magnificent promises, in order that by them you might become partakers of the divine nature. (2 Pet. 1:2–4 NASB)

In Orthodoxy ethics and soteriology are bound together. For example, ethics cannot be done without particular attention to sacramental and liturgical theology. For through the sacraments of the Church Christ, who is the Life, enters the person and takes the person into his life. "The Bread of Life Himself changes him who feeds on Him and transforms and assimilates him into Himself," wrote Cabasilas.[10] The spiritual life is both an ascetical striving to do good and a mystical reception of transforming grace. "Those who imitate, as it were by picture, by means of certain signs and symbols, the death of which He [Christ] died for the sake of our life, He renews and recreates by these very acts and makes them partakers of His own life." Ethical striving or *askesis* has one end only, deification and union with God. But that end is realized only when "Christ is Himself present . . . implant[ing] the very essence of life into our souls."[11]

The image of God is restored in a person, the likeness achieved, only when by grace the divine life flows within the person. "Baptism confers being and in short, existence according to Christ,"[12] Cabasilas concluded. The elements of water and oil and the very act of immersion are symbols which, true to the etymological meaning of the word *symbol*, work together the ascetical and the mystical and unite the human and the divine. The imitation of Christ is not merely the striving to attain an external model, it is an event in which *the doing is a happening* and the model is an image which transfigures from within.

LOVE: THE SUPREME VIRTUE

"To love anything besides Him [Christ] . . . is a manifest aberration from duty and a turning aside from the first principle of our nature,"[13]wrote Cabasilas. Thus charity is the supreme virtue and also the summation of all the virtues natural and theological. Gregory of Sinai echoes this persuasion when he states, "Virtues are equal in the sense that they all reduce themselves to one, all leading to the same end and, in their totality, forming one complete image of virtue." That "image of virtue" is Christ, "the origin and the basis of all virtues, in Whom we stand and by Whom we perform every good action".[14] The love manifested in Jesus Christ is a love which does not negate but sublimates and transforms all so-called natural or human loves. This explains why such Greek writers as John Chrysostom and Nicholas Cabasilas used *philanthropia* and *agape* (or *caritas*) interchangeably. In the hands of these theologians *philanthropia* transcends its Hellenistic connotation as a merely human love exchanged between human beings and redounding to them. It is defined as a divine love for humanity manifested in Jesus Christ and returning to God through loving human acts toward the neighbor. This is also how the Greek fathers reinterpreted *eros*. *Eros* no longer is simply a human yearning for the divine. It is a divine-human love, the ascending mode of charity itself, whereby the mind "ravished by divine knowledge"[15] seeks God but in so doing discovers from a divine point of view the infinite value and perfect equality of all human persons. *Agape* is yet another way of speaking of charity. It is the prevailing mode of love since it more properly expresses love from the divine point of view. *Agape* knows the other as subject, as Thou. It is out-flowing and seeks a communion with the other. The human modality of *agape* images the divine life of the triune Godhead. That life is personal, relative, and communicative, and the energy which keeps the three Persons of the Godhead in relation and communion is love. Here we would do well to remember that the divine life remains a mystery. "To say: 'God is love', 'the divine Persons are united by mutual love', is to think of a common manifestation, the 'love energy' possessed by the three hypostases, for the union of the Three is higher even than love," wrote the twentieth-century Russian theologian Vladimir Lossky.[16] We can speak of *agape* as a descending and self-emptying love since it is revealed as such in the condescending and kenotic act of the Second Person of the Holy Trinity whereby he stooped to become "flesh" and humbled and sacrificed himself for our redemption. Yet *agape* is a love which descends in order to elevate, unite, and transfigure. Paradoxically, as self-emptying love *agape* fills all things with the divine life. "Out of love for man," wrote Nicholas Cabasilas, "He [Christ] received all things from us, and out of even greater love He joins what is His to us. The first means that God has come down to earth, the second that He has taken us from earth to heaven."[17]

The Trinity and the Incarnation provide the only sufficient understanding of the true character and meaning of Christian love. Love is revealed through each doctrine as a unitive energy. In the doctrine of the Trinity this is a union of Persons and in the case of the Incarnation a union of natures. On the basis of the trinitarian formula Orthodox theology makes a definite distinction between personality and individuality. Individuality is strictly an attribute of the creature. Personality is ascribed to God and in humankind is an image of the tripersonal life of the Godhead. Personality is spiritual and transcendent freedom; individuality is material (or physical) and rooted in determinate nature.[18] While careful to recognize that human persons are created as individuals of a species and that the divine Persons are uncreated and unindividuated, Orthodox theology insists that the communion in love which is the goal of the moral life is a harmonious relation of human beings in their personhood, not as mere individuals. In nature the individuals of a species are reducible to number. Yet the three Persons of the divine essence are not reducible to number. The Kingdom of God is the fulfillment of personality but transcends individuality and number, i.e., the natural individuation of humanity which sets material and psychological limitations upon personal communion. The Kingdom of God marks an end of that sinful division of our human nature into selves which are endemically at cross purposes with each other.

Our natural individuation is not an evil in itself. It serves a good according to its created purpose. However, due to the Fall, sin rules the "flesh" and has made from this individuality the "detestable self." This self is distinguished by its so-called self-will. While many ethics have taken this self as natural and normative, Orthodoxy considers it unnatural and radically abnormal. This division of our common human nature into selves which assert themselves over and against other selves represents the deprivation of love, the loss of genuine freedom, and the disintegration of personality.

We must not equate the person with the self, the ego whose character is determined by an autonomous will. The doctrine of the Trinity does not attribute autonomy to the respective Persons of the Godhead. And, on the basis of the Church's Christology, *will* is defined as a property of nature and not person.[19] Persons, therefore, are distinguished not by will but by origin, creative purpose, and free, loving relation with others. A deprivation of love accounts for humanity's attraction to the polar extremes of either an anarchy of competing autonomous selves or a totalitarian order in which the person is diminished to a mere individual and part of the social organism. Love unites persons; it does not reduce them to parts of a whole. Love is freedom, but it is also the transcendence of autonomy. Love is the very energy or movement in the person which renounces the self. Love seeks a communion of persons who are of one nature and united in will.

The Incarnation leads to an understanding of love as a unitive energy, accomplishing a union of human and divine natures. Through a supreme act of kenotic and agapic love, the Second Person of the

Trinity — the very Word of God — became "flesh", atoned for sin, and redeemed human nature, wedding it with the divine nature. This union of the human and divine natures was intended by God even at the Creation. The human person, wrote Maximus the Confessor, is called "to reunite by love created with uncreated nature, showing the two in unity and identity through the acquisition of grace."[20] The capacity to communicate with God and grow increasingly more in communion with the divine life was given to human beings at the Creation but was diminished severely by the Fall. Love is finally powerless and meaningless outside of personal relation and reciprocity. The Incarnation was a perfect act of love in its descending and ascending movements. First, while preserving the integrity of the human nature and its distinction from the divine, God in Christ restored by grace the human capacity to reciprocate God's love. Second, Christ in his humanity completed the human movement toward a full communion with the Godhead.

Trinitarian love is an inner inseparableness and consubstantial unity of three divine Persons. In Jesus Christ love achieves an inner inseparableness and hypostatic union of two natures. In Christian *koinonia* love becomes the inner inseparableness and consubstantial union of two or more persons who in their common human nature are united by grace with the divine life.[21]

LOVE AND LAW

In his study *Byzantine Theology* John Meyendorff observes that "the main characteristic of Eastern Christianity, in its ethical and social attitudes, is to consider man as already redeemed and glorified in Christ." Such an outlook he contrasts with Western Christianity's more pessimistic assumption that, "though redeemed and 'justified' in the eyes of God by the sacrifice of the cross, man remains a sinner."[22] This difference in perspective between Western and Eastern Christianity should not be taken to mean that Orthodox theology assumes that after the Incarnation and Resurrection humankind is no longer in a sinful state or that original sin no longer afflicts personal existence. But it does indicate a disposition toward anthropology and soteriology which has important ramifications for the Orthodox understanding of the relationship between love and law.

Put very simply, Orthodoxy regards the experience of law as externally imposed rules and commandments as peculiar to the psychology of the old Adam. The Incarnation exposes the Law for what it is, a creature of sin. Sin itself is not at root the breaking of an externally imposed command but the contradiction of that inner spiritual law of human nature which impels persons toward a harmony and unity of life with God and fellow human beings. Only as a result of sin do human beings experience law as externally imposed codes and commandments, usually in the form of prohibitions which indicate when the harmony and unity of life are lost, not how they might be restored. An incarnational faith, however, upholds love as the unitive energy which restores that harmonious relationship between God and humankind of which the Law as prohibition takes negative measure.

Ernst Benz has suggested that Orthodoxy's ethic is a love ethic "for which a sense of mystical union of all the redeemed in their participation of the resurrected Lord"[23] is the cardinal intuition. This slant of vision, I would judge, accounts for the relatively underdeveloped state of natural law theory in Orthodox thought. The natural law is counted as an image in human beings of the divine love which draws them toward the fulfillment of their nature, i.e., deification and union with the Godhead. Basil expressed this point of view in the following fashion:

> Instruction in divine law is not from without, but simultaneously with the formation of the creature — man, I mean — a kind of rational force was implanted in us like a seed, which, by an inherent tendency, impels us toward love.[24]

Eastern fathers such as Clement of Alexandria, John Chrysostom, and Basil of Caesarea agree that the fundamental moral law is expressed in and through the creature in several forms. Besides the special case of Scripture (e.g., the Decalogue), the eternal law is imprinted in the rational creature as the natural law and it is reflected in the customs, codes, and positive laws of nations. But natural law, the law of nations, and civil law are, after all, only creaturely expressions of the one eternal divine law. The natural law does not have an independent life of its own. Nature is not an autonomous plane of existence. The Logos was present at Creation, and the Incarnation commences an infusion of grace into nature and a transfiguration of it that destroys the wall of separation between God and creature which was built up by sin.

A deified human existence already has begun in the life of the Church. Lastly, Orthodox theologians have not articulated the precise ways in which the various forms of law — divine, natural, and civil — are ordered hierarchically or otherwise correspond with each other, because they have not made the sharp distinctions between nature and grace which gave rise to such questions in the West.[25]

In view of Orthodoxy's approach to natural law it is not surprising that love predominates over law as the ruling aspect of Orthodox ethics. *Oikonomia* is interpreted as " 'an imitation of God's love for man' and not simply an 'exception to the rule.' "[26] *Oikonomia* preserves the freedom of human personality in a synergistic movement toward *theosis*. Rules and commandments are relative to God's plan of salvation. But that plan is not the possession of any one person. It belongs to the mind of Christ, which is the mind of the Church.

Rules and commandments are important in Orthodox ethics, but they have taken on a new cast and meaning in the glorious light of Easter morning. The Law is no longer a taskmaster. Christians know not to fix their attention so closely on the letter of the Law that they lose sight of God's salvation plan. "The true fulfillment of the commandments," wrote Gregory of Sinai, "does not require merely forebearance from excesses or defects, it also demands an aim acceptable to God, that is the fulfillment in everything of God's will alone."[27] Christ fulfilled the Law and having done so made it spiritual. The person in whom Christ abides experiences the Law not as externally imposed rules and commandments but as an inner call to theanthropic life. Such a person is also one in whom the Spirit is present and sanctifying, and in whom the practice of virtue is being transformed into an essential disposition of the heart. " 'The law of the Spirit of life' of which the Apostle speaks (Rom. 8:2) is such as acts and speaks in the heart."[28] According to God's plan of salvation all things will be made to work for good. The person of faith is one who knows from within that this is true. Rules and commandments will indicate those modes of behavior which are in accord with the Word of Life and appropriate to the sanctifying work of the Spirit both in persons and in the Church.

THE KINGDOM OF GOD

In Orthodoxy the Kingdom of God is not primarily an ethical ideal.[29] Primarily it is an eschatological datum and sacramental event of faith. The Kingdom of God is "beyond ethics" because the moral law is fulfilled in a free, loving concert of personality which transcends all experience of duty, right, or obligation. Yet, in a world for which the Kingdom is not fully present, the perfection of persons in their social relations is the appropriate goal of human striving.

All ethics which are even vaguely Christian have affirmed this, and yet Christians have differed over how to go about this striving and what to expect from it. These disagreements derive from the various interpretations which Christians have given to the fundamental Christian experience of the two communities. The new reality into which Christians find themselves born of water and Spirit, the *ekklesia*, the Church, is a community which while in this world is not of it. And while it is certain that the Church and the world are not the same, the nature of their terrestrial relationship is much less clear. Orthodox theology offers no conclusive explanation for this mystery or final answer to the problem it poses for every Christian. In the past some Orthodox mistakenly have thought a final solution was reached in Byzantium or in imperial Russia. But Orthodoxy is not wed to theocracy. The Byzantine and Russian political theologies have come and gone without changing significantly Orthodox theology or the Orthodox Church's understanding of its mission. And there are other relationships which the Orthodox Church has had with the world that bear recalling. For much of its historical journey the Orthodox Church has been a church either under siege or in captivity, first under the Ottoman conquest and empire and presently under Soviet rule. Also there is the most recent experience of Orthodoxy in the pluralistic and democratic societies of Western Europe and North America. Yet in all of this it is possible to identify a typically Orthodox response to the mystery and problem of the two communities. That response is fundamentally sacramental and eschatological while not otherworldly. The Church must not be explained in terms of the world; rather, the world is understood, its origin, value, meaning, and end grasped, only from within the life of the Church.

An Orthodox social ethic rests in three fundamental perceptions about the world.[30] The first is that the world is God's creation. Whatever value it has or is given through humankind's creative action cannot be considered apart from God's goodness, wisdom, and purpose. Second, the resurrected and sanctified life which is already present in the Church shows the fallen condition of the world. But fallen is not confused with evil. The essential goodness of the world is not lost in its fallenness. The Fall has brought about, however, the radical distinction between this world and the Kingdom of God. Where there should have been immortal life there is decay and death. Where there should have been communion there is conflict amidst coerced order. The fragmenting and disintegrating effects of sin set this world and the Kingdom of God apart and at war with each other. Lastly, from the standpoint of the Incarnation and Resurrection, the Church experiences and intends the world as "the 'matter' of the Kingdom of God, called to be fulfilled and transfigured so that ultimately God may be 'all in all things.' "[31] It is the mission of the Church as the bearer of the Spirit to sanctify all things, making it known that there is no final polarity of nature and grace, state and church, world and Kingdom of God.

This makes Orthodox social ethics consistently transformationist or conversionist.[32] The mission of the Church is to make the Kingdom of God present by redeeming and transfiguring the world. This mission is not reserved solely to priestly and monastic vocations. For example, the monastic vision as it developed in the East did not include any notion of a "grading in the scale of 'perfection.' "[33] St. Basil and St. Theodore of Studium thought of the monastery as a place in which those standards of the Kingdom which were binding on all Christians would be put into effect. They did not suggest that there were two sets of standards for the Christian life, one for laity and one for the monastics.

Byzantine monasticism was inspired by an ascetical ethos which was both social and transformationist. The initial impetus of this asceticism was exodus from a world which fell terribly short of meeting the requirements of the Kingdom. Yet this exodus was not a contemptuous renunciation of the world. As Georges Florovsky said: "True asceticism is inspired not by contempt, but by the urge of transformation. The world must be re-instated to its original beauty from which it fell into sin. . . . Ascetism [is an] 'eschatology of transfiguration'."[34] The monastic community is to be a community "founded on love and mutual affection, on a free realization of brotherly love."[35] Love, not law and force, gives life to the Kingdom of God. The Kingdom of God is a social reality, albeit one that transcends any society of this world. "Nothing," wrote Basil in *The Long Rules*, "is so compatible with our nature as living in society and in dependence upon one another and as loving our own kind." The "seeds of these qualities" God planted within human beings in "anticipation" of their germination and fruition in the Kingdom of God. For this reason, he explained, "[God] says: 'A new commandment I give unto you: that you love one another' " (1 John 13:32).[36]

In rejecting any notion of a dual standard for Christian life, Orthodox theology affirms a certain continuity of nature and grace and of history and the Kingdom of God. Politics does not belong to the Kingdom, but love does; and without the leavening presence of love in the world freedom and justice, which are the appropriate ends of all political activity, would not be possible. Therefore, the Christian must neither underestimate the value of the imperfect achievements of political life nor equate them with the values of the Kingdom of God. The Bible is not a set of ethical principles or injunctions for political action. But neither are Christianity and the Church irrelevant to political life, particularly the constant struggles against oppression and injustice. The relevance of Christianity to political life is guaranteed by the salvation accomplished in Jesus Christ—his life, death, and Resurrection. The perfect love which Christ manifested in his humanity proves that humankind's struggles in history for social justice will be fulfilled and transfigured. The rough and measured equality and harmony which is all that justice can bring into this world is but an imperfect image of that *agape* which enlivens the Kingdom of God.

More importantly, to say that Jesus Christ accomplished our salvation is to say that he alone is our true Liberator.[37] This puts in right perspective all of our political efforts to overcome tyranny and injustice. We learn that the source of all social, economic, and political injustice is our radical alienation from God and enslavement to sin. Politics is a mark of the Fall because it reflects the efforts of the old Adam to control the disintegrating effects of sin and because, tragically, institutions which were made to free human beings tyrannize over them. The Church, not politics, is salvation. But this is not to say that political life and the life in Christ are two autonomous realms with their own separate ends. Christ took on our whole human nature and redeemed it. The political life is part of that material of the Kingdom which the Church must take within its own life, sanctify, and return to God.

Politics reforms; the Church transfigures. *Metanoia*, the reversal of the psychology of the old Adam and the division, conflict, and suffering which it stamps on the world, is realized in the Church. Politics presupposes the old Adam. The root source of collective injustice, however institutionalized, remains the same, a damaged will turned against its own nature. While institutions can be reshaped, reorganized, "cleaned up," or even abolished and replaced by new ones, the artificer is disoriented and the artifacts are inevitably flawed. Thus, the political art at its best will practice prudence and do what it can with an imperfect fabric. But without Christ, statecraft is inherently tragic.

It is the Church's mission to transform the human life of *persons*. The Church's primary although not exclusive concern is with persons. It is the responsibility of the Church to follow the example of the perfect love of Christ by giving alms and shelter to the poor. Without charity the Church counts for nothing. Yet there is a proper distinction to be made between charity and social welfare. Charity is person-directed. Social welfare sees groups and institutions as it looks out upon the common life. It is a creature of politics and requires all the coercion and power of the state. Social welfare is not the free giving which charity is, and it is no substitute for charity. Nevertheless, it is probably a necessary remedy — not to be confused with a cure — for the inevitable injustices which sin has introduced into the world. Yet the Church's support or opposition to social welfare programs will not depend upon a utilitarian or hedonistic calculus. It will issue, instead, from a judgment about whether such social welfare strengthens or debilitates personality.

Certainly, the Church is summoned to voice prophetic criticisms of collective injustices, calling the world back to its divinely ordained end. Within its sacramental life the Church proclaims and pursues this vocation. It must not forget that the world, including its political life, is truly the "matter" of its sacraments. If need be, this prophetic witness and work includes martyrdom. The world, which is the object of the Church's mission, hates the Church precisely because the Church puts its faith in Christ rather than in the world's claim to being an end in itself. The highest expression of the Church's affirmation of the noblest goals of political life is when members of its body endure even death at the hands of political authorities, as did Christ. When the Church suffers with all the suffering children of God, politics may yet be redeemed by love and humankind can hope with assurance for the coming of the Kingdom of God.

CONCLUSION: ORTHODOX THEOLOGY AND ETHICS

My underlying thesis in this essay has been that the distinctiveness of Orthodox ethics is derived from Orthodox theology. The most significant observation to be made about Orthodox theology is that it has never been rigorously systematic, not having had such systematicians as Calvin or Aquinas. Indeed, Orthodoxy has consistently resisted such systematics. For instance, Vladimir Lossky argued that theology which "constitutes itself into a system is always dangerous. It imprisons in the enclosed sphere of thought the reality to which it must open thought." In other words, theology which properly begins with the word of God in Scripture, and proceeds from prayer and worship, must remain true to the living experience of faith and not replace or close itself off from such experience through the construction of "mental schemata."[38] The symbols of faith should not be mistaken for the life of faith from which these symbols arise and to which they continually must remain open.

Orthodoxy has understood theology as a coherent worded expression of the life of faith in its responsiveness to God, that life comprising a catholic unity in revelation, prayer, worship, and loving acts. Orthodox ethics must be done in a similar fashion. Therefore, it seems fair to say that even as Orthodox theologians do ethics as a deliberate activity, their ethical reflection is not likely to be formally systematic. Yet ethics done in an Orthodox mode will, nevertheless, be guided by some well defined theological concepts.

The theological concepts of *theosis*, image and likeness, and love lie at the heart of the ethic outlined here. And these cardinal concepts of Orthodox theology in turn rest upon a distinctive Orthodox spirituality. Orthodoxy experiences the world as creature, mystery to itself and epiphany of God. The world is valued as sacrament of communion with God. This way of experiencing the world is also a special way of intending the world. The world is intended as God intends it, not as an end in itself but as a milieu in which and through which human persons translate natural dependency and determinacy into creative and free communion among themselves and between themselves and God. Orthodox theology rejects all forms of utilitarian, deontological, or teleological ethics which intend the world as either utility, law, or unfolding rationality. An Orthodox ethic does not rely on a utilitarian calculus or on a formal or conscientious adherence to rules and a dispensing of duties. Rather, it is concerned primarily with the realization of love, righteousness, and divine similitude in persons and social institutions. In this aim, I think, Orthodox theologians and ethicists will remain steadfast, believing that the goal of Christian morality is, after all, salvation.

2

Love in Orthodox Ethics:

Trinitarian and Christological Reflections

ERNST BENZ DESCRIBED ORTHODOX ethics as a love ethic,[1] and Sergius Bulgakov argued on one occasion that "humility and love are the supreme characteristics"[2] of Orthodoxy. While one rightly might question the capacity of such rubrics as love ethic or virtue ethic to describe adequately a living ethos, there is little doubt that serious reflection on the meaning and activity of love in the Christian life is a fundamental concern of Orthodox spirituality and theology. Orthodoxy regards the Trinity and Incarnation as the only realities in which full knowledge of love is revealed. Two important points need to be made in this regard: (1) love has its source and end in the very being of God who is personal and triune; and (2) the Incarnation is the concrete proof of the meaning and possibility of Christian love.

THE TRINITARIAN STRUCTURE OF LOVE

"The Trinity," writes the contemporary Roumanian Orthodox theologian, Dumitru Staniloae, "is the culmination of the humility and sacrifice of love."[3] The Father, who is the causality[4] of the Godhead, surmounts both monad and dyad by "a total gift of His divinity to the Son and to the Spirit."[5] Vladimir Lossky adds, "The Father would not be a true person if He were not this: *pros*, towards, entirely turned towards other persons, entirely communicated to those whom He makes persons, therefore equals, by the wholeness of His love."[6] God's love transcends the philosophical distinction between love as a virtue and love as relation. The love which is of God does not in the creaturely sense empower persons to accomplish a fullness of being. "Love is the 'being of God'; it is his 'substantial act,' " Staniloae reminds us.[7] Neither is God's transcendent love a cooperative relation of individuals who are otherwise not so disposed or situated. Within the Godhead three utterly distinct divine Persons—Father, Son, and Holy Spirit—dwell as one in nature, will, and energy; they thereby form what Gregory of Nyssa described as "a sort of continuous and indivisible community."[8] The God who is love is an inexhaustible, dynamic self-communication of being.

The structure of perfect love, says Orthodox theology, is trinitarian.[9] Even the love shared between two is incomplete and imperfect. Even the most self-giving and self-communicating relation between two is inherently egocentric and limited in its horizons, always subject to the erotic fixation of one upon the other and the "absorption of two 'I's' into a mutual love which is indifferent towards the presence of any other."[10] But with the presence of a third subject conditions arise in which the two need not fall into the selfish subjectivity of a self-contained mutual love. There comes an invitation for the two to participate in a truly intersubjective and pleromic communion.

In the Armenian Rite of Holy Matrimony the priest prays over the couple:

> We beseech Thee, O Lord, bless this marriage, as Thou didst bless the marriage of the holy patriarchs, and keep them spotless in spiritual love and in one accord during their lives in this world.
>
> Bless, O Lord, and make their marriage fruitful with offspring, if it be Thy will, so that they may inherit a life of virtuous behavior for the glory of Thy all-holy name. Grant them a peaceful life and lengthen their time in this world to a ripe old age, and make them worthy to attain the undespoilable joys of the heavenly nuptials, together with all Thy saints, by the grace of the loving-kindness of our Lord and Savior, Jesus Christ, with whom Thou art blessed, O Father Almighty, together with the life-giving and liberating Holy Spirit, now and forever and unto the ages of ages. Amen.[11]

This ordering of the goods of marriage is entirely consistent with the Orthodox understanding of love in its trinitarian structure. Spiritual love is unitive love, making the two "of one accord." But such love is also overflowing, self-emptying, and creative, bringing into existence an *other* toward whom this love might be directed and in whom might be engendered a loving response. More important, the child, who is a third for the two in their mutual love, becomes the second for each spouse in his or her personal relation with the child. In this relation each of the spouses experiences the other spouse as a third whose love is born and reflected in the child. When the spouses return to one another in love, that love for one another as well as their love for the child has been "rekindled."[12] The child as completion of a trinity corresponds to the Holy Spirit, both as the subject who bears the love of the Father to the Son and the love of the Son to the Father and as the "object" in whom Father and Son transcend all duality and opposition and the self-containment of their common subjectivity. The third born of conjugal love is not an obligation of the nuptial union but a felicitous outcome of it. The presence of the third is the occasion in which those virtues can be exercised which enable persons and make them worthy to enjoy "the heavenly nuptials" of the communion of all the saints in the divine life of the Trinity. This is the proper trinitarian sense in which the Orthodox speak of marriage as the beginning "of a small kingdom which *can* be something like the true Kingdom."[13]

The Trinity is the archetype and goal of the "We" of I-Thou-He/She in Christian marriage and family, as well as human society. The good of Christian marriage as a loving relation of three is only such insofar as it is a symbol of entrance and means of participation in the eternal "We" of the divine life. This love is perfectly unitive in its total self-giving. The eternal love which is God is the reciprocal gift of personal divinity between Father, Son, and Holy Spirit. The Father, in an eternal act of self-giving and self-communication, begets the Son and "breathes" forth the Spirit. It is the Father, observed Vladimir Lossky, "who distinguishes the hypostases 'in an eternal movement of love'."[14] The Son, in whom the Father eternally forgets himself as his very Image, offers himself back to the Father in a kenotic act of perfect self-sacrifice through which the Father is glorified and the Spirit shines forth. The Spirit, who eternally proceeds as the life-giving "breath" of the Father, allows himself to be sent by the Son in a perfectly hidden and self-eclipsing manner in order to impart the gifts of knowledge of the Father and Son to liberate for participation in the divine life of the three Persons.[15]

The divine essence, Staniloae emphasizes, is "a relation-unity,

or conversely, . . . a unity-relation."[16] This is to say that the perfect
love of the Godhead is a complete reciprocal interiority (*perichoresis*)
of the three. "For the subsistences," wrote John of Damascus, "dwell
in one another in no wise confused, . . . For as we said, they are made
one not so as to commingle, but so as to cleave to each other, and
they have their being in each other without any coalescence."[17] Love
in the Trinity is the inner inseparableness and consubstantial unity of
three Persons. Quoting John of Damascus once again: "For each one
of them [divine Persons] is related as closely to the other as to itself:
that is to say that the Father, the Son, and the Holy Spirit are one
in all respects, save those of not being begotten, of birth and of procession. . . . For we recognize one God: but only in the attributes of
Fatherhood, Sonship and Procession, both in respect of cause and effect and perfection of subsistence, that is, manner of existence, do we
perceive difference."[18]

Human beings, unlike the divine Persons, are naturally indi-
viduated and do not attain by reason of material and psychological
attributes of their common nature a complete coinherence or interiority
to one another like that of the Trinity. Yet, if the archetype and goal
of humanity is the life of the Trinity, are these human attributes, is
this individuality, an evil? The Orthodox answer is that there is nothing
evil in these things. Human individuality serves a good according to
its ordained purpose. The material and psychological attributes of our
common human nature which individuate us do serve the limited
autonomy that befits a creature made to have, as Gregory of Nyssa
said, "a self-ruling and independent principle, such as to enable the
participation of good to be the reward of its virtue."[19] As a result of
the Fall, however, the "flesh" is ruled by sin. Our individuality becomes
the instrument and *expressivity* of a sinful self determined by its so-
called self-will or autonomous will.

Adam's first act was the object of divine condemnation not because
he acted in a self-determining manner but because he chose to make
himself (i.e., self-gratification) the sole end of his self-determination.
"Although all things are made in their individuality," observes George
H. Tavard, "they are not autonomous but theonomous. God is all in
all. His relationship to his creature is analogous to the inner relationship by which God is one and three. Divine love sustains the world
in being. This being is itself love" (Eph. 1:10, Col. 1:11).[20] Adam's
sin inherited by all his heirs was one of self-love to the very denial

of divine love. It was a refusal of his (Adam's) priestly vocation of taking into his own life the whole of creation, material and spiritual, and returning it to God transfigured by his loving knowledge of it (not self-gratifying possession and use of it). "Self-love . . . separate[s] men from one another . . . and split[s] the single nature (of those endowed with a single nature) into many parts." Self-love, said Maximus the Confessor, is "the origin of that hardness of heart which possesses everyone and through this quality . . . set[s] nature against itself."[21] Thus, human beings originally created in the image of the triune God are moved by an egocentric (self-possessive and self-assertive) principle which separates persons from one another in an atmosphere charged with conflicting purposes.

Humanity, insists Orthodox theology, was created with the liberty (self-mastery and self-determinancy), virtue (capacity to participate in the good), and dispassionate (selfless and pure-hearted) disposition suited for a loving union of human and divine natures. "Personhood," Lossky wrote, "is freedom in relation to nature."[22] Personality does not divide up the nature and possess a part of it for itself (concupiscence), nor does it define itself in opposition to other persons (irascibility). Rather, it contains within it all of what that nature is and by directing that nature to its proper end attains its own distinctive identity. Personality is distinguished by its origin, creative purpose, and free, loving relation with others. Humanity created in the image of God is a multiplicity of hypostases of a common nature in loving relation with one another. The deprivation of personality is a weakening of this image of God and the *graced* capacity of the human being to translate natural determinancy into a transcendental and free communion of human and divine persons. The weakening of the image of God is accompanied by the diminishment of that capacity to love which was bestowed upon humanity at Creation. This leads to what Athanasius called a corruptible death — the complete disintegration of the human person into its constituent elements of body and soul. The evidence that death rather than love rules over human life is that human beings are drawn universally to the polar extremes of an anarchy of competing autonomous selves and a totalitarian order in which the human being is reduced to a mere individual and part of the social organism. In both cases love is overruled; in the former by an autocratic and unnatural *self-will* and in the latter by the tyranny of a *collective will*. "That which is the result of compulsion and force cannot be virtue," said Gregory of Nyssa.[23] And love is the supreme virtue.

INCARNATE LOVE

"Sacrifice is the most natural act of man," wrote Alexander Schmemann.[24] Adam's vocation at his creation was to act as priest of creation, receiving it from God as the "food" of communion with God and returning it to God with thanksgiving as his very "body." Adam freely rejected that vocation. He refused to locate his identity and that of creation in the life of God. Instead, he became disposed to use and consume creation for himself alone. His will was characterized by a self-love which was in contradiction to *agape*—the "inner law" of his being. Sin is at root the contradiction of this "inner law" of love rather than the breaking of an externally imposed command. It is making the world an end in itself instead of the matter of the sacrament of the Kingdom. It is making one's own life the absolute center of one's existence, loving it and valuing it above all other human beings and thus setting oneself at enmity with God and others.

As a result of the Fall, love as sacrifice became *self*-sacrifice, with *self* understood as an ego characterized by a self-will and claiming to be its own law (autonomous). Thus, sacrifice in a fallen world becomes "the rejection of all selfishness as the very form of sin." But such sacrifice cannot be the same perfect sacrifice of which Adam was capable at Creation. For "wherever sin exists there no pure sacrifice can be found."[25] It remained for the sinless One, Jesus Christ, to make the pure sacrifice and fulfill that vocation given to humanity at Creation.

Jesus Christ was the complete revelation that love is sacrificial (is sacrifice) and as such the "inner law" of human nature. "Therefore be imitators of God, as beloved children," wrote St. Paul (Eph. 5:1–2 RSV). "And walk in love, as Christ loved us and gave himself up for us, a fragrant offering and sacrifice to God." Christ is God's total gift of himself to the creature. While the initiative is God's, this act of perfect love in Jesus Christ is both human and divine because it is a perfectly reciprocal love of God for the creature and of the creature for God. In Jesus Christ, God and humanity are reconciled, not by some substitutionary formula or measure of infinite satisfaction in the mind of God or the human being, but by the *metanoia* of the creature — a total conversion or turning toward God. Thus, in Jesus Christ both God and humanity are glorified — as it was meant to be at the creation of humankind — in the intimacy of their good will toward one another. Such is the perfection of Christian love. It is Emmanuel, God-with-us. This is celebrated exquisitely in the Hymn of the Kiss of Peace of the Armenian liturgy sung at the beginning of the Great Entrance, immediately after the bread and wine — symbolizing Jesus Christ and the whole world — have been placed on the altar.

> Christ in our midst hath been revealed,
> He-who-is God is here seated.
> The voice of peace hath resounded,
> Holy greeting hath been enjoined.
> Here the church is become one soul,
> The kiss given for bond of fullness.
>
> The enmity hath been removed,
> And love is spread over all.
> Now, ministers, raising your voice,
> Give ye blessing with one accord
> To the consubstantial Godhead,
> To whom seraphs hagiologize.[26]

Self-sacrifice is neither the sufficient reason for a moral act nor an end in itself. To be sure, it is correct to say that belonging to the character of Christian love is the disposition to do good toward the other without thought of reward. But this is not the full account of Christian love, even if the parable of the good Samaritan has suggested to some that it is. On this parable Protestant writers, especially, have rested their case for Christian love as self-sacrifice exclusive of all regard for reciprocity or mutuality. The Orthodox understanding of *agape* conflicts with such an interpretation. The Armenian hymn cited above testifies to this. An alternative reading of the good Samaritan parable might help show what is at stake.

Gilbert Meilaender makes a friendly sparring partner for this purpose precisely because, while he argues in his book *Friendship: A Study in Theological Ethics* that Christian love is also inclusive of reciprocity and mutuality, he takes the lead of Anders Nygren and Reinhold Niebuhr when interpreting the parable of the good Samaritan. Thus he derives from the story the lesson that the love which the Samaritan shows for the stranger is an unqualified and more or less complete specification of *agape* understood as pure benevolence. I will not enter into a critique of Meilaender's somewhat strained efforts in the book as a whole to hold together such an interpretation of *agape* with a view of love as reciprocity and mutuality. Leave it to say that, at this particular point in his discussion, Meilaender adopts a Niebuhrian definition of *agape* as a love "which seeks simply to affirm and serve the well-being of the neighbor without any thought of fellowship or communion with the other as the fruition of that service."[27]

Two objections must be raised about Meilaender's interpretation: first, concerning the definition of *agape* which he proposes, and second, over the use of the Samaritan story as a specification of such a definition. It is correct, certainly, to say that the Samaritan, by helping the wounded traveler, has acted out of a profoundly disinterested love for the other as a person *qua human existent*. But it is a mistake to describe such love as *agape*. St. Luke, in fact, says the Samaritan "had compassion" (*splanchnizomai*), no more or less (Luke 10:33). This compassion is a fundamentally human response, even viscerally human response, of pity or mercy toward another who is suffering and quite helpless. The priest and the Levite show no such compassion and for that they can be held morally accountable.

Meilaender also describes the act of the Samaritan as one of "Franciscan Love," by which he means a love "not . . . fitted for society."[28] He says that this is supported by the fact that the Samaritan writes a "blank check" for the innkeeper—hardly a prudent thing to do for someone whose goal it is to live in society with responsibility for self, friends, or relations. Yet the "blank check" hardly can be the heart of the matter in this story. Indeed, we can assume that the Samaritan likely knew the innkeeper.

Contrary to Meilaender's conclusions, I would argue that the compassion which the Samaritan showed toward the traveler is a necessary prerequisite for human community. Such compassion also is the basis upon which truly agapic relations between persons are established. To act with compassion for another human being is to recognize the human worth of the other on the affective level of empathy. It is the first step toward befriending and knowing that person in God.

The query which introduces the parable of the good Samaritan is that of the young Pharisee who wishes to know what he must do to inherit eternal life. The proper answer is to "love the lord your God with all your heart, with all your soul, and with all your strength, and with all your mind; and your neighbor as yourself" (Luke 10:27 RSV). Then the question turns to who is one's neighbor. Now the anwer is not so simple as many interpreters, including Meilaender, would have it: that the wounded traveler is the neighbor. In fact, the traveler is a stranger, a Jew, not a neighbor of the Samaritan, at least not yet. Rather it is the Samaritan, in his willingness to help the wounded traveler, who defines himself as a neighbor to this stranger (Luke 10:36–37 RSV). Having responded compassionately toward this man whom he did not know and obviously could not have helped out of any preferential love, the Samaritan also has made it possible for the stranger to respond with gratitude as neighbor toward the Samaritan. Such a mutuality even between two strangers is the love to which Christ calls human beings. That such a reconciliation of all who were once at enmity with one another is also part of this process of *agape* is confirmed by the identities of traveler as Jew and helper as Samaritan. Compassion and self-sacrifice are on the way to *agape*, in the process of *agape*, but they are not *agape* and should not be mistaken as such. The relation of bonded fullness which is perfect love is only hinted at, not described, by the parable. *Agape*, by this understanding, has not so much the character of a noun proper as of a gerund. *Agape* is more like a relationship in process than a state of being.

The story of the good Samaritan is not the whole story of Christian love. It is not shorthand for *agape*. The story does not tell us whether the traveler responded with friendship (*philia*) toward the Samaritan and opened up the possibility for mutual love in God. However, in the life of the teller of the story, Jesus Christ, the Christian knows that this must be so.[29] The work of Incarnate Love is not ended on the Cross. It is finished only when all who are of good will toward God and humankind are gathered together in the resurrected life. Its work is completed only when the sin which has brought mortality and desolateness to life is defeated and replaced by everlasting life and the unity of fellowship in Jesus Christ. As St. Paul wrote:

> Do you not know that all of us who have been baptized into Christ Jesus were baptized into his death? We were buried therefore with him by baptism into death, so that as Christ was raised from the dead by the glory of the Father, we too might walk in newness of life.

For if we have been united with him in a death like his, we shall certainly be united with him in a resurrection like his. We know that our old self was crucified with him so that the sinful body might be destroyed, and we might no longer be enslaved to sin. For he who has died is freed from sin. But if we have died with Christ, we believe that we shall also live with him. For we know that Christ being raised from the dead will never die again; death no longer has dominion over him. The death he died he died to sin, once for all, but the life he lives he lives to God. So you also must consider yourselves dead to sin and alive to God in Christ Jesus. (Rom. 6:3–11 RSV)

In Orthodox worship, baptism is followed immediately by chrismation and presentation before the altar for first communion. The new life in Christ of which St. Paul spoke is one in which human beings have been set free from the Law as condemnation to death to enter into communion with God. This freedom is the gift of the Spirit. For "the Lord is the Spirit, and where the Spirit of the Lord is, there is freedom" (2 Cor. 3:17 RSV). And this liberty is the indwelling of love in the creature "because God's love has been poured into our hearts through the Holy Spirit which has been given to us" (Rom. 5:5 RSV). This freedom is the "law of Christ" (Gal. 6:2 RSV) come alive by the action of the Spirit dwelling within the human being. It is the image of God restored in the person. It is the person once again "rooted and grounded in love" (Eph. 3:17 RSV) and *graced* with the self-determining capacity to attain "to mature manhood, to the measure of the stature of the fullness of Christ" (Eph. 4:13 RSV).

That same love which defeats sin frees persons for communion. Love, wrote St. Paul, "binds everything together in perfect harmony . . . in the one body" (Col. 3:14–15 RSV) which is Christ. Jesus is the *autobasileia*—the "Kingdom in Person"—said Origen.[30] In Christ all opposition or contradiction between love as self-sacrifice and love as mutuality or reciprocity is overcome.[31] And since Christ is the archetype and perfection of our humanity, the same is true of perfect human love. The Cross leads to the Resurrection and Pentecost. The three are, indeed, one act of divinity made human in Jesus Christ. Christian *koinonia* (1 John 4:7–12) is the revelation of that love through which persons are joined together in communion by grace with divine life.

Christian love is a disposition of character toward all human beings which, though not shared by all, always belongs to more than one. Such love is established in the character of one Person recognized, by those who know him, as their nearest neighbor in whom they are reconciled with God and their fellows and in whom also they are called into loving company (fellowship) such that they are "being changed into his likeness from one degree of glory to another" (2 Cor. 3:18 RSV).[32]

THE DIVINITY OF HUMAN LOVE

"God is love," wrote St. John (1 John 4:8 RSV). So the question arises: "What then is man?" Perhaps we need not look to the theologians alone for the answer. Was it not the argument of Fyodor Dostoevsky, speaking out of the spiritual riches of Russian Orthodoxy, and Flannery O'Connor, calling out from the heart of a transplanted Roman Catholicism, that the human being is defined by his or her *eros*? "For where your treasure is, there will your heart be also" (Matt. 6:21 RSV). Dostoevsky and O'Connor went on to argue that the fullfillment or goal of our humanity is divine love—*agape*. *Agape* and *eros* are, as Martin D'Arcy skillfully pointed out, both united and distinct.[33] This conclusion is based upon the Incarnation. In the words of Augustine: "The very same person is at once God and man, God our end, man our way."[34] *Eros* without *agape* degenerates into carnal desire and finally a God- and man denying narcissism. *Agape* absent *eros* is itself replaced by a benevolent self-interestedness and finally a God- and man denying egotism.

Two characters of modern literature in whom one finds a radical disjunction of *agape* and *eros* are Flannery O'Connor's Rayber in *The Violent Bear It Away* and Fyodor Dostoevsky's Ivan Karamazov. Both suffer from similar spiritual maladies. Both are haunted by a yearning for a transfigured world against which their reason rebels. Both, persuaded that an active present concern for the improvement of this world is threatened by this yearning for a transfigured world, reject their irrational love and decide for the immediate good that might be accomplished by the complete rationalization of human affairs.

Rayber, the schoolteacher and secular humanist, is distraught and terrified by the "outrageous" love aroused within him by his idiot son, Bishop. "He was not afraid of love in general. He knew the value of it and how it could be used." But this love was not a controllable and reasonable benevolence. "It could not be used for the child's improvement or his own." This love had no reason to be, no utility or predictable end. "It was completely irrational and abnormal. . . . It appeared to exist only to be itself, imperious and all demanding."[35] Rayber senses that this love has no limits. "He could control his terrifying love as long as it had its focus in Bishop, but if anything happened to the child, he would have to face it in itself. Then the whole world would become his idiot child."[36] Rayber's love culminates in a yearning for his great-uncle, Mason Tarwater, with his hunger for the Bread of Life and his "vision of a world transfigured." "The longing was like an undertow in his blood dragging him backwards to what he knew to be madness." Rayber practices "a rigid ascetic discipline," vigilantly guarding his reason against this love and keeping "himself upright on a very narrow line between madness and emptiness, and when the time came for him to lose his balance, he intended to lurch toward emptiness and fall on the side of his choice."[37]

Ivan Karamazov is a more complex character than Rayber. More acutely than Rayber, Ivan senses that the way beyond this present tragic human lot is a "love" which defies "the rules of logic" of his "earthly Euclidean brain." During a conversation with his younger brother, Alyosha, Ivan exclaims:

> Alyosha, my boy, so I want to live and go on living, even if it's contrary to the rules of logic. Even if I do not believe in the divine order of things, the sticky young leaves emerging from their buds in the spring are dear to my heart; so is the blue sky and so are some human beings, even though I often don't know why I like them. . . . I'll get drunk on my own emotion. I love those sticky little leaves and the blue sky, that's what! You don't love those things with reason, with logic, you love them with your innards, with your belly.[38]

This *eros* is the source of Ivan's intuitive non-Euclidean sensibility and his recognition of the transcendent worth of every human being. Ivan's "rebellion" originates in a heart mortified by the offense of human suffering and ends in an intellectual hubris which will not trust in the mystery of divine love and its promise of universal reconciliation. Speaking to Alyosha in the chapter entitled "Rebellion," Ivan states:

I believe in justice and I want to see justice done with my own eyes; if I should be dead by that time, I want to be brought back to life, because the idea that, when justice finally does triumph, I won't even be there to witness it is too abhorrent to me. Why, I certainly haven't borne it all so that my crimes and my sufferings would be used as manure to nurture the harmony that will appear in some remote future to be enjoyed by some unknown creatures. . . . I can imagine what a universal upheaval there will be when everything up in heaven and down in the entrails of the earth come together to sing one single hymn of praise and when every creature who has lived joins in, intoning, "You were right, O Lord, for Your way has now been reavealed to us! The day the mother embraces the man who had her son torn to pieces by the hounds, the day those three stand side by side and say "You were right, O Lord," that day we will at last have attained the supreme knowledge and everything will be explained and accounted for. But that's just the hurdle I can't get over, because I can't agree that it makes everything right. And while I am on this earth, I must act in my own way. . . . No, I want no part of any harmony; I don't want it out of love for mankind. I prefer to remain with my unavenged suffering and my unappeased anger—*even if I happen to be wrong.* I feel, moreover, that such harmony is rather overpriced. We cannot afford to pay so much for a ticket. And so I hasten to return the ticket I've been sent.[39]

Ivan's refusal of a transcendent world transfigured by *agape* and the ticket to that world has the unhappy consequence of also leaving him unable to believe that *agape* is a possibility even in this world. "In my opinion," says Ivan to Alyosha, "Christ's love for human beings was an impossible miracle on earth. But he was God. And we are no gods. . . . The idea of loving one's neighbor is possible only as an abstraction: it may be conceivable to love one's fellow man at a distance, but it is almost never possible to love him at close quarters."[40]

Both Rayber and Ivan are characters unable to accept the God-man who is the coincidence of *agape* and *eros*. Rayber mocks the faith of old Tarwater even in his thoughts about Bishop, whom he looks upon "as an *x* signifying the general hideousness of fate. He did not believe that he himself was formed in the image and likeness of God, but that Bishop was he had no doubt. The little boy was part of a

simple equation that required no further solution, except at the
moments when with little or no warning he would feel himself over-
whelmed by the horrifying love."[41] Yet this very love that Rayber resists
is the key that would unlock for him the legitimate status of Bishop's
humanity. It is this love that testifies to the true image and likeness
of God not only in Bishop but in Rayber as well. Through this love
Rayber, if he would allow himself, could affirm Bishop in his personhood and eternal value. Through it Rayber could discover within himself
and others a potentiality for good uncharted by any of the psychological
theories he has learned and beyond the measure of any of the educational tests he has contrived or administered in his job at the high
school.[42]

Eros united with *agape* belongs to the original image of God in
humanity. "God," wrote the Byzantine theologian Nicholas Cabasilas,
"has emplanted the desire into our souls by which every need should
lead to the attainment of that which is good, every thought to the
attainment of truth. . . . For those who have tasted of the Savior, the
Object of desire is present. From the beginning human desire was made
to be gauged and measured by the desire for Him, and is a treasury
so great, so ample, that it is able to encompass God." *Eros'* repose
is Christ, in whom it is translated into a universal love. "Those, therefore, who attain to Him are hindered by nothing from loving to the
extent that love was implanted into our souls from the beginning."[43]
In Christ the creature's inner "movement" toward the Godhead is completed and humankind's capacity to reciprocate God's love is perfected.
The christic human being is characterized by a "burning love of his
charity for God" and, in Christ, for fellow human beings — even all
creation.[44] Such love is not a grace infused from *without*. Rather it
is the original image of God restored from *within* by the express Image
of God himself, Jesus Christ.

THE CHARACTER OF LOVE

In Orthodox theology *agape* is not described as a single principle of the moral life. It is a total disposition toward life. John Chrysostom wrote that love is "the mother of every good, and the badge
of His [Christ's] disciples, and the bond which holds together our whole
condition."[45] Due to human finitude and sin, however, the one divine

agape is experienced and expressed in a variety of temporal modes (e.g., commandments, rules, virtues) and does not attain a complete hypostatic embodiment or wholeness of character in human beings. Yet *agape* is the "inner law" of our humanity, even though it is experienced by sinful humankind as commands or laws, imposed from without, which are disagreeable and even threatening to well-being and happiness. Those who trust in Christ, however, have the knowledge and experience of this "law" of human nature as the Life of life. For the person of faith the requirements of love are experienced as the qualities of a near and particular Person. "It is possible," wrote Cabasilas, "to discern in the character of the only Savior the whole of righteousness. . . . He alone has exhibited a character totally pure from all that is contrary to virtue, for 'He committed no sin' (1 Pet. 2:22)."[46] Christ is divine love (*agape*) hypostatically incarnate. Thus is he not only the perfect model of our humanity but its goal as well. By becoming our human neighbor in love, the Word has acted consistently with the intentions of the Father, who created within humankind not only a capacity for self-determination but a self-transcendent "movement" toward him who is the good of its being. The Incarnation was the ultimate strategy of divine love precisely because by having become a human being the Word was able to replace the Law as external command with a personal invitation for human beings to achieve the full potentialities of their nature and fulfill their theanthropic vocation. When the Word established himself as our neighbor by becoming "flesh," it was inevitable that he also would be our nearest neighbor, since he, the express Image of the Father, is the archetype of the image of God in us. Thus it is that he is able to evoke from within persons those virtues by which they can attain their full stature as human beings. As John of Damascus commented:

> Now, the virtues are natural, and they are also naturally inherent in all men, even though all of us do not act naturally. For, because of the fall, we went from what is according to nature to what is against it. But the Lord brought us back from what is against nature to what is according to it—for this last is what is meant by "according to his image and likeness" (Gen. 1:26). Now, asceticism and the labors connected with it were not intended for the acquisition of virtue as of something to be introduced from outside, but for the expulsion of evil, which has been

introduced and is against nature—just as the steel's rust, which is not natural but due to neglect, we remove with hard toil to bring out the natural brightness of the steel.[47]

However, the restoration of the image of God in human beings by the exercise of virtues natural and theological is also growth into freedom, "a coming up to a state which owns no master and is self-regulating," said Gregory of Nyssa. "It is that," he went on to observe, "with which we were gifted by God at the beginning" but which was obscured by sin.[48] For it is the good of a human being to become by the practice of virtue a free being in possession of herself. This is to become in the likeness of God—for God is a perfectly free subject—by a grace which does not compel from without but transfigures from within.

"Christ," states Gregory of Sinai, is he "Whom we have as the origin and the basis of all virtues, in Whom we stand and by Whom we perform every good action."[49] Blessedness (or perfection) in all virtue is attained only when one makes the life and character of Christ one's own. This cannot be a solitary achievement; it is possible only within the body of Christ. *Unus Christianus—nullus Christianus* ("One Christian—no Christian"). "Be imitators of me as I am of Christ," wrote St. Paul to the Corinthians (1 Cor. 11:1 RSV). The imitation of Christ is a corporate remembrance of one Person. This Person is in those who remember, and in him they remember all who have lived faithfully in him. Thus, in the Divine Liturgies of the Eastern churches, Christ is petitioned "to direct their will [the will of those living and at rest] . . . as well as our will [the will of those present] to what is right and is abounding in salvation, and reward . . . all with thy blessed bounties that pass not away."[50] The remembrance *must* be eucharistic because the imitation is not possible or complete "unless grace transforms" all the virtues "into an essential disposition of the heart."[51]

Christ, having fulfilled the Law, showed for all who would follow him a way to eternal life. So we are told in the Gospel of St. Matthew.

> And behold, one came up to him saying, "Teacher, what good deed must I do, to have eternal life?" And he said to him, "Why do you ask me about what is good? One there is who is good. If you would enter life, keep the commandments." He said to him, "Which?" And Jesus said, "You shall not kill, You shall not commit adultery, You shall not steal, You shall not bear

false witness, Honor your father and mother, and, You shall love your neighbor as yourself." The young man said to him, "All these I have observed; what do I still lack?" Jesus said to him, "If you would be perfect, go, sell what you possess and give to the poor, and you will have treasure in heaven; and come, follow me." When the young man heard this he went away sorrowful; for he had great possessions" (Matt. 19:16–22 RSV).

"One there is who is good. . . . Follow me." So says Christ to the young man. Yet, like Pharisees of all ages, the young man had mistaken the law for the good and was unable to recognize the good as One who-is-with-us. Orthodox theology has understood divine commandments, especially those of the Sermon on the Mount, not as counsels of perfection reserved for monastics,[52] nor as impossible ideals relevant as symbols which point to the Kingdom of God, nor as a literal blueprint (or set of laws) for a new Christian society. The beatitudes have been interpreted as traits of character, the whole disposition of a Person who perfects humanity-in-relation-to-God.

Thus the first and final act of the conscientious Christian is to "Remember the Lord thy God." By prayer, worship, and all forms of loving acts Christians are to remember Christ and invite him into their hearts. In this sense the beatitudes are themselves "reminders of the kind of people we must be"[53] in order to make the Kingdom present. Yes, the beatitudes are a glimpse into the Kingdom — but in the form of a Person in whom it is already present. They are the details of a living icon which is a Person. Together the beatitudes form the image of One whose mind and heart are perfectly disposed toward God and humanity. It is in this sense, particularly, that the double love commandment — "You shall love the Lord your God with all your heart, and with all your soul, and with all your mind. . . . You shall love your neighbor as yourself," (Matt. 22:37–40 RSV) — sums up the Law and all the commandments. Indeed, in all the beatitudes we find the character of the one praised in the ancient hymn of Philippians, "who, though he was in the form of God, did not count equality with God a thing to be grasped, but emptied himself, taking the form of a servant, being born in the likeness of men." Christ is the one who, being perfect in all virtue, represents in his person all the promises of the beatitudes as well. He in whom poverty, humility, gentleness, mercy, and purity of heart reigned and who was himself reconciler and peacemaker, suffering "even death on the cross" for righteousness' sake, is also he whom God "has highly exalted" "and on whom God has bestowed . . . the name which is above every name, [so] that . . . every knee should bow, in heaven and on earth and under the earth, and every tongue confess that Jesus Christ is Lord, to the glory of God the Father" (Phil. 2:5–11 RSV).

Thus, in Christ all the virtues turn out to be one complete character of kenotic and agapic love. Through this christic disposition of love which intends all things for God, and through the refinement and perfection of the image of God in the neighbor, persons achieve blessedness. Absent this character and intentionality of love all virtues are what Augustine called splendid vices, or even worse. Or, in Maximus the Confessor's words:

> The world has many poor in spirit, but not as they should be; many that mourn, but for bad bargains, or for loss of children; many meek, but in the face of impure passions; many hungering and thirsting, but to seize others' goods and to gain unjustly. And there are many merciful, but to the body and its comforts; many clean of heart, but for vanity's sake; many peacemakers, but they subject the soul to the flesh. The world has many that suffer persecution, but undisciplined; many that are reviled, but for shameful sins. Only those are blessed who do and suffer all these things for Christ and after His example. Why? Because *theirs is the kingdom of heaven*, and *they shall see God*, and what follows. So then, not because they do and suffer such things are they blessed (for the men just mentioned do the same), but because they do and suffer them for Christ and after His example.[54]

According to Orthodox ethics, Christ's rules and commandments are obligatory not because he is an authority whose reason and purpose are external to us, but because they belong as virtue to the total character of him who shares the same ontological status with us as a human being in whom that humanity has reached its full maturity. The great emphasis upon obedience to these commandments in Orthodox theology is not a commitment to a myriad of rules for the sake of duty to some objective, extrapersonal, moral order. Rather, it reflects a faithfulness to the theanthropic vocation of human persons and to the one Person who fulfilled that vocation — the one in whom was revealed in the fullness of time God's plan of salvation (Eph. 1:9–10 RSV).

Love "supplies perfect discernment," wrote Symeon the New Theologian, "and by itself is a good guide . . . which carries us across the spiritual sea (cf. Wisd. 10:18). It is this that I pray may be granted you by God, . . . that you may discern your affairs in a manner pleasing to God."[55] Symeon pointed out that such discernment is not guaranteed by a formalistic adherence to rules and commandments. Obedience to Christ's commandments must be a *spiritual* observance which disciplines the mind and purifies the heart so that the Word himself is "acquired . . . as our indweller and teacher" who gives us reasons to act which no single commandment or rule, person or authority, alone can provide. "One should abide in the commandments of our Lord and God and await His command (to undertake one service or another)."[56]

All rules and commandments are relative to Jesus Christ in whom God's salvific work is completed. As such, rules and commandments indicate those modes of behavior which are consistent with Christ, the model of our salvation, and the sanctifying work of the Spirit. That which is the good is God and, therefore, unchanging and absolute. That which is right and good conduct shares the mutability and contingency of the creature, even as it serves God's eternal plan of salvation. Discernment of God's will and the knowledge of that which is right and good in each occasion is available to a person only when the person puts to death self-will and responds in total obedience to God.

As St. Paul wrote to the Romans:

> Therefore, my brothers, I implore you by God's mercy to offer your very selves to him: a living sacrifice, dedicated and fit for his acceptance, the worship offered of mind and heart. Adapt yourselves no longer to the pattern of this present world, but let your minds be remade and your whole nature thus transformed. Then you will be able to discern the will of God, and to know what is good, acceptable, and perfect. (Rom. 12:1–2 NEB)

The mark of a loving, christic disposition is a power of discernment which has reasons of mind and heart that already belong to eternal life. Such a power of discernment is the gift of the Spirit obtained in that very activity of worship by which persons render themselves totally dedicated to God's purpose. The true hermeneutic and discipline of Orthodox morality is that catholic mind of the Church which is the *telos* of every person who offers himself "a living sacrifice" to God.

In this activity the person *"widens the scope of . . . his personality"* and begins to include within himself the many which are the fullness of Christ's body, the Church.[57] This vision of Orthodox ethics makes no sharp distinction between the activity of worship and morality. The two come to the same loving service toward and identification and union with one's brothers and sisters. Orthodox ethics does not identify a general or universalizable principle of right conduct as the criterion for determining how and when such loving service and union are accomplished. Such an ethic looks to the Spirit himself "communicating to each member of the Body of Christ the faculty of hearing, of receiving, of knowing the Truth in the Light which belongs to it, and not [simply] according to the natural light of human reason." This, Vladimir Lossky said, is "the pure notion of Tradition."[58]

PART II

Liturgical Ethics

3

Seeing Worship as Ethics

In the introduction to his landmark book on Eastern Orthodox ethics, *Toward Transfigured Life*, Stanley S. Harakas argues that while there is room within the Orthodox tradition for a distinction between ethics and theology, there is no warrant for a separation of ethics from dogma and religious practice.[1] Harakas sets out this rule for himself at the beginning of his book because he, like other Orthodox writers, detects a separation, if not an outright divorce, of worship, belief, and ethics in much of American religious discourse — which even has affected Orthodoxy.[2] This essay is prompted by that concern. I will not seek to prove here that a separation or divorce of ethics from worship exists in contemporary Christian ethics. Suffice it to say that the near total disregard by Christian ethicists of the *lex orandi* as source or resource for ethics testifies to such a separation or divorce of ethics from dogma and religious practice. In view of this omission in religious ethics, my purpose is to explore the relation or correlation of worship with right conduct and good works as understood from within the Orthodox tradition. Furthermore, I seek to indicate some ways in which worship seen as ethics enables Christians to engage the culture both critically and constructively.

Paul Ramsey spoke accurately several years ago when he described Orthodoxy as a tradition in which the "shaping influence" on persons runs "from liturgy to faith and life"; in other words, in which *lex orandi* is regnant over *credendi* and *bene operandi*.[3] But Ramsey's statement requires several qualifications. The Orthodox understanding of the relation of the three "does not imply a reduction of . . . faith [or works] to liturgy or cult." Indeed, faith is the "source and cause" of worship, but faith needs worship "as its own self-understanding" and translator into loving acts.[4] It would be a mistake, therefore, to describe the

Orthodox tradition as ordering the *lex orandi, lex credendi*, and *lex bene operandi* in a rigid hierarchy. The Orthodox interpretation of the three relies less upon a ranking of the *lex orandi, lex credendi*, and *lex bene operandi* than upon their unity, continuity, and commensurability under the life of worship. The human being is, above all else, a worshiping creature whose very act of worship, if it is not perverse, is to establish or deepen belief and to do good. There is not a necessary "one-directional influence from one to the other, or derivation of one from the other,"[5] as Ramsey suspects might be the case in Orthodoxy, but rather the process, once worship is present, of each mode of activity informing, influencing, and strengthening the other.

A SPECIFIC CASE

In recent years, American religious ethics has become locked needlessly in a set of religious and philosophical categories and questions which defy the mutually informative and constitutive relationship between belief and ethics which I have just described. Stanley Hauerwas has brought this to the attention of those in the discipline of religious ethics. For example, he has pressed people in the field away from an obsessive concern with the objective evaluation of acts toward an "analysis of the actual development of the virtue" and character in the agent, and beyond a scholastic quandary over "the relation of law and gospel, creation and redemption, faith and works" toward discussion of "the kind of moral concerns and issues that constitute how men and women in fact live." But it is not surprising that in order to do this Hauerwas also has seen fit to argue that there are no biblical grounds for a sharp distinction or separation "between religious belief and practice." He has challenged the idea of ethics as "an independent discipline," preferring to define it as "one aspect of theology," that which seeks to depict what we must do and become in order to complete our journey to God. Finally, Hauerwas defines Christian ethics as "a form of reflection in service to a community, . . . [which] derives its character from the nature of that community's convictions."[6]

This last claim is one which seems obvious. Yet it is consistently ignored by religious ethicists. It is hardly surprising, therefore, that ethics' relation or correlation to worship has not been adequately clarified or demonstrated by Protestant or Roman Catholic ethicists. The word *liturgy* derives from the Greek *leitourgia*. The Greek connotes an action through which persons come together to become something corporately which they were not as separate individuals. It means a gathering whose unifying purpose is to serve (minister to) the world on behalf of God. The churchly community ethic sought by Hauerwas arises precisely when ethical reflection is liturgically grounded and informed. For liturgy is that primal activity by which the Church becomes a holy ministry to the world and bears testimony to Christ and his Kingdom. When ethicists ignore this fact they risk the surrender of their reflection—which rightly ought to express and interpret the Church's journey toward the Kingdom—to an academic agenda of questions and problems more often than not unrelated to the primal Christian life of prayer and worship.

Allow me just one example of how this happens and the confusion it creates. In the above-cited article by Paul Ramsey, Ramsey states that he is "distressed by somewhat 'scholastic' articles—some referring to my writing, and some in *JRE*—that assume *agape* to be a sort of philosophical concept to be tested like any other, say, by the universalizability principle." Ramsey insists, "The notion of steadfast 'covenant' love, or *agape*, in Christian ethics must obviously be constantly nourished by liturgy, and the entirety of Biblical narrative, or else it loses its meaning and becomes a mere 'concept' . . . If *agape* means only benevolence or equal regard or the universalizability-principle, then I see no particular reason for taking the trouble to be a Christian in the present age or any age."[7] In his own fashion Ramsey has raised the issue of this essay through this one example. Whether, for example, *agape* can be proved rationally or intuited as a valid ethical principle is a legitimate philosophical question which can have vital bearing on religious self-understanding. But such inquiry cannot grasp the whole Christian meaning of the word. The presumption that this is possible puts *agape* in jeopardy of being interpreted as simply the theologian's version of the philosopher's benevolence or equal regard.

Agape, however, is incomprehensible as a norm, virtue, or principle of the Christian life apart from its manifestation, realization, and fulfillment through the liturgy of that eschatological community which is the Church. If it is at all correct to speak of a warrant for or proof of *agape* in Christian ethics, such a warrant or proof is manifest during the Church's very activity of worship and service to the living Lord. There *agape* is experienced, first and foremost, as a sign of the Kingdom present among, indeed binding, those who have gathered to worship as Church. Perhaps this is what John Chrysostom had in mind when he observed: "Charity is a sacrament. So shut your doors, so that no one can see the objects that you could not put on show without giving offence. For our sacraments are above all God's charity and love."[8] Or in the words of the author of the Epistle to the Hebrews: "Through him let us continually offer up a sacrifice of praise to God. . . . Do not neglect to do good and to share what you have, for such sacrifices are pleasing to God" (Heb. 13:15–16 RSV). The injunction of Jesus, "You shall love the Lord your God with all your heart, and with all your soul, and with all of your mind. . . . You shall love your neighbor as yourself" (Matt. 22:37–40 RSV), is a religious injunction. It is a call to service, to a *leitourgia*, which brings into being the new eschatological community peopled by those born anew of water and Spirit whose love for God, for one another, and for all of creation is a foretaste of the Kingdom.

If what I have said about the liturgical context of Christian *agape* holds true, then it is also fair to caution against abstract discussions of Jesus' words regarding love of God and neighbor which would equate *agape* with the philosophical concept of benevolence, testable by a universalizability principle. Such reductions of *agape* to a bare rational principle hazard, if they do not already commit the error of, severing Christian ethics from Christian worship and belief, and from the very people in whom only that ethic is possible.[9] Once that error is committed, the further quandary will arise inevitably as to whether there is such a thing as a distinctively Christian ethic. Forgotten in such questioning is the experience of the new eschatological creation, Christ and his Kingdom, which is the primal reason (warrant) for *agape* and the source of that which makes not only Christian ethics but Christian worship and belief distinct.

THE SACRAMENTALITY OF CHRISTIAN ETHICS

Christian ethics is possible because a new people has come into existence by baptism and chrismation, is reconstituted and nourished in eucharistic celebration, is diversified and deepened in agapic union by the sacraments of marriage and orders, and is reconciled and healed through penance and anointing.[10] Since a comprehensive discussion of Christian liturgy and sacraments is not possible here, I have taken recourse to the traditional mystagogic pattern of baptism, chrismation, and eucharist as a vehicle for discussion. In the Orthodox Church these three sacraments remain intimately joined. Unlike Western churches, such as the Roman Catholic and Anglican, which have marked off infant baptism from adult (or adolescent) confirmation and reception to the eucharist, the Orthodox Church holds that baptism leads directly to chrismation and reception at the eucharistic table for Holy Communion. Thus there is a peculiarly Orthodox inner logic to my movement from a discussion of a baptismal (and chrismational) ethic to a eucharistic ethic of the Great Supper.

Baptism is, as the creeds say, for the remission and forgiveness of personal sins. And it is a rite whose principal effect is to bestow new and immortal life upon the individual. Yet beyond that, baptism is also a corporate and public act. It is performed by the Church. Its efficacy is not, according to Orthodox theology, guaranteed by the faith of the individual, but by the faith of Christ, which is that of the Church.[11] The virtues, especially of humility and love, and the freedom into which baptism and chrismation inaugurate persons are the very same qualities to which the Church as a whole is called in eucharistic assembly as the Body of Christ and sacrament of the Kingdom. The movement from baptism and chrismation to the eucharistic table is a symbol of the Church's journey through this world of darkness, slavery, and desolation to the Kingdom of light, liberty, and love.

BAPTISMAL ETHICS

"Water is at the origin of the world, the Jordan is at the origin of the Gospels,"[12] wrote Cyril of Jerusalem. Baptism is the beginning of the Christian life. It is the primal action by which Christian character is formed. The reduction of baptism within the Orthodox Church to a private rite hidden from public view and the ongoing worship of the people of God is a tragedy which obscures its centrality to Orthodox ethics and threatens its efficacy as a world-transforming event. For as Alexander Schmemann observed, "Baptism is the *confirmation* of Christ's Resurrection, the only 'existential' *proof* that Christ is risen indeed and communicates His risen Life to those who believe in Him."[13] In the early baptismal practice of the Church the newly baptized moved in a procession from the *baptisterion* (a building separate from the church) into the church where they were greeted by the assembled community. Baptism was a *public* proclamation of the Resurrection and the newly baptized were a sign to the world of the momentous redemptive meaning of the Church's presence. And if we add to this that in the early Church baptism took place at the climactic moment in the Christian calendar of Christ's Resurrection, we can appreciate its significance as a witness to the coming of the Kingdom.

Whatever may be the state of decadence of baptismal practice in the Orthodox Church or in other churces, the importance of baptism for Christian ethics is great. Baptism is where reflection upon Christian ethics ought to begin. The Eastern rites of baptism abound with Scriptural narrative and imagery, setting the Christian *kerygma* in such a context of activity and symbolism that there is left no doubt as to what sort of people Christians ought to be and by what standards Christians are to engage the world. Most important these baptismal rites keep in clear perspective the fact that Christian ethics is a discipline of discipleship for the Kingdom. It is not accidental that the Lord's Prayer appears fully six times in the Armenian Rite of Holy Baptism — at the beginning of the rite before the enrollment of the catechumens and at the end of the enrollment; after the exorcisms, renunciation of Satan, and the confession of faith; after the baptism; and at the end of the rite following the chrismation and again after holy communion. Six times in this ancient rite the Church prays that the Kingdom will come, before and after each redemptive action by which new persons are initiated into the Church and consecrated as priests, prophets, and kings of the Kingdom.

However mistaken Walter Rauschenbusch may have been about the actual meaning obtained in the catholic rites of baptism, he was correct when he asked in *A Theology for the Social Gospel*: "Why not connect baptism with the Kingdom of God? It has always been an exit and an entrance; why not the exit from the Kingdom of Evil and the entrance into the Kingdom of God?"[14] Baptism is that. Rauschenbusch's understanding of baptism turns out finally to be a reduction of the rite to a service of moral dedication to the Kingdom-building imperative. But his description of the role baptism should play in Christian ethics, however lacking in sacramental realism, is very much worth recalling. He wrote:

Scarcely any Christian institution has experienced such changes and deteriorations as baptism, but of them all the loss of outlook toward the Kingdom of God was one of the most regrettable. Could the social gospel — at least in some instances — fill baptism with its original meaning? We could imagine a minister and group of candidates who unite in feeling the evil of the present world-order and the promise and claims of the impending Christian world-order, together using baptism to express their solemn dedication to the tasks of the Kingdom of God, and accepting their rights as children of God within that Kingdom.[15]

"Blessed art thou, O Lord God almighty, who hast chosen for thyself a new people unto priesthood and kingship to be a holy nation,"[16] read the opening words of the prayer over the oil (chrism) in the Armenian Rite of Holy Baptism, thus affirming the biblical realism about baptism. Through baptism of water and Spirit, not by natural generation, social reform, or revolution, a new people and the Kingdom come into being. Christian ethics begins with the affirmation of the goodness of creation as it came from the hand of God and returns to his bosom through the eucharistic action of the Church. Yet, it also moves directly to a recognition of the evil which afflicts that creation. The recitation of the Lord's Prayer at the very beginning of the Armenian baptismal rite affirms the goodness of creation. It also reminds those assembled that something has gone wrong in us and in the world. The prayer at the reception of the catechumens in the Byzantine rite and the presence of Psalms 51 and 131 before the enrollment in the Armenian rite emphasize that those to be baptized and indeed the entire created order are in need of redemption. The prayer in the Byzantine rite proclaims that henceforth Christ will take possession of the whole person. Baptism itself is declared to be a flight from the fallen order "unto thy holy Name, . . . to take refuge under the shelter of thy wings."[17]

More important for Christian ethics is the review at the very beginning of the Orthodox rites of those virtues belonging to Christian character. These qualities set Christians apart from the world. In the Armenian rite humility is the most prominent virtue. "The sacrifice acceptable to God is a humble spirit; a humble and contrite heart, O God, thou wilt not despise" (Ps. 51). "I did not go with the great ones; nor with them that are more marvellous than myself. / But I have humbled myself like a child, who is weaned away from his mother's breast and then returns to the same. / If I had indeed made my soul proud; that would be my retribution" (Ps. 131).[18] This is what it means to put on Christ and to be born again in his likeness. The almost singular concern among some Christian theologians with love as the primary or summary virtue of Christian ethics receives an important corrective in this rite. Christian love is possible only after the pride of the Evil One is destroyed in us by the baptismal waters and is replaced by the humility of Jesus Christ "who, though he was in the form of God, did not count equality with God a thing to be grasped, but emptied himself, taking the form of a servant, being born in the likeness of men. And being found in human form he humbled himself and became obedient unto death, even death on a cross" (Phil. 2:6–9 RSV).

Walter Rauschenbusch argued that the Christian meaning of baptism had degenerated into an "individualistic interpretation of it as an escape from damnation."[19] He strongly implied that, in fact, the catholic rites of baptism had of themselves taken on such signification in their language and actions. Nothing could be further from the truth. Rather, a religious piety developed in East and West alike that tended to minimize the *ordo's* Kingdom signification and to interpret the sacramental action of the Church as a deliverance of the individual from the profane for his or her personal sanctification. But the *ordo* itself, at least in the East, retained its objective eschatological content.

The exorcisms of the Byzantine rite are proof of this. These exorcisms provide the basis for a powerful social ethic. The spirit of evil is exorcised not only from the catechumen but from the air, water, and oil as well. From this vantage baptism is a proleptic re-creation of the entire cosmos.[20] Exorcism is a *necessary* action of Christian ethics because there is a demonic reality which obstructs the way of return to God. Exorcism is *possible* because the Lord of all creation has waged a successful struggle against Satan and has redeemed us by conquering death through his submission to it on the cross. No twentieth-century writer was more impressed with this Christian conviction than Flannery O'Connor. In the "Fiction Writer and His Countryside" she observed:

> St. Cyril of Jerusalem, in instructing catechumens, wrote: "The dragon sits by the side of the road, watching those who pass.

Beware lest he devour you. We go to the father of Souls, but it is necessary to pass by the dragon." No matter what form the dragon may take, it is of this mysterious passage past him, or into his jaws, that stories of any depth will always be concerned to tell.[21]

A Christian ethic, like the good stories which Flannery O'Connor told, always will pay heed to the surd of evil in the Christian story which makes all forms of Pelagianism and ethical idealism impossible and the Incarnation, death, and Resurrection of Christ necessary.

The three exorcisms of the Byzantine rite set out a vision of the Christian life as struggle against sin, triumph through the creative, destructive, and restorative action of God, and transfiguration in the eschatological time of Christ's Second Coming. Allow me to quote in full the first of these prayers of exorcism.

> The Lord layeth thee under ban, O Devil: He who came into the world, and made his abode among men, that he might overthrow thy tyranny and deliver men; who also upon the Tree did triumph over the adverse powers, when the sun was darkened, and the earth did quake, and the graves were opened, and the bodies of the Saints arose; who also by death annihilated Death, and overthrew him who exercised the dominion of Death, that is thee, the Devil. I adjure thee by God, who hath revealed the Tree of Life, and hath arrayed in ranks the Cherubim and the flaming sword which turneth all ways to guard it: Be thou under ban. For I adjure thee by him who walketh upon the surface of the sea as it were dry land, and layeth under his ban the tempests of the winds; whose glance drieth up the deep, and whose interdict maketh the mountains to melt away. The same now, through us, doth lay thee under ban. Fear, begone and depart from this creature, and return not again, neither hide thyself in him (her), either by night or by day; either in the morning, or at noonday: but depart hence to thine own Tartarus, until the great Day of Judgment which is ordained. Fear thou God who sitteth upon the Cherubim and looketh upon the deeps; before whom tremble Angels and Archangels, Thrones, Dominions, Principalities, Authorities, Powers, and many-eyed Cherubim and the six-winged Seraphim; before whom, likewise, heaven and earth do quake, the sea and all that therein is. Begone, and

depart from this sealed, newly-enlisted warrior of Christ our God. For I adjure thee by him who rideth upon the wings of the wind, and maketh his Angels spirits, and his ministers a flaming fire: Begone, and depart from this creature, with all thy powers and thine angels.

Exclamation

For glorified is the Name of the Father, and of the Son, and of the Holy Spirit, now, and ever, and unto ages of ages. Amen.[22]

Alexander Schmemann described this prayer as "a *poem* in the deepest sense of this word, which in Greek means creation." Schmemann insisted upon the utter realism of this sacramental action. "It truly manifests and *does* that which it announces; it makes powerful that which it states; it again fills words with the divine energy from which they stem. And exorcism does all this because it is proffered in the name of Christ; it is truly filled with the power of Christ; who has 'broken' into the enemy territory, has assumed human life and made human words his own, because He has already destroyed the demonic power from within."[23] Such a sacramental realism does not allow for an ethical idealism which would interpret evil as a function or valence of ignorance or as the mere absence in nature of some perfection achievable in an indeterminate future. Neither does it permit a Pelagianism which would define the Christian life and the virtues and values belonging to it as products solely of human freedom. Human freedom is not a power or state of being autonomous of divine initiative. Human freedom is a divinely bestowed ability to cooperate with God to his glory and purpose. Prayer and worship are, as Karl Barth said, "literally the archetypal form of all human acts of freedom in the Church."[24] And as such those who do pray and worship are bound to discover that, before they act, God, who is the absolute ground of freedom, already has acted.

For the Christian, baptism is proof that the great history of divine initiative to redeem humankind from the destructive power of Satan is fulfilled. The Matthean account (Matt. 3:13–17) of Jesus' baptism in the Jordan comes at the end of the baptism in the Armenian rite, just preceding chrismation. The location of the story at this point in the rite emphasizes that not only is this the fulfillment or antitype of all God's previous deeds by which he has sought out a free human response to his gracious redemptive purpose, but also Jesus' baptism is the paradigm of all future baptisms. The *autexousion*, or self-determining freedom of persons, of which the Greek fathers speak, is a freedom whose right use is for human beings to make full claim of themselves. It is the *graced* capacity of a creature made in the image and likeness of God to become a son or daughter of God. Such sonship or daughterhood is not by nature but by grace. Yet it is entirely dependent upon whether or not human beings freely accept the divine invitation to attend the heavenly banquet as sons and daughters of the Father. Baptism rehearses the story of how even that self-determining freedom bestowed upon Adam at his creation was lost when he chose to place himself in bondage to Satan. Baptism is the restoration of that freedom as well. Thus St. Paul is moved to say: "For freedom Christ has set us free; stand fast therefore, and do not submit to a yoke of slavery" (Gal. 5:1 RSV).

But how is this new freedom mentioned by St. Paul attained? How is it to be used and to what purpose? Furthermore, what acts make good deeds, and by what doings do human beings become that which they are purposed to become by God and enabled to become by baptism? Finally, what attributes belong to that character which is befitting human beings as creatures made in the image and likeness of God? These are questions raised by the Eastern baptismal rites and answered by them as well. In the Orthodox tradition they are also the fundamental concerns of Christian ethics.

Baptism is a renunciation of Satan. But what is more, it is a pledge and promise of oneself to Christ. The pledge or adhesion to Christ is in the form of a profession of faith in his divine sonship, Incarnation, baptism, Crucifixion, and Resurrection. What we become is dependent upon what we believe to be true. The sixth chapter of St. Paul's Epistle to the Romans is a key scriptural passage in the Byzantine and the Armenian rites of baptism. There St. Paul gives the content of the catholic conviction about the truth of baptism. Baptism is a participation in Christ's death, burial, and Resurrection. "We were buried therefore with him by baptism into death, so that as Christ was raised from the dead by the glory of the Father, we too might walk in the newness of life" (Rom. 6:4 RSV). This "newness of life" is Christian ethics, not narrowly defined as reflection upon what is right behavior or good character but in the full sense as an *activity* by which free beings purposefully do the right and become the good.

In his second baptismal homily, John Chrysostom has the following to say about the meaning of having pledged oneself to Christ:

> Then once you have made this covenant, this renunciation and contract, since you have confessed his sovereignty over you and pronounced the words by which you pledge yourself to Christ, you are now a soldier and have signed on for a spiritual contest.[25]

Once baptized, Christians are prepared to *pursue* the "newness of life" to which St. Paul refers. They have been freed for the freedom which is Christian ethics. Through baptism persons are incorporated into a new structure of life. Their being has been changed, as has their ethics, from that of the world—premised in a fallen *gnomic* freedom,[26] which the world celebrates as the freedom to choose—to the *graced* freedom to serve God and his Kingdom with praise and thanksgiving. Neither baptism nor chrismation, however, guarantees that persons will live the "newness of life." Baptism liberates persons from evil to strive to obtain this goal by imitation of Christ. Chrismation confers the seal of perfection upon persons and the promise of sanctification by the Holy Spirit. But the freedom to neglect or reject the divine call and the possibility of failure to win the spiritual struggle ahead remain. Thus the prayer of chrismation in the Armenian Rite of Holy Baptism is not a declaration that the child has been made perfect but rather a petition that he who has been prepared for perfection will pursue righteousness to the glory of God and the Kingdom.

> Thou hast enlightened thy creatures, O Christ our God, making the light of the knowledge of God shine forth in our hearts. And now thou hast made this thy servant free and hast sanctified and justified him and has given him the honour of adoption as thy child. Grant to this child, O Lord, also harmony of life and give him continuous purity, joining him with the righteous in thy sight and mingling him with the number of thy saints with whom may he glorify thee together with the Father and the Holy Spirit, now and always and unto the ages of ages. Amen.[27]

As shown above, in his second baptismal homily John Chrysostom used a military analogy to introduce the theme of *askesis* or ethical struggle belonging to St. Paul's "newness of life." Later in the same text he mixes metaphors and uses the analogy of "athletes of Christ . . . [in] a spiritual arena."[28] But the meaning is not ambiguous. "God," he says, "has given you great assurance. You were once slaves; he has enrolled you among the chief of his friends. You were once captives; he has raised you up and adopted you as sons. He will not refuse your demands; he will grant them all, true again in this to his own goodness."[29] The distinctiveness of Christian ethics is in this covenant and promise and in this liberation and adoption as sons and daughters of the Father and friends of and in the Son. Christian ethics is a spiritual *askesis* in total service to God and to one's fellow humanity for the sake of the Kingdom. It requires the dedication of one's entire being and the special virtues of the Kingdom.

This is indicated in the prayer over the oil of the Armenian rite.

> And now we pray thee, O Lord beneficent, send down the gift of the all-holy Spirit together with this oil, so that this may be to him who will be thereby anointed for holiness of spiritual wisdom, for courage to struggle and triumph over the Adversary, for strength to keep the commandments that enjoin virtuous deeds, for perfect discipline and for the exercise of godliness, to the end that being enlightened in mind he may live in this world for the salvation of his soul and glory of the all-holy Trinity, and may be worthy to enter into the inheritance of the state of the saints in the light, glorifying the Father, the Son and the Holy Spirit, now and always unto the ages of ages. Amen.[30]

And to underscore and amplify these qualities which belong to Christian character, life, and conduct, the rite includes these words which the priest says as he anoints the newly-baptized with the holy chrism:

> Sweet ointment in the name of Jesus Christ is poured upon thee as a seal of incorruptible heavenly gifts.
> The eyes:
> This seal in the name of Jesus Christ enlighten thine eyes, that thou mayest never sleep unto death.
> The ears:
> This holy anointing be unto thee for the hearing of divine commandments.

The nostrils:

This seal in the name of Jesus Christ be to thee a sweet smell from life unto life.

The mouth:

This seal in the name of Jesus Christ be to thee a guard for thy mouth and a strong door for thy lips.

The hands:

This seal in the name of Jesus Christ be to thee a cause for good works and for all virtuous deeds and conduct.

The heart:

This seal establish in thee a pure heart and renew within thee an upright spirit.

The back:

This seal in the name of Jesus Christ be to thee a shield of strength thereby to quench all the fiery darts of the Evil One.

The feet:

This divine seal direct thy goings unto life everlasting that thou mayest not be shaken.[31]

There is a markedly ethical imperative in the Armenian baptismal rite. The actions and words of this rite bestow upon persons (ontologically) and call them to (ethically) a certain disposition and character. If the baptized conscientiously strive to cultivate this character within themselves, it will mark them off radically from the selfishness, pride, vengefulness, will to power, and violence of this fallen world which condemn it to death unless it, like they, be transformed. A baptismal ethic develops persons of humility, purity of heart, contrition, gratitude, and peacefulness. These virtues constitute that christic character which Christians must make their own through constant and conscientious spiritual struggle. Because their old selves have been drowned in the baptismal waters and they have been resurrected with Christ, Christ himself becomes the pattern of their lives to which they are called by him to conform.[32]

THE ETHICS OF A EUCHARISTIC PUBLIC

Through baptism persons are placed within that pattern of divine activity by which God brings us out of the darkness and slavery of sin into the light and liberty of his Kingdom. That pattern is corporate and relational. Baptism is an initiation of persons into the witnessing Body of Christ in the world. A baptismal ethic is incomplete apart from the eucharistic action by which persons gather and constitute themselves as Church. Christ entered the sinful and desolate human community in order to draw persons into the holy and enlivening fellowship of the Trinity. Those who would pattern their lives after the one who joined himself to our flesh in order to die and return that flesh to new life are invited to sup together at the great banquet in God's Kingdom. As the Word became "flesh," the "flesh" becomes like God by supping on the Bread of Life. Those who have been cleansed in the baptismal waters also require nourishment. By feeding at the Lord's table they are not only nourished from within by the bread and wine but they are assimilated into the very body of the one with whom and upon whom they feast. As that body they become the very presence and action of God's reign in this world.

Contemporary theology has gotten into the habit of speaking of the Church as a community. And so it is in many ways. Still, the use of this term is somewhat troublesome. It needs to be qualified with the adjective *peculiar*. The Church, if it is any kind of community at all, is a rather *peculiar* community. It is a community whose character, as indicated above, ought to contrast markedly with that of the world. Though it is a peculiar community, paradoxically it is one for all humanity. The Church is catholic. And it is catholic because it is an eschatological and sacramental manifestation of the Kingdom of God. The Orthodox theologian George Khodre has stated, "The Church is not a society but rather a gathering."[33] Khodre might have gone one step further and said, "As the Church is not a society but a gathering, so the Kingdom of God is not a community but a public." This is the move that William J. Everett makes in several provocative articles. Everett has written:

> The public is not an institution, like the government, university, or family. Nor is it simply a collection of cultural values and visions. It is not the same thing as a community either, for it has a distance from the emotional bonds of kin and neighborhood. It is, as Sennet says, a pattern of interaction in which strangers can participate.[34]

Everett argues that the term *public* is useful to indicate that the "redeemed existence" of the Church transcends the "communalism, kinship and monarchy that have dominated Christian symbolism during its penetration of the European tribes."[35] The meanings of Khodre and Everett are similar. Neither denies that the Church, since it is in the world, includes worldly forms of human association and organization ranging from the most "organic" ties of kinship and family to the most "artifactual" bureaucratic arrangements. Community and society can be used to describe the Church, but certainly not exclusively so. The Church is also a "gathering" whose fundamental reason for being is to make the Kingdom of God present. If the Church were merely a society or community it could not be for the world an icon of the Kingdom. It would look and act no differently from the family, political state, or corporate business. The Church indeed must be an eschatological and sacramental gathering which pays no ultimate heed to the organic and organizational forms of historical communities or societies, though it will "use" these "elements" of the world to build up the Kingdom. Similarly, the Kingdom of God must not be confused with "social order" or "dominion." The Kingdom of God is a trinitarian, therefore a perfect, public. It is not a "social order" or "dominion" in the political sense because it is not threatened by the breakdown of mutuality. Rather it is a "network of relations" characterized by total trust, complete knowledge and perfect liberty and justice. A public is "a pattern of action that is evoked, not commanded," writes Everett. "Otherwise the participants would lack that essential equality requiring them to affect each other through words and persuasion."[36] The Kingdom of God is that perfect public in which the love of God draws but does not compel persons into perfect harmony of will and purpose.

Everett's championship of the term *public* as a means of both clarifying the nature of the Church and the Kingdom of God and articulating an ethic which will effectively in-form and transform the world is bound up with a critical — I believe quite correct — evaluation of the structure and dynamics of our secular, pluralistic society. He refuses to define the ethical significance of liturgy merely as a "means for orienting individuals towards 'society.' " Liturgy is not just "a didactic exercise for persons." Liturgies "dispose us . . . to be public beings. As expositions of our law of action, they not only legitimate institutions but also maintain the conventions by which a public can exist. Not only do we rehearse the stories of the past action in worship, we project new scenarios to test the judgments of the public realm." Christian liturgy is intimately, indeed vitally, connected with ecclesiology and eschatology. Its subjects are the Church and the Kingdom of God. All of the Eastern liturgies declare, as Everett suggests they do, that the Kingdom is the "perfect public — a place of light, of open disclosure, of persuasive truth, of judgment in light of all the facts."[37] God calls us out of the darkness, falsehood, desolation, bondage, and abyss of death which is the fallen condition of humankind into his divine public.

During the prologue of the Eucharistia in the Armenian liturgy before the singing of the Sanctus and the Anemnesis, the celebrant prays:

> It is verily meet and right with most earnest diligence always to adore and glorify thee, Father almighty, who didst remove the hindrance of the curse by thine imponderable and fellow-creator Word, who having taken the Church to be a people unto himself, made his own those who believe in thee and was pleased to dwell amongst us in a ponderable nature, according to the economy through the Virgin, and as divine master-builder building a new work, he thereby made this earth into heaven.
>
> For he, before whom the companies of vigilant-angels endured not to stand, being amazed at the resplendent and unapproachable light of thy Godhead, even he, becoming man for our salvation, granted unto us to join the heavenly ones in spiritual choirs.[38]

In this prayer several important things are said which are in turn amplified in word, song, and gesture through the rest of the liturgy. Clearly, the prayer acknowledges that God in Christ has invited us, who are under the "curse" of this fallen existence, to participate in this creative activity of building heaven out of his earth. The Church does this each time it offers the bread and wine as symbols of the Word's Incarnation and one holy sacrifice. Liturgy, therefore, is not a private pedagogy without a stake in creating and legitimating public institutions and values. Indeed liturgy does not make a final distinction between private and public. It is an action which seeks to re-create the world through the formation of a eucharistic public which is sent out into the society to transform it into the image of God's Kingdom of light, liberty, and love. The truth which the liturgy publicizes is inseparable from the vision of that Kingdom which the Church prays will come.

Such liturgy defies the privatization of religion which this pluralistic, secular society promotes. It evades the place that society provides for religion among a panoply of alternative ideologies good for private consumption but discouraged in the name of tolerance from public enactment. The degree to which the American churches have allowed themselves and the truth they would proclaim to be defined this way is a measure of these same churches' forgetfulness of what they are. It is a sad indication of their inability to act decisively and publicly upon that which they profess to be true.

Allow me to speak of the Orthodox churches in America for the sake of illustration. First, these churches have confused the exclusive togetherness of family or ethnic group with the inclusive togetherness of the Kingdom. They have forgotten that the Church is, as Khodre rightly insists, not a society but an ever-growing gathering. These are churches also that have not yet come to terms with the fact that in a pluralistic, secular society such as America a Constantinian sociology of the Church as sacramental organism of the political society is an anachronism. A church which insists upon viewing itself as such cannot hope to have a transformative influence upon the greater society. Though it was not an entirely accurate description of the working arrangements of Byzantine society, the theory of *symphonia* was then at least a practicable vision. But it is not practicable for the publicization of the truth in Jesus Christ and the transformation of values and institutions in this society. The theory fails to take into account a plurality of publics which, in most instances, are speaking different languages and envisioning different worlds than that of an out-of-mind and out-of-memory Christendom. A liturgy which in the Byzantine context had developed within its rubrics a practicable social vision and the capacity to criticize as well as legitimate public values and institutions merely legitimates cultic existence when conducted by a church with the mind and self-image of the Orthodox Church in America today. The Orthodox Church in America has effectively allowed itself to be reduced to a religion which is neither public nor has a public.

The present minority status of the Christian churches in America does not allow Christians to bethink themselves in a Constantinian world. But neither must they allow it to distract them so much that they forget why they are in the world. The Church is not in the world as one additional God-blessed voluntary or welfare agency or advocacy group in service of the world's agendas for progress or prosperity. Christians need look no further than the rites of holy baptism to be reminded that the world is in the grip of sin. Even the good which it pursues becomes either the pretext or the victim of the pride, vengefulness, greed, will to power, and hatred which divide it against itself and bring dissolution and death upon humankind everywhere. The reason why the Church is in the world has not changed, even if the social, economic, and political structures of modernity and postmodernity may differ radically from those with which the Church was so familiar for fifteen hundred years. The Church remains the Body of Christ in the world, offering a holy service to God and seeking to create unity where there is division, to bring forth reconciliation where there is alienation, to heal and restore a sick and dissipated human nature, and to free persons from the spiritual and physical violence of evil.

Stanley Hauerwas has written that

> The task of the church [is] to pioneer those institutions and practices that the wider society has not learned as forms of justice. (At times it is also possible that the church can learn from society more just ways of forming life.) The church, therefore, must act as a paradigmatic community in the hope of providing some indication of what the world can be but is not. . . . The church does not have a social ethic, but rather is a social ethic. That is, she is a social ethic inasmuch as she functions as a criteriological institution—that is, an institution that has learned to embody the form of truth that is charity as revealed in the person and work of Christ.[39]

Hauerwas is correct, though one would hope that he could be more concrete about just how the Church "pioneers" new "institutions and practices" and "functions as a criteriological institution." For Orthodoxy the answer is that this social ethic originates in baptism and is continued in all of the Church's liturgical and sacramental acts. As Everett suggests, the eucharistic worship of the Christian churches remains the primary context out of which Christians must publicize the truth they profess and fulfill the role Hauerwas assigns to the Church. But this is more easily said than done. It requires, above all else, an imaginative pedagogy of eucharistic judgment, forgiveness, reconciliation, and *philanthropia*.

AN ETHICS OF THE GREAT SUPPER

And men will come from east and west, from north
and south, and sit at table in the kingdom of God.
Luke 13:29 RSV

At heart Christian ethics should be an invitation to the great banquet. "Blessed is he who shall eat bread in the kingdom of God" (Luke 14:15 RSV). If the Christian churches were to take these words ascribed to Christ by St. Luke seriously as well as the parable which follows in that Gospel, what a difference it would make. Perhaps Christian ethicists' quandary about what is distinctive in Christian ethics is merely a reflection of the Church's own inability to make the supper it serves compelling, not only to those who are invited by reason of baptism but to those in "the streets and lanes of the city, . . . the poor and maimed and blind and lame" and to those in "the highways and hedges" (Luke 14:21, 23 RSV). St. Paul instructs the Corinthian church that prophesy spoken in Christian assembly should be directed to the believers "for their upbuilding and encouragement and consolation" (1 Cor. 14:3 RSV). Yet he also exhorts, "But if all prophesy, and an unbeliever or outsider enters, he is convicted by all, he is called to account by all, the secrets of his heart are disclosed; and so, falling on his face, he will worship God and declare that God is really among you" (1 Cor. 14:24–25 RSV). Christian worship is for Christians. The same holds true for Christian ethics. Both are possible only when two or three have gathered in Christ's name and is in the midst of them (Matt. 18:20 RSV). Yet the stranger always should be welcome to the supper. "Then the King will say to those at his right hand, 'Come, O blessed of my Father, inherit the kingdom prepared for you from the foundation of the world; for I was hungry and you gave me food, I was thirsty and you gave me drink, I was a stranger and you welcomed me" (Matt. 25:34–35 RSV).

However, to come to the table in the Kingdom is not like stopping at a fast food drive-through for a hamburger and fries. To eat at the heavenly banquet requires a certain disposition toward the King and all who have gathered at his table. "The kingdom of God does not mean food and drink but righteousness and peace and joy in the Holy Spirit" (Rom. 14:17 RSV). St. Paul's admonition to the Roman Christians is about their behavior and character and just what it is that they must believe, express, and become when they gather together for food and drink. The Orthodox churches in America have failed to make the Lord's banquet compelling because they have made the eucharistic meal a privilege of independent ethnic cults (one can substitute social or economic class or race where appropriate for other churches) rather than the public expression of the virtues, values, character, and hope of the Kingdom of God. The cults work strenuously at being ethnic Greek or Russian or Armenian, and ethnic in a respectably American fashion. The most noticeable meal which such churches offer is the annual food bazaar. And it is to this meal, not the heavenly banquet, to which those on the highways, streets, and hedgepaths are invited. Celebrated are the commercial values and ethnic heritage of the American nation — all, of course, for a price. As for the banquet at the Lord's table, these churches hardly exact a price. If these churches are incapable of asking their members whether "they can pray, whether they live as disciples and servants of other members of the local church, whether they know how to make their occupations and professions a ministry for justice in the world, or whether they can give a real account of the hope that is in them,"[40] how can it be expected that such churches be what their liturgies declare them to be and do what their liturgies declare them to be doing — "a people" of the "creator-Word" who with him is "building a new work," making "this earth into heaven."[41]

Christian ethics begins when the people of God gather to worship. Everett is undoubtedly correct when he observes that "the liturgies of the civil religion or of the sports-university-entertainment 'media triad' "[42] have become the most powerful liturgies in our society. The liturgists of our age are the writers of advertising jingles and television "sitcoms" and the choreographers of football half-times (witness also the pageant of civil religion staged at the 1984 Los Angeles Olympics and the Statue of Liberty Centennial celebration of 1986). These are liturgies and liturgists, however, without a church. There is not room here to discuss the liturgical revival which is needed desperately in the Christian churches. Leave it to quote Metropolitan Emilianos Timiados when he writes that the "greatest enemy" of the Church is the "enemy among us" of "the lack of an adequate and substantial communion."[43] Christian ethics, I repeat, should start in the sacred rites of the Church. If ethics as a discipline is to bear any concrete or effective relationship to the action of the people of God upon the world, it must begin its reflection in those rites as well and bring a critical eye to the religious practice of Christians when they are at home worshiping and praying together.

Earlier I proposed that Christian social ethics must attain the character of an imaginative pedagogy of eucharistic judgment, repentance, forgiveness, reconciliation, and *philanthropia*. I would like to close this essay with some observations regarding the shape which such a pedagogy might take. In his *Doxology*, Geoffrey Wainwright argues that, contrary to the usual emphasis placed by anthropologists and sociologists on the stabilizing or legitimating functions of ritual, Christian liturgy can also function as a criteriological activity which brings judgment—even radical judgment—to bear on a particular social order. There is no better contemporary example of just how this can happen than in present-day Poland. The mere gathering of the people of God in eucharistic assembly serves in that nation as a judgment upon and criticism of the injustice and brutal power of the present Communist regime. Why this is possible is not explained simply by the fact that the Roman Catholic Church maintains an imposing presence as an alternative institution for human allegiance in that society—though that is true. Deeper than this sociological phenomenon is the powerful symbolism of the Catholic liturgy itself. In Wainwright's words: "Even relatively good governments are exposed to critique by the absolutely good rule of God in his kingdom. By keeping open the vision of a divine kingdom which transcends anything yet achieved, the Christian liturgy is to that extent subversive of all *installation dans le provisoire*."[44] But in Poland the Roman Catholic Church has succeeded also in assuming a role as a reconciling, community-binding public and as a philanthropic presence consistent with the liturgical vision of its worship. I am not suggesting that the example of Poland is directly transferrable to Christian social ethics in North America. However, that modern example, along with others, such as the criteriological role the Roman Catholic Church has assumed in Latin America and appears to be assuming in the Philippines, can be instructive if not always to be emulated. Similarly the ability of the National Conference of Catholic Bishops to argue as forcefully as they did in their 1983 Pastoral Letter—*The Challenge of Peace: God's Promise and Our Response*—for a peacemaking vocation of Christians in the world is a reflection of the power of the Roman Catholic Mass to shape the character and behavior of a people. As the bishops said:

The Mass in particular is a unique means of seeking God's help to create the conditions essential for true peace in ourselves and in the world. In the eucharist we encounter the risen Lord, who gave us his peace. He shares with us the grace of the redemption, which helps us to preserve and nourish this precious gift. Nowhere is the Church's urgent plea for peace more evident in the liturgy than in the Communion Rite. After beginning this rite of the Mass with the Lord's Prayer, praying for reconciliation now and in the kingdom to come, the community asks God to "grant us peace in our day," not just at some time in the distant future.[45]

But the judgment, repentance, forgiveness, reconciliation, and *philanthropia* of Christian ethics is not a program for social progress, reform, or revolution. Nor are these elements of Christian ethics planks in a platform which the Church proposes as items to be taken or left by the rest of society as the agenda for the address of issues of racial or economic justice, environment, or nuclear armaments. This, of course, is how all special interests and parties in the American pluralist society are expected to present their particular concerns. The Church, however, offers its social ethic as an expression of its own inner being. Judgment, repentance, forgiveness, reconciliation, and *philanthropia* are not mere principles to be applied. They are a way of life. "Christians, certainly we Orthodox Christians," writes Thomas Hopko, *"have nothing to offer people and the world but Christ and the Church.* And it is our conviction that there is nothing else to be offered and nothing else that is necessary. Our witness is to this conviction; our service, to this end."[46]

Hopko stands firmly within the Orthodox tradition on this score. The Church is at its best as a criteriological and transformative institution when it speaks and acts with a firm sense of its true identity as the Body of Christ in the world. Once again, this means that Christians must derive their ethics from the experience of God's Kingdom and truth which is found in the Church's worship. Before the Church judges it is judged; before it can call the world to a proper sense of contrition it must repent; before it can bring forgiveness to the world it must be forgiven; before it can reconcile it must be reconciled; and before it can bring love to humankind it must gratefully accept and reflect God's *philanthropia* in holy service. By using the preposition *before* I am not suggesting a temporal sequence as if the Church must keep itself separate from the world until it gets itself in order. *Before* simply stands for the primal action of prayer and worship without which the Church has no true knowledge of itself and, therefore, is incapable of discriminating between the world's standards and those which belong to the Kingdom of God. Christian ethics is an ethics of the Great Supper because it is in eucharistic assembly, not in private prayer or study, that judgment, repentance, reconciliation, and God's love are experienced in their full Kingdom signification. The eucharistic prayers of the great Christian liturgies express this realization by the Church of its true identity. The following prayer is the first of three said before communion in the Armenian liturgy. It is said aloud and addressed to the Father. The second and third prayers amplify the meaning of the first and are said silently by the priest.

> Holy Father, who hast called us by the name of thine Only-begotten and hast enlightened us through the baptism of the spiritual font, make us worthy to receive this holy mystery for the remission of our sins. Impress upon us the graces of the Holy Spirit, as thou didst upon the holy apostles, who tasted thereof and became the cleansers of the whole world.
>
> And now, O Lord, Father beneficent, make this communion part of the supper of the disciples by dispelling the darkness of sins. Look not upon mine unworthiness and withold not from me the graces of the Holy Spirit, but according to thine infinite love of man grant that this communion be for the expiation of our sins and the loosing of our transgressions, as our Lord Jesus Christ promised and said that whosoever eateth my flesh and drinketh my blood shall live forever.
>
> Therefore make this to be unto us for the expiation of our sins, so that they who shall eat and drink of this may give praise and glory unto the Father and the Son and the Holy Spirit, now and always and unto ages of ages. Amen.[47]

One striking aspect of this prayer is that baptism is immediately recalled. (This is not found, for example, in Byzantine liturgies of St. Basil or St. John Chrysostom). Baptism is recalled as the primal divine-human action by which those gathered as church were brought out of the darkness and slavery of this fallen world and into the light and liberty of the Kingdom. That action also has conferred upon Christians "the graces of the Holy Spirit," making them people of the same vocation and having spiritual gifts like those of the "holy apostles" whose calling it was to be "the cleansers of the whole world." The "graces of the Holy Spirit" are those virtues listed in the already cited prayer over the oil in the Armenian baptismal rite and the words spoken as the newly-baptized is sealed by anointment with the holy oil.[48] These virtues of holiness, spriritual wisdom, courage, discipline, purity of heart, and humility enable the Christian to take up the vocation of the apostles. By prayer together and eating and drinking together Christians have a foretaste of the Kingdom. Christians, therefore are moved by gratitude to bring spiritual enlightenment, forgiveness, reconciliation, and love into a world in "the darkness of sins" and under the condemnation of death. These are qualities of the Kingdom of God. The Kingdom is indeed a realm of light, liberty, and love as revealed by the very actions of God who enters into dialogue with Christians as their prayer becomes his as well, and he reveals himself as the "Father beneficent" whose "infinite love of man grant[s] . . . this communion [to] be for the expiation of our sins and the loosing of our transgressions."

The shape of the pedagogy which is required for there to be an evangelical, churchly Christian ethic which challenges the world with the standards of the Kingdom is nothing other than the shape of the Divine Liturgy. As they offer themselves to God "a living sacrifice, dedicated and fit for his acceptance, the worship offered by mind and heart," Christians also constitute themselves a living social ethic "able to discern the will of God, and to know what is good, acceptable, and perfect" (Rom. 12:1–2 NEB). Thus St. Paul exhorts:

> Love in all sincerity, loathing evil and clinging to the good. Let love for our brotherhood breed warmth of mutual affection. Give pride of place to one another in esteem.
>
> With unflagging energy, in ardour of spirit, serve the Lord.
>
> Let hope keep you joyful; in trouble stand firm; persist in prayer.
>
> Contribute to the needs of God's people, and practice hospitality.
>
> Call down blessings on your persecutors—blessings, not curses.
>
> With the joyful be joyful, and mourn with the mourners.

Care as much about each other as about yourselves. Do not
be haughty, but go about with humble folk. Do not keep thinking how wise you are.

Never pay back evil with evil. Let your aims be such as all
men count honorable. If possible, so far as it lies with you, live
at peace with all men. My dear friends, do not seek revenge, but
leave a place for divine retribution; for there is a text which reads:
"Justice is mine, says the Lord, I will repay." But there is another
text: "If your enemy is hungry, feed him; if he is thirsty, give
him drink; by doing this you will heap live coals on his head."
Do not let evil conquer you, but use good to defeat evil. (Rom.
12:9–21 NEB)

There is no such thing as a Christian ethic which is the exclusive
possession of the individual. Apart from the Church there is no Christian ethic. St. Paul makes this clear when he prefaces his instructions
for Christian behavior with the claim that through the eucharistic
celebration believers become "united with Christ, [to] form one body"
(Rom. 12:5 NEB) and that when they act, whatever their individual
gifts, they act as members of that one body. Seeing Christian ethics
as worship is recognizing that no movement for justice, reconciliation,
or peace apart from the Church can achieve all that it promises. This
does not exclude Christians from participation in political movements
or government services which respond to genuine and specific injustices
or needs of persons. It does indicate, however, that Christians will find
their ultimate reasons — even their proximate reasons oftentimes — for
engaging or not engaging in such action not in the ideologies or plat-
forms of parties and interests of the day but from within the prayerful
and worshiping life of the Church. When the tormented voices of the
world call out for freedom, justice, and peace, Christian ethics will
refer those demands and principles to the Christian experience of the
Kingdom. Freedom has a specific context and meaning for Christians
different from, for example, the liberal social-contractarian description of freedom as a possession of the individual or the Marxist-Leninist
interpretation of freedom as a property of the socialist state. In Christian ethics freedom is not a right of the autonomous individual to do
what she would do so long as her use of it does not offend the rights
of others. Nor is it a condition of liberation from an oppressive social

order for a total obligation to the new order and its program for justice. Rather, for Christians freedom is a gift of faith granted by a gracious and loving God to those whom he forgives of their sins and enables to serve others as he served them through the life, death, and Resurrection of his Son. Freedom is the grace-filled construal of one's life as an adopted son or daughter of God ready (i.e., prepared) to serve God and neighbor for the sake of the Kingdom. Thus St. Paul exhorts the Christians of Corinth: "Do you not know that your body is a shrine of the indwelling Holy Spirit, and the Spirit is God's gift to you? You do not belong to yourselves; you were bought at a price. Then honour God in your body" (1 Cor. 6:19–20 NEB). It is on the basis of this understanding of freedom discovered, demonstrated, and affirmed to be true in Christian worship that the Church must engage that society in which it happens to be placed. As such the Church will always, until the end of time, serve as witness to the world that it is indeed fallen and needs correction even in its understanding of the highest ethical goals. And it will send out into the world a people who, having worshiped and prayed for the world together, are prepared to plant and nurture the seeds of the Kingdom in every walk of life.

This is the commission given to the people of God at the close of the Divine Liturgy. In a psalm of dismissal (Psalm 34) in the Armenian liturgy, the people of God are instructed: "Keep thy tongue from evil, and thy lips that they speak no guile. / Eschew evil and do good; seek peace and ensue it. / The eyes of the Lord are over the righteous; and his ears are open unto their prayers."[48] Within the context of the Divine Liturgy this Hebrew hymn obtains a special meaning. For the worshiping Church true goodness, peace, and righteousness have been achieved by one man whose liberating sacrifice has become the reason for the Church to be. That sacrifice is at the same time the service rendered in his behalf by the Church for the sake of humankind so that that which is the fullness of truth and righteousness in his life might be fulfilled in all. Christ contextualizes and personalizes all virtues, principles, and values by which Christians conduct their lives. The Kingdom is inseparable from Christ himself. Thus Christian worship glorifies him in whom the virtues, principles, and values of the Kingdom are alive. Through worship Christians envision the Kingdom concretely. Through worship the Church juxtaposes present realities to the pattern of actions by which God seeks to establish communion between himself and humankind. It evaluates those same realities by the values which sustain that communion and, in light of all this, brings what action is necessary into the world for the sake of the Kingdom. Indeed, Christian ethics is possible only because the Church prays the prayer of the Son of God himself, "Thy kingdom come, thy will be done on earth as it is in heaven."[49]

4

An Ethic of Marriage and Family

THIS IS AN ESSAY about normative Orthodox marriage and family.[1] It also is a critique of the actual state of these institutions as their distinctively Christian character is threatened within the American culture. For this reason, careful thought is given to empirical and social scientific studies which have addressed that which is referred to popularly as "the problem of the family." Such analysis provides a context within which to address a facet of the problem of the family largely overlooked by these writers. Instead of asking, as they often do, how and why the family has become a problem for society, I propose that the family has become a problem for the Church and that an Orthodox ethic of marriage and family must take account of this.

Furthermore, I invoke the Orthodox rites of matrimony which are rich in instruction about the moral meaning and purposes marriage and family ought to obtain in Christian living. These rites are vital to an Orthodox ethic of marriage and family.

THE PROBLEM OF THE FAMILY

Recently a team of social scientists headed by Robert Bellah published *Habits of the Heart*. The book is an inquiry into American mores and institutions based upon field studies of Americans selected from representative communities and groups within the society. Marriage is among the institutions discussed. The authors identify some troubling trends in this sphere of human relations, concluding their chapter "Love and Marriage" with this critical assessment of American marital and family relations.

The family is no longer an integral part of a larger moral ecology tying the individual to community, church, and nation. The family is the core of the private sphere, whose aim is not to link individuals to the private world but to avoid it as far as possible. In our commercial culture, consumerism, with its temptations, and television, with its examples, augment that tendency. Americans are seldom as selfish as the therapeutic culture urges them to be. But often the limit of their serious altruism is the family circle. Thus the tendency of our individualism to dispose "each citizen to isolate himself from the mass of his fellows and withdraw into the circle of family and friends," that so worried Tocqueville, indeed seems to be coming true.[2]

Others also have worried over the privatization of the American family and the reduction of its values and purposes to hedonistic and narrowly self-serving ones.[3] These studies conclude that that which ails the American family is symptomatic of cultural trends which are potentially destructive of viable community and American democratic values. In their book *The War Over the Family: Capturing the Middle Ground*, Brigitte and Peter Berger observe that in the past the American family transmitted to children the virtues "enjoined by . . . bourgeois-Protestant morality . . . : hard work, diligence, discipline, attention to detail, frugality, and the systematic (not sporadic) cultivation of willpower."[4] They argue that this type of family prepared "autonomous individuals imbued with an ethic of responsibility."[5] Such a family structure, they conclude, remains *"the necessary social context for the emergence of the autonomous individuals who are the empirical foundation of political democracy."*[6] The Bergers fear that this character of the American family now is endangered. They speak of the "hollowing out" of the old symbols and values once cultivated from within church and culture "by which the family was legitimated and sustained in the actual lives of individuals."[7] The result is that reasons for living out the norms of constancy, mutuality, fidelity, and indissolvability are no longer apparent and the actual behavior of families and the individuals within them contradict such symbols and norms. "The family ceases to be an objective given and becomes a locale where miscellaneous subjective motives intersect. Put differently, the family ceases to be an institution in the full sense of the word; instead it becomes a project of individuals, thus always susceptible to redefinition, reconstruction—and obviously termination."[8] As indicated in the sub-title of their book, the Bergers believe that the fate of American culture and the retention of this society's liberal democratic character is linked to the survival of the besieged bourgeois family. They are not com-forted by the emergent alternatives to the normative bourgeois family structure. Like the authors of *Habits of the Heart*, the Bergers con-tend that those alternatives are hyperindividualistic and narcissistic,[9] subversive of community, and a threat to political democracy.

MARRIAGE AS AN ECCLESIOLOGICAL PROBLEM

Now this concern expressed by serious social scientists over the fate of the family gives reason for pause. As the Bergers say, "The family has become a problem."[10] By a "problem" they mean that persons within the culture have observed that the family, as that primary in-stitution of society within which occur very important human relations, interactions, and socializing activities, seems to have "gone out of joint" or lost its "fit" and institutional role within the flow of society. And they certainly have got something here. Yet as I indicated at the start of this essay, I wish to redescribe the problem of the family. The real Orthodox critique of marriage and family does not come from these institutions' failure within the culture as described by the social scien-tists. Rather, the critique rests in their failure to be what they are called to be by the Church. The warrant for arguing this way is that Orthodox theology regards marriage as fundamentally an ecclesiological reality. The issue is not primarily sociological, *it is an ecclesial one*. Conse-quently, my first normative concern here is not with the recovery of stable or healthy family life for the sake of the good of American pluralism or democracy—though this might be a worthy goal. My aim is to retrieve from within the tradition of the Orthodox faith the norms, values, and virtues of marriage as a sacrament and as a calling to Chris-tian mission. The problem the family poses for the Orthodox Church (and other churches) parallels but is not the same as that identified by the Bergers in a societal context. Rather it is that many Christians lack a clear sense of why they are married and raising families as church members. Indeed, in so far as contemporary Christians even try to ex-plain a social purpose for marriage they tend to do so primarily in sociological or secular political terms. They have lost sight of the significance of Christian marriage and family as a form of human community in service to the Church and the Kingdom of God.

Orthodox are no exception. They frequently have joined in the chorus of those who insist that family is the backbone of society and that for this reason it needs to be strengthened or rehabilitated. In his *Contemporary Moral Issues*, a book intended for pastoral use and general lay Orthodox study, Stanley S. Harakas includes a section entitled "Under Attack: The Family." Harakas's treatment of the crisis of marriage and family is indicative of the confusion in perspective and language which typifies much of the Christian, certainly the Orthodox, discussion of this issue. Harakas observes, "The family is understood to be the 'building block' of society, [yet] the developments of our laws and the legal interpretations of existing laws during the past several years seem to be directed at its dissolution." He continues, "The basic institution of the family is the idea of life-long marital bonds between one man and one woman. Anything which attacks that firm foundation, cuts away at the roots of our society,"[11] Yet is, as Harakas suggests in these passages, the preservation of a stable social order the primary reason why Orthodox should strive to have good marriages and raise families? It does not seem wise, nor is it consistent with Orthodox ecclesiology, to make the question as to whether Christians are up to the task of saving the social order or guaranteeing its success by having good marriages and families the starting point for an Orthodox ethic of marriage.

Harakas does mention the primary reason why Christians should strive to have good marriages and families. Unfortunately, he subordinates this *ecclesiological* reason to sociological concerns. He rightly states that " the family . . . [is] under attack . . . [especially since] from our Orthodox Christian viewpoint, . . . the family is understood as a network of sacramental relationships: marriage, baptism, confirmation, family preparation and participation in Holy Communion, the forgiveness and reconciliation of the sacrament of Holy Confession [being regarded as] closely tied to the family."[12] Indeed, an Orthodox ethic of marriage and family originates in the sacramental nexus of marriage with the rest of the Christian *leitourgia*, identifying also the significance of marriage as vocation and mission. Christian marriage is, as St. Paul said, marriage "in the Lord" (Col 3:18,1 Cor. 7:39). As a sacrament, Christian marriage is supposed to expose nothing less in its own life than the character of God's reign.

Unfortunately Harakas does not develop the ethic in this fashion. Rather, he returns to the prejudice that the primary context of the ethic is the social order and its primary purpose the maintenance of that same order. The following passage typifies this misconstrual of the context and purpose of Orthodox marriage and family:

> The upshot of the situation is that with the family most of the important values of our nation are being lost. . . . When the family weakens, the whole society weakens. The faithfulness which makes monogamy possible is the same kind of attitude which makes the dependable worker, the dedicated professional and the committed soldier. . . .
>
> We need the restoration of family life. The old values must be recovered and put back into force. . . . It is needed now and in heavy application, if we are to save ourselves and this nation from decay and ultimate destruction.[13]

This analysis contains several serious cultural and theological miscalculations. First, Harakas's plea for a return to traditional values in marriage and family assumes that the values it evokes in the minds of Americans are consistent with Christian, specifically Orthodox, values. American society, however, is not a Christian order. It is a highly secularized, pluralistic society, informed by a variety of religious and philosophical traditions. Harakas's plea would make more sense were there presently a social consensus on the values of marriage and family sympathetic to Christian morality. But even this seems a doubtful proposition presently. It would be more acccurate to say that in the wake of an increasingly ritualized uncertainty about which of the conflicting standards of life circulating in the American bloodstream are or ought to be normative, Americans prize tolerance often to the degree of a near-dogmatic cultural relativism and adhere to a utilitarian and often hedonistic individualism at the expense of any authoritative institutional morality. Thus it is not at all evident to this writer that the laws and legal interpretations which Harakas judges to be subversive of traditional monogamous marriage—I assume he has in mind the state and federal statutes and court decisions over the past fifteen years which have liberalized divorce and abortion laws and undercut parental authority over children under the banner of children's rights— conflict with the beliefs and values held by most Americans. It might very will be that the legislatures and courts are reflecting prevalent and

emerging values of their constituencies. For example, the authors of
Habits of the Heart have noted that "Americans . . . are torn between
love as an expression of spontaneous inner freedom, a deeply personal,
but necessarily somewhat arbitrary, choice, and the image of love as
a firmly planted, permanent commitment, embodying obligations that
transcend the immediate feelings or wishes of the partners in a love
relationship."[14] The latter image is quite consistent with a biblical and
Orthodox understanding of marriage as a sacrament and permanent
relationship whose purposes are greater than those of the two who enter
into it. In such a conception of love there is room for relatives who
are not chosen but "inherited" and children who, while begotten, are
not "made to order." In the former attitude, however, one detects a
highly subjectivistic romanticism spilling over into narcissism. Romantic
love always has focused on choice and glorified the arbitrary element
of sexual passion. Narcissism concentrates even more exclusively on
love as the expression — even fulfillment — of individual freedom and
means to immediate personal gratification. Narcissism radically sub-
jectivizes love. It severs love from the values of long-term commitment
and expansive regard for others. If Christopher Lasch's analysis in *The
Culture of Narcissism* and *Haven in a Heartless World* is anywhere
near correct, then it is this latter view of love and marriage which is
threatening to replace the more traditional bourgeois ethos of American society.

Second, and following from this possible cultural miscalculation,
Harakas makes a mistake common to Constantinian Christianity past
and present, including its Orthodox, Roman Catholic, and Protestant
expressions, East and West. Just as Christians since the age of Constantine got used to thinking of social ethics as a special branch of the
politics of the empire or nation and not a teaching and practice applicable in the lives of all persons who confess a faith in Jesus Christ,
Harakas manages to depict the primary context of an Orthodox ethic
of marriage and family as that of nation (power) rather than the community of faith (evangelical witness). Third, and related, by tying so
closely his plea for a renewed Christian marital and family morality
to an appeal to the patriotism of Orthodox Christians, Harakas puts
at risk the transcendent judgment which Christian marriage and family
should bring to the social order. Lastly, Harakas places an unnecessary
responsibility for the survival or success of the society upon the family. Unwittingly, he leaves the impression that the Christian family is

able to mediate the whole fabric of Christian values directly to society. Harakas does not emphasize strongly enough the fact, otherwise acknowledged in Orthodox theology, that the strength of Christian marriage is not autonomous or self-explanatory. The meaning of marriage is comprehensible and its efficacy as an institution of Christian witness possible only in the context of a particular community, the Church, whose own significance for the world is not instrumental but sacramental and eschatological.

Perhaps because Orthodox carry the weighty baggage of a Byzantine past, they have not thought to separate out such sociological concerns as those expressed by Harakas, legitimate in their own right, from the ecclesiological issues raised by the New Testament writers and by the fathers of the Church. John Chrysostom's description of Christian marriage and family is a case in point. His interest in the Christian family was fundamentally *ecclesiological*. He wrote in his *Homilies on Ephesians*: "Seek the things which belong to God, and those that belong to man will follow soon enough. . . . If we thus regulate our own houses, we shall be also fit for the management of the Church. For indeed a house is a little Church. Thus it is possible for us by becoming good husbands and wives, to surpass all others."[15] According to Chrysostom, Christian marriage is in service to the Kingdom of God. It is a training ground for the proper maintenance of church polity. Similarly, Clement of Alexandria drew out the ecclesiological dimension of Christian marriage by referring the conjugal unit to Matthew 18:20. "But who are the two or three gathered in the name of Christ in whose midst the Lord is? Does he not by the 'three' mean husband, wife and child? For a wife is bound to her husband by God. . . . Through his Son, God is with those who are soberly married and have children."[16] St. Paul's teachings on marriage, especially in Ephesians 5, stress the ecclesial nature of the conjugal community.

There is no question that in the life of the Church, as Christians no longer experienced themselves as a persecuted minority but as the norm-setting community in society, the value of the household as a stabilizing force for the secular society achieved greater prominence in their thought. Chrysostom himself recognized this value and function and exhorted his listeners to take up their civic responsibility as households and members of such. But there is a distinct difference between even Chrysostom's exhortations about the social responsibilities of family and the instrumentalist fashion in which contemporary Christian spokespersons often make a defense of marriage and family in the name of democracy or the American Way. The call to social responsibility of a Chrysostom (or an Augustine in the West) issues rather unambiguously from the perspective of the life of faith within the community of God's people.

Christian theologians and churchpersons need to be much clearer than they have been about why the state of marriage and family, particularly among those who identify themselves as Christians, is of matter to the Church. This goal will not be served by immediately raising the cry that Christians need to have good marriages, raise children properly, and not divorce, because if they fail to do so the foundations of society will crumble. Christians who worry about the triumph of secularism or cultural relativism in American society would do well to direct their attention first to ecclesiology. There is nothing new in the observation that this world is fallen, however one puts it. The crucial issue for the Church always has been to maintain the well-being and good functioning of its own polity. This is an obligation owed to Christ who, for the world's sake, is married to the Church. Marriage, St. Paul tells us, is bound up with a profound mystery, that of "Christ and the church" (Eph. 5:32 RSV).[17] If marriage has become a problem for the Church—if, from within the very life of the Church, marriage looks as if it is "out of joint" with the Church's norms—then it is incumbent upon Christians to deal with this problem as a vital ecclesiological matter. The Church, which is the gathering of Christ's faithful, is itself "made up of kinds of conduct that congeal into relationships and then sub-societies of the inclusive society." As Theodore Mackin goes on to observe:

> Marriage is the most substantial of these sub-societies. If the Church does not understand marriage in its nature she does not understand her own. For the Church's nature is to be a society in which the belief, the trust and the caring love absolutely necessary for happiness are learned and carried on. But these are learned and carried on in families first and more than in any other relationship.[18]

When Christian marriages and families lose their sense of belonging and purpose within the community of faith, the Church is weakened; and lessened is its ability to witness to Christ and his Kingdom. This is a great loss to a world in need of redemption.

THE NATURE OF MARRIAGE

John L. Boojamra has observed that "even monasticism makes sense only in the context of family as a mutualistic paradigm and is justified only in the context of a fallen world, a world misshapen by sin and separation. In a world whose purpose was clear and undirectional . . . the family would be the norm as the Genesis account (Gen 2:18) makes clear."[19] This basic theological affirmation about human sociality provides the source for an Orthodox ethic of marriage and family. The second chapter of Genesis illumines marriage (and the family) as a natural institution of human life rooted in the creative activity of God. Through marriage and family God enables human beings to participate in his creative activity and redemptive purpose. There belongs a "natural" sacramentality to marriage even in its fallen condition. This sacramentality, like the image of God in humankind, was not lost entirely with the primal act of disobedience and deviance from the normativity of being human. Marriage need not be reinvented by Christians. Its character and intentionality, however, must change from selfishness, carnality, and possessiveness to being married "in the Lord." Marriage must be reconnected with the divine purpose through its full integration into the sacramental life of the Church, centered, as that life is, in the renewing and nurturing actions of baptism and eucharistic assembly.

Marriage, it is true, is grounded in the natural sociality of the human species. This sociality is unthinkable without rationality and the freedom of the will peculiar only to human beings. But marriage derives also from natural and biological necessity (e.g., sexual attraction, the lengthy dependency of human offspring). As Basil wrote in his *Long Rules*, we need one another because no one of us " is self-sufficient as regards corporeal necessities, . . . God, the Creator, decreed that we should require the help of one another, . . . so that we might associate with one another."[20] However, marital community, unlike the monasticism which Basil sought to found, is fixed in human sexuality. Human sexuality is no simple instinct for perpetuation of the species either. It is itself compounded of human freedom and *eros*. Sexual exchange is integral to marital love and the union which marriage signifies. In human life "love penetrates to the very root of instinct and 'changes even the substance of things' " [1 Tim. 2:15].[21] The Orthodox Church describes sexual intercourse as *synousia*, a term

which means consubstantiality. Husband and wife are joined together
as *one* in holy matrimony. They are an ecclesial entity, one flesh, one
body incorporate of two persons who in freedom and sexual love and
through their relationship to Christ image the triune life of the Godhead and express the great mystery of salvation in Christ's relationship to the Church.

Thus, according to Orthodox teaching, marriage is founded in
a sexual love which, when not deviant, aspires toward perfect union
with the other. This union is the primary good of marriage. "Indeed
from the beginning," wrote John Chrysostom in his homily on Ephesians 5:22–23, "God appears to have made a special provision for this
union; and discoursing of the twain as one."[22] This means that marriage is no mere agreement or contract between two individuals. As
Basil exhorts in the *Hexaemeron*,"May the bond of nature, may the
yoke imposed by the blessing make as one those who were divided."[23]
This union may be understood as an ethical imperative of marriage
even as, paradoxically, it is also a divine gift, a blessed bond. Those
who are married have an obligation to live a life together consistent
with this norm of union. And this is not an obligation that the spouses
owe only to themselves. It is an obligation owed to the Church which
marries them. Marriage is not, as some contemporary views have it—
e.g. the new "contractual marriages"—an utterly private, mutually
agreed-upon relationship regulated by certain claims of one spouse upon
the other and rights to certain goods or benefits which derive from
living together. Such views deny the norms of unitive and communicative love as well as expansive community in marriage and replace
them with a norm of separateness together for the sake of personal
psychic satisfaction, self-fulfillment, and autonomous activity. An Orthodox ethic of marriage denies all claims of normative so-called natural
egoism, self-interest, or autonomy. The first chapter of Genesis introduces the very first man and woman as one conjugal being, com-
plementaries of one complete humanity.[24] This is declared to be good.
Only with the intrusion of the demonic is this conjugal community
of being, this "Adam-Eve," divided into two who are alienated from
one another and their relationship disrupted by sexual shame and an-
tagonism. Nevertheless, conjugal union and communion become fundamental analogues and metaphors in the Old Testament prophets
for the alliance between God and his people and the restoration of
humanity's original relationship to God. In the New Testament mar-

riage is a symbol for the personal, pleromic communion of God's Kingdom (Rev. 19).

Such an ethic of marriage is not limited to natural law. For that nature known through empirical science, however much it might yet reveal about its origins and inner workings, is fallen and deranged. As Christos Yannaras has said, "[Christian] marriage draws its identity not [only] from the natural relationship, but from the relationship in the realm of the Kingdom."[25] It is important to the Orthodox understanding of marriage as sacrament that the Gospel of John—a reading from John 2 is included in all Eastern rites of matrimony—begins with the wedding at Cana where Christ transforms the water into wine, foreshadowing the Last Supper where wine becomes the blood of Christ.[26] In Orthodox theology natural marriage founded in *eros* is translated into an image of the Kingdom of God, a way of witnessing to the Cross and participating in the communion of saints. "If the monk converts eros by sublimation, conjugal love effects its transformation by opening onto divine love,"[27] writes Paul Evdokimov. Conjugal union, the primary good and norm of marriage, is achieved as natural *eros* transcends itself in a movement of reciprocal self-gift of one spouse to the other. *Eros* enters into the dynamic of *agape* which, as Basil described it, " 'seeketh not her own' . . . [and is not] concerned only with . . . private interests," but is in service "to many that they might be saved."[28] Conjugal union makes agapic love possible. Marriage (as well as Basilian cenobitic monasticism) is a way in which human beings are enabled through the grace of God to overcome their *unnatural* separateness and to perfect that mutual love for which humanity was created.

In the Armenian Rite of Holy Matrimony two prayers are said immediately following the crowning of the bride and groom and just before their enthronement. In these prayers the norms of conjugal union and communion are evoked and their relation to the other goods of marriage is established. The clear meaning in word, symbol, and action is that the union of two who were once separate serves a social—even public—end, has its being in an ecclesiological setting, and prepares persons for the eschatological advent of God's Kingdom. The first prayer reads in part:

> We beseech Thee, O Lord, bless this marriage, as Thou didst bless the marriage of the holy patriarchs, and keep them spotless in spiritual love and in one accord during their lives.

Bless, O Lord, and make their marriage fruitful with off-spring, if it be Thy will, so that they may inherit a life of virtuous behavior for the glory of Thy all-holy name. . . . And make them worthy to attain the undispoilable joys of the heavenly nuptials, together with all Thy saints.[29]

In this prayer spiritual love and a mutual accord are singled out as the highest goods of marriage. But conjugal union and communion are not ends in themselves. They are described as the basis for a virtuous life whose context is community with others. Children are a gift and blessing which will deepen and extend this agapic community. The family is a school for that personal and virtuous life which prepares persons of a character willing to do service to others and fit for the Kingdom of God. Through the gift of children God forges husband and wife into persons they never imagined they could be. Children teach their parents humility, tolerance, patience, and how to deal with their own limitations. But a child's presence is also the opportunity which God provides parents for discovering within themselves the capacity to love without measure, to forgive and redeem the lives of others.

The second prayer of the Armenian rite begins with a recollection of the marriages of "Abraham and Sarah, of Isaac and Rebecca, of Jacob and Rachel, of Joachim and Anna, of Zacharia and Elizabeth." These marriages the Lord blessed and by them God kept his covenant and promise. These righteous were forerunners of the Kingdom by whose example those being married not only are instructed in the virtues of the Kingdom but are assured of God's steadfast love and intention to make them also heirs of the Kingdom of God. "We pray Thee [bless] the crowning of these Thy servants into marriage, as Thou didst bless the crowns of Thy righteous. For Thou hast made these Thy servants to arrive at Thy sweet blessing and hast placed upon their heads a crown of precious gems." The wedding at Cana is then mentioned as proof that Christ brought marriage into the orbit of his priestly service to the Kingdom.[30] And this is followed by the invocation of those virtues appropriate to marriage. But rather than citing the Armenian rite it would do well to quote a portion of the Coptic prayer of crowning. It is a powerful example of the intimate link between ethics and eschatology within Eastern Christianity's vision of marriage.

Holy Lord, who crowned your holy ones with untainted crowns and joined things heavenly with things earthly in unity, . . . bless these crowns, which we have prepared, in order to place them on your servants; may they be for them the crown of glory and honour. Amen. The crown of blessing and health. Amen. The crown of rejoicing and good fortune. Amen. The crown of jubilation and gladness. Amen. The crown of virtue and justice. Amen. The crown of wisdom and understanding. Amen. Grant lavishly on your servants who wear them the angel of peace and the bond of love, deliver them from every wicked thought, and evil assaults of the devil; may your mercy be over them, hear the cry of their prayer; set fear of you in their hearts, rule their lives, so that they may live to a long old age, may they rejoice in gazing upon sons and daughters, and whoever they may bring to birth may they be useful in your one and only holy Catholic and Apostolic Church, confirmed through Orthodox faith.[31]

This prayer expresses a powerful sense of the presence of God in Christian marriage and of marriage being "in the Lord." The first blessings which God is asked to bestow upon the married couple are dispositions of joyfulness, gladness, and well-being. These blessings invoke the image of the great banquet of God's Kingdom and the wedding of the Lamb. Marital blessedness is a foretaste of that eschatological event mentioned in Revelation: " 'Alleluia! The Lord our God, sovereign over all, has entered on his reign! Exult and shout for joy and do him homage, for the wedding-day of the Lamb has come.' . . . 'Happy are those who are invited to the wedding supper of the Lamb!' " (Rev.19:7–9 NEB). Marital union is the very image of that last day when, as the author of Revelation states, "I saw a new heaven and a new earth, for the first heaven and the first earth had vanished, and there was no longer any sea. I saw the holy city, new Jerusalem, coming down out of heaven from God, made ready like a bride adorned for her husband. I heard a loud voice proclaiming from the throne: 'Now at last God has his dwelling among men! He will dwell among them and they will be his people, and God himself will be with them' " (Rev. 21:1–3 NEB).

There is no question in the Coptic prayer that the blessed bond of marriage is a matter of both personal and corporate destiny. "Is marriage an end in itself—or is it part of a nurture fitting us more ably for larger purposes?"[32] asks Donna Schaper. Her answer is the same as that given in the Coptic prayer and in similar prayers of the Eastern rites of matrimony. Marriage *is* a preparation for larger purposes. Were marriage an end in itself, the suffering and tragedy, the boredom and anxiety, the spitefulness and psychological laceration of self and others which it also often includes would be intolerable, a sure sign of the futility, meanness, and meaninglessness of life. However, "the church," as Schaper observes, "historically has understood marriage as a sacrament, an adventure into impossible commitment which has divine sanction, encouragement, and blessing."[33] Perhaps "impossible" is too strong a word. But certainly marriage is from the standpoint of Orthodox theology an eschatological commitment and venture in faith.

Orthodoxy understands sacramental marriage to be a gift bestowed upon the couple by God through the Church. The sacrament of marriage is a passage from natural and fallen marriage into the new order of Christ's Kingdom. Marriage which is of this order would be impossible indeed, were it dependent solely upon human will. But Christian marriage is itself a medicine which heals the ruptured relationship of men and women by uniting them through grace within the eschatological community of the Church. One great failure of the Western, particularly Roman Catholic, theology of marriage, is that it lost sight of this eschatological promise in marriage and the Christian vocation bestowed upon the couple by the Church. Roman Catholic moral theology went far toward reducing marriage to a legal contract, a guarantee of certain rights and privileges between the contracting individuals, which terminates in death. The language of the Coptic prayer insists upon the extralegal spiritual reality of marriage as communion with God and service to his Kingdom. God bestows upon the married couple the dispositions and virtues necessary for building up his Kingdom. And in all the Eastern rites children are counted as spiritual blessings which strengthen the little church of the family, increasing its service to God and extending it from one generation to the next until Christ's Second Coming. Lest there be any confusion about it, the force of this logic is not utilitarian; it is eschatological.

Again in contrast to earlier Roman Catholic moral theology, the Eastern theology could never define procreation as the primary purpose of marriage. Procreation obtains a fully human value only when it occurs within a relationship which is characterized by *unselfish and unitive love*. One of the oldest prayers of the Byzantine rite orders the goods of marriage with special clarity. "Unite them in one mind:

wed them in one flesh, granting unto them of the fruit of the body and the procreation of fair children."[34] And in typical Eastern fashion the Coptic prayer refers the blessing of children to the greater service to God to which all those married and "familied" "in the Lord" are called. "May they rejoice in gazing upon sons and daughters, and whoever they bring to birth may they be *useful in your one and only holy Catholic and Apostolic Church* [my emphasis], confirmed in Orthodox faith."[35]

In the Armenian rite these ecclesiological and eschatological themes are phrased in the imagery of the Psalms. The prayer following the crowning beseeches God to "plant them [the couple] as a fruitful tree, in the House of God, . . . living in righteousness, in purity, and godliness." Such marriage is the context in which children ought to be raised and a family nurtured whose activity becomes a service to the Church. The Armenian prayer speaks of children as a fruit or blessing of marriage and asks that the spouses "live to an age that they may see the children of their children and [that] they may be a people unto Thee and glorify Thy holy name, and bless the all-holy Trinity."[36] Thus the special insight of the Armenian prayer is not only that children are gifts of God but that covenanted marriage "in the Lord" is the sort of relationship most fit for the nurture of children who will become heirs to God's promise of salvation which he made to the patriarchs and revealed fully in Jesus Christ. Children are a gift and blessing, a human reflection within the union of husband and wife of the power and plenitude of the divine nature. And children who become "a people unto God" are an even greater gift and reward of marriage well lived. Christian marriage is the beginning of a "small church," the smallest and most important social unit of Christ's Body in the world. Marriage envisioned as sacrament, lived out in marital fidelity, gives hope for steadfast love and enduring communion even beyond the brokenness of all human relationships, including marriage itself. Christian family is a promise, enfleshed in the form of children, of a future filled with joy.

WHEN MARRIAGE FAILS

A Methodist colleague once remarked to me that he stood puzzled by persons who habitually describe Orthodox Christianity as an optimistic faith in a sort of counterpoint to Western Christian realism.

He realized that Orthodoxy holds very high expectations for human perfection, but that this perfectionism is also the source of a profound recognition in Orthodox theology and practice of human weakness, failure, and sin. Nowhere in Orthodox theology is my colleague's observation better exemplified than in the Orthodox attitude toward divorce and, particularly, remarriage. Yet even the argument I am prepared to make in this regard will not be readily apparent to all. For Orthodoxy does view marriage in high sacramental perspective. And this is likely to lead some observers to the conclusion that in this area of theology, as in others, Orthodoxy lacks sufficient realism and appreciation for the persistence of sin. After all, such a sacramentalism risks overdrawing the analogy of marriage with the Church and too quickly speaking of marriage as if it already has been transfigured into the new relationships of the Kingdom. Yet such critics are still left with the notable fact that the Orthodox Church will accept divorce (under limited reasons) and provides for remarriage in its canons and rituals.[37]

In his insightful book on marriage, *Blessed Be the Bond,* William J. Everett notes this phenomenon and tries out an explanation for it. He writes: "Eastern Orthodox theology seems to have a 'two levels' approach [to marriage] in which the religious reality exists as a heavenly permanence but the equally valid human and natural experience of marriage and divorce goes its own way without impugning the sacramental realities. This verges on an effort to hold them paradoxically together."[38] This interpretation suggests a nature/grace — even ideal/real — dichotomy in Orthodox theology which simply does not exist. The Orthodox approach to marriage is not "two-leveled." There is no such dualism in it. It does not propose such a thing as a natural marriage which is distinguished from a heavenly religious reality of marriage. There may be paradox, certainly tension, between the fallen institution of marriage and its norms of unitive, communicative, and self-sacrificial love. Yet even this tension is not between "two marriages," one spiritual and the other temporal. If the breakdown and dissolution of marriage does not ultimately impugn its sacramentality, this is because God has shown himself as willing to forgive marital failure and even make out of such failure persons fit for his Kingdom.

Nevertheless, one could ask, what, according to Orthodox teaching, precisely are the sacramental realities of marriage and where are they located? I have alluded to this question earlier in the essay, having said that this sacramental reality is made of the very stuff of so-called natural marriage.[39] The Orthodox use of this term natural is not in contradistinction to grace. Marriage is the primal human community. As such it is natural in the same way that human nature is. The two, man and woman were created as *one*. Humanity in its *two-in-oneness* is created *grace-in-natured*. Grace is not something external to human nature. It is a God-bestowed dynamism, an energy for growth toward perfection (*theosis*). This is how Orthodox tradition has understood the biblical concept of humanity being created in the image and likeness of God (Gen. 1:26). In some real sense the sacramental realities of marriage are located in "every marriage of persons who are in communion with God."[40] In the Byzantine rite, during a prayer of crowning, the priest asks that God bless this marriage as he has the marriages of Abraham and Sarah, Isaac and Rebecca, Jacob and Rachel, Joseph and Aseneth, Moses and Zipporah, Joachim and Anna, and Zechariah and Elizabeth.[41] The first marriage of Adam and Eve was blessed with the presence of God. When the primordial pair sinned, that presence was withdrawn. However, God did not abandon humankind. The marriages mentioned in the Byzantine rite were marriages which became "a locus and vehicle of the holy presence of the living God"[42] and were in that sense truly sacramental. Christ does not change marriage suddenly from natural to sacramental; he simply reveals marriage in its true essence. From this time on marriage is called out by Christ to participate in the "newness of life" (Rom. 6:4 RSV).

Everett's quandary, however, is over a church which marries people for eternity in the most emphatic of ways and yet accepts divorce — and what is more — will remarry persons, not only once but twice. The simple explanation for this is that the Eastern churches have never viewed marriage as a legal contract given the character of indissolubility by the Church. Orthodox faith understands marriage as a blessed union for eternity *in via* along with the whole Church toward redemption and perfection. But this gift of grace bestowed upon the couple is not magical or compelling to the extent of denying free will. It may be that the couple are unable (or unwilling) to accept and "use" that grace as seal of the permanent bond which God intends for all marriages.[43] Orthodox theology includes in its view toward marriage the human realities mentioned by the Roman Catholic theologian Leonard Boff. Boff writes: "Marriage as a sacramental reality shares in the ambiguity common to every condition of fallen humanity; it is love, but also domination; it is self-sacrifice, but also a power structure; it is

giving, but egoism at the same time." Marriage not only brings together
two persons, it is constructed out of the material of their personal
histories, material which inevitably is burdened with psychological fail-
ings and deep, often open and yet festering, spiritual wounds inflicted
from earliest childhood through adulthood. "Because of this," Boff
continues, "marriage, more than the other sacraments, is under the
aegis of the cross of Christ."[44]

In the Armenian Rite of Matrimony — indeed unique to it among
the Eastern rites of matrimony — the best man stands as a brother-in-
the-cross. During the crowning ceremony he holds a cross over the heads
of the bride and groom. The meaning of this action is clarified in the
closing prayer of the rite: "Guard us O Christ, under the shadow of
Thine holy and precious Cross in peace. Deliver us from enemies visible and invisible, make us worthy to give thanks to Thee and to glorify
Thee with the Father and the Holy Spirit, now and forever and unto
the ages of ages. Amen."[45] In these actions and words the Armenian
Church recognizes that the destructive power of sin threatens all marriages, while also declaring that Christ has provided a way for marriage to overcome this threat. A church with such a ritual and prayer
is bound to recognize the possibility that some marriages will fail.

Not all marriages are entered into by persons who are compatible, willing, or able to make the blessing fructify. In the case of some
marriages the ends of marriage are hopelessly frustrated. Under such
circumstance the marriage is dissolved; the two, as it were, have "died"
to one another. The Church can admit this and allow divorce and even
remarriage. Since marriage in the Orthodox Church is not defined
primarily in legal contractual terms — consent alone does not make marriage, nor does any defect in consent annul it — the fundamental issue
is not how one goes about breaking or voiding a contract but rather
how the Church can provide other ways for persons for whom marriage has failed to continue the journey toward God's Kingdom.[46] The
crucial problem which marital failure raises, therefore, is not juridical.
It is soteriological. How can the salvation of the lives of those who
have failed in marriage be yet secured? Orthodox Christianity has not
encouraged remarriage but it has found an answer to this question in
a second rite for remarriage. The rite is sufficiently penitential in
character to distinguish it from the normative marriage rite, yet also
sacramental and consistent with the Orthodox norm of marital permanence even as it recognizes that the norm has been broken.

The Byzantine Order of Second Marriage contains two rather lengthy penitential prayers. Interestingly, these prayers replace the prayer of betrothal of the first rite. Perhaps no great significance need be attached to this substitution. But, for the purpose of exposing the ethical content of these rites, it is interesting to note which values and virtues of Christian living are emphasized in them respectively. In the betrothal prayer of the rings *fidelity* is the virtue emphasized. The prayer reads in part:

> O Lord our God, who didst accompany the servant of the patriarch Abraham into Mesopotamia, when he was sent to espouse a wife for his lord Isaac; and who, by means of the drawing of the water, didst reveal unto him that he should betroth Rebecca: Do thou, the same Lord, bless also the betrothal of these servants, N. and N., and confirm the word which they have spoken. . . . O Lord our God, who hast sent forth thy truth upon thine inheritance, and thy covenant unto thy servants our fathers, even thine elect, from generation to generation: Look thou upon thy servant, N., and upon thy handmaid, N., and establish and make stable their betrothal, and in oneness of mind, in truth and love. For thou, O Lord, hast declared that a pledge should be given and confirmed in all things. By a ring was power given unto Joseph in Egypt; by a ring was Daniel glorified in the land of Babylon; by a ring was the uprightness of Tamar revealed; by a ring did our heavenly Father show forth his bounty upon his Son; for he saith: Put a ring on his hand, and bring hither the fatted calf, and kill it, and eat, and make merry. By thine own right hand, O Lord, didst thou arm Moses in the Red Sea; by the word of thy truth were the heavens established, and the foundations of the earth were made firm; and the right hands of thy servants shall be blessed also by thy mighty word, and by thine upraised arm. Wherefore, O Lord, do thou now bless this putting-on of rings with thy heavenly benediction; And let thine Angel go before them all the days of their life.[47]

God has been *faithful* to his chosen ones throughout all his creative and redemptive activities. The rings which the couple exchange are symbols of that history and the assurance it brings that he will be powerfully present in their marriage as well. And it is because God in his character is faithful toward those whom he loves that the two who are betrothed can and must also carry that disposition of fidelity toward one another in their marriage.

The penitential prayers of the Order of Second Marriage reveal God as *forgiving* and *compassionate* even toward those who have fallen far short of his expectations of human character and behavior. The first prayer begins:

> O Master, Lord our God, who showest pity upon all men, and whose providence is over all thy works; who knowest the secrets of man, and understandest all men: Purge away our sins, and forgive the transgressions of thy servants, calling them to repentance, granting them remission of their iniquities, purification of their sin, and pardon of their errors, whether voluntary or involuntary. O thou who knowest the frailty of man's nature, in that thou art his Maker and Creator; who didst pardon Rahab the harlot, and accept the contrition of the Publican; remember not the sins of our ignorance from our youth. . . . For thou only art righteous, sinless, holy, plenteous in mercy, of great compassion, and repentest thee of the evils of men.[48]

The Church can beseech confidently such a merciful, forgiving, and compassionate God—one who, in the history of his people, has shown that these qualities belong to his character—to bless a second marriage of persons who were unable to go on living alone either after the death of a spouse or after the termination of a previous marriage due to divorce. The prayer continues:

> Do thou, O Master, who has brought together in wedlock thy servants, N. and N., unite them to one another in love; vouchsafe unto them the contrition of the Publican, the tears of the Harlot, the confession of the Thief; that, repenting with their whole heart, and doing thy commandments in peace and oneness of mind, they may be deemed worthy also of thy heavenly kingdom.[49]

The second prayer of this rite focuses on Christ himself who, though he was sinless, "wast lifted up on the precious and life-giving cross, and didst thereby destroy the handwriting against us."[50] God in the flesh has shown that his mercy and forgiveness are without measure. He became the remedy for our sin. And the clear implication in this prayer is that this second marriage likewise can serve as a remedy for sin. As mentioned above, the sacrament of marriage not only takes the good material of natural marriage and makes it the matter of the Kingdom of God; it also is medicine for the broken condition of a fallen humanity.[51] In the Byzantine Rite of Holy Matrimony the Church states that God thought "it is not good for man to be alone on the earth."[52] In the Order of Second Marriage, it can pray with equal conviction: "Cleanse thou the iniquities of thy servants; because they, being unable to bear the heat and burden of the day, and the hot desires of the flesh, are now entering into the bond of second marriage, as thou didst render lawful by thy chosen vessel, the Apostle Paul, saying for the sake of us humble sinners, It is better to marry in the Lord than to burn."[53] Clearly such a second marriage does not on its own merit meet the Church's norm, given to it by Christ, for permanence and perfect fidelity in marriage. It would be better for those who by death or divorce have been separated from their spouses to witness to that norm by remaining single afterwards. But the Church, having the example of Christ to emulate, is allowed to condescend to human weakness and assist brothers and sisters, whatever their mistakes or failing, toward salvation. This rite sets forth *contrition, humility, compassion* and *forgiveness* as virtues and dispositions which ought to characterize the relations of Christians toward one another. Indeed, failed marriages and second marriages are a lesson to all persons married or "familied" "in the Lord" about the universal frailty of human nature and the sin which attaches to everyone. In this regard Paul Ramsey astutely has observed that "interlaced in these prayers [of the Order of Second Marriage] are a general confession that we are all sinners with *specific* confession connected with the undertaking of second marriage."[54] Thus the apparent harshness of this rite, with its allusions to "Rahab the harlot" and the "Publican," is another example of the great tension the Church itself experiences between the hope of human perfection represented in the biblical figures and saints whose names are invoked in the Rite of Holy Matrimony and the initial, but not necessarily final, failure to achieve that end represented by the biblical figures mentioned in the several penitential prayers of the Order of Second Marriage. An institution which is already under the aegis of the Cross becomes under the conditions of second marriage a special reminder to married and single people alike that, as Christ humbly and compassionately reconciles himself with sinners and them with him, they too in contrite recognition that no one is sinless must act forgivingly and with compassion toward one another in order that their marriages and ministries bear the fruit of the Kingdom.[55]

THE ASCETICAL MEANING OF MARRIAGE

Unlike the Roman Catholic Church, the Orthodox Church has not established formally a hierarchy of Christian life in which celibacy is designated a higher state of Christian living than marriage. In fact, married life and the raising of a family has been described at times within the Orthodox tradition as a more difficult and courageous vocation than that of celibacy.[56] The Russian dissident priest Dmitri Dudko has stated in one of his famous dialogues with the faithful, translated in the West under the title *Our Hope,* "So build your domestic church—the family—together. This is the great ascetic feat of Christianity."[57] The tradition supports this affirmation of the high ethical value of Christian marriage. Clement of Alexandria wrote in book 7 of the *Stromateis*:

> And true manhood is shown not in the choice of a celibate life; on the contrary the prize in the contest of men is won by him who has trained himself by the discharge of the duties of husband and father and by the supervision of a household, regardless of pleasure and pain—by him, I say, who in the midst of his solicitude for his family shows himself inseparable from the love of God and rises superior to every temptation which assails him through children and wife and servants and possessions. On the other hand he who has no family is in most respects untried. In any case, as he takes thought only for himself, he is inferior to one who falls short of him as regards his own salvation, but who has the advantage in the conduct of life, in as much as he actually preserves a faint image of the true providence.[58]

As Clement emphasized the ascetical struggle which is a component of the married state and the divine similitude which a husband obtains through selfless giving to wife and children, so John Chrysostom made it clear in his homily 7 on Hebrews that the highest Christian virtues are not the exclusive reserve of monks. People who are married are called by Christ to a life no less virtuous than that of those who have chosen a monastic life. Addressing married persons who would make excuses for their behavior by invoking their married state, Chrysostom said: "And if these beatitudes were spoken to solitaries only, and the secular person cannot fulfill them, yet He [Christ] permitted marriage, then He has destroyed all men. For if it be not possible, with marriage, to perform the duties of solitaries, all things have perished and are destroyed, and the functions of virtues are shut up in a strait." Chrysostom's argument is not just about the morality of Christians, married or celibate, either. It is an argument which dismisses all notions that the institution of marriage is inferior in God's plan of salvation or fails in its nature to serve his purpose. "And if persons have been hindered by marriage state, let them know that marriage is not the hindrance, but their purpose which made an ill use of marriage. Since it is not wine which makes drunkenness, but the evil purpose, and the using it beyond due measure. Use marriage with moderation, and thou shalt be first in the kingdom."[59]

Nowhere in Orthodox tradition or practice is the high ascetical value and significance of marriage more strongly affirmed than in the central action of the rite of matrimony, the Service of Crowning. The crowns (or garlands) placed on the heads of the bride and groom have been understood in the Pauline sense as a proleptic sign of the victory of life over death, as Christians are compared to athletes who run a race under a strict discipline (I Cor. 9:24–25). The Eastern rites of matrimony identify the highest virtue of this discipline as chastity. God is asked in an opening prayer of the Service of Crowning in the Byzantine rite to "bless this marriage, as he blessed that in Cana of Galilee: That he will grant unto them [the bride and groom] chastity, and of the fruit of the womb as is expedient [of good benefit] for them: That he will make them glad with the sight of sons and daughters."[60] Marital chastity obviously does not exclude sexual love. This is evident from the link between chastity and the blessing of children in the Byzantine prayer. Chastity purifies and transforms human love into the abundance, richness, pleromic communion, and joy of the Kingdom, just as Christ transformed the water into wine for the wedding banquet. True marriage requires giving up the sinful desire to possess, to control, and to use others for self-gratification or self-glorification. But conjugal chastity is not so limited or negative as continence. It is not primarily a remedy for sin or concupiscence as continence is in much of medieval Western moral theology. Conjugal chastity is understood in the Orthodox theology of marriage as an *askesis* of the spirit which elevates our nature and transforms the life together of husband and wife into a true communion. In the Armenian rite the prayer of crowning asks God to unite the couple "in the spirit of meekness, loving one another with modest behaviour, pure spirit, without giving cause for shame, without impudence always ready for good works."[61] Conjugal chastity is compared in the Byzantine rite to the virginal purity of Mary in her perfect obedience to God and to the holiness of the Church as the Bride of Christ.

William Faulkner captured this ascetical meaning of marriage with a striking metaphor in *Go Down Moses*. In the story "The Bear," Isaac McCaslin, after having come of age, renounces his inheritance of the Macaslin plantation and gives it up entirely to his cousin Macaslin Edmunds. Isaac's renunciation does not derive from a hatred of the land, of what grows on it, or of its inhabitants animal and human. Rather, he cannot accept the legacy of slavery left by his grandfather and his father who used human beings and nature to aggrandize themselves. Isaac concludes that the only way to "enjoy"the inheritance is to relinquish it, that it might revert back to being held in that "communal anonymity of brotherhood."[62]

With this background Faulkner tells the story of Isaac's marriage to the daughter of his partner in carpentry—the trade Isaac takes up after renouncing his inheritance. As with every marriage, theirs bore the possibility of becoming that yearned-for ideal union in love and the beginning of a new creation: "They were married and it was the new country, his heritage too as it was the heritage of all, out of the earth, beyond the earth's long chronicle, his too because each must share with another in order to come into it, and in the sharing they become one."[63] But on their wedding night she, who had already learned of the inheritance, linked her love for him with her desire to possess the land. "And he saw her face then, just before she spoke: 'Sit down': the two of them sitting on the bed's edge, not even touching yet, her face strained and terrible, her voice passionate and expiring whisper of immeasurable promise: 'I love you. You know I love you. When are we going to move?' " With her body and her love she sought to exact from Isaac the promise that he would reclaim the inheritance and move her to it. " 'No,' he said. . . . 'No, I tell you, I won't. I cant. Never:' . . . and still the steady and invincible hand

and he said Yes and thought, *She is lost. She was born lost. We were all born lost.*"[64]

Faulkner's account of Isaac's marriage and his relationship to the land is a parable of the ascetical nature of marriage and thus the Kingdom and how it is won or lost. On that wedding night, when his wife undressed with the intention of using her naked body and their shared love to obtain possession of the plantation, lost was the promise of marriage as a chaste union of two. Lost also was a future filled with the joy of children who might one day inherit—as Sam Fathers, the old Indian chief (half Negro, half Chickasaw) had said one could—the land, not as property or possession but as gift and freedom to learn "humility and pride" ("pity and tolerance and forebearance and fidelity and love of children") through suffering, sacrifice, and endurance.[65] For, while marriage might include possessions, it is not *about* possessing. If the love of one spouse for the other is prefaced by the will or desire to possess others (spouse and children) or things (house, belongings, land), there can be no true marital union.

On their wedding night Isaac "wanted to see her naked because he loved her and he wanted her but after that [after she forcibly drew him into their bed to get what *she* wanted] he never mentioned it again, even turning his face when she put the nightgown on over her dress to undress at night and putting the dress on over the gown to remove it in the morning and she would not let him get into bed beside her until the lamp was out."[66] And in time, when "he stopped thinking and even saying Yes [that he would reclaim the plantation], . . . with a movement one time more old than man she turned and freed herself and on their wedding night she had cried and he thought she was crying now at first, into the tossed wadded pillow, the voice coming from somewhere between the pillow and the cachinnation: 'And that's all. That's all from me. If this don't get you that son you talk about it won't be mine:' lying on her side, her back to the empty rented room laughing and laughing."[67] Thus, he "lost her, ay, lost her even though he had lost her in the rented cubicle before he and his clever dipsomaniac partner had finished the house for them to move into it; but lost her because she loved him. But women hope for so much. They never live too long to still believe that anything within the scope of their passionate wanting is likewise within the range of their passionate hope."[68] True, his wife loved him, but with a love not purified by chastity's fire nor elevated to the greater comprehension of the promise in their marriage because it belonged to the land and not the land to it.

Yet in the solitary life which Isaac chose after his wife's death, Isaac retained the true vision of marriage as dispossession and communion, of chaste love, of the promise of creation and re-creation. We hear of that vision in "Delta Autumn" through a dream the old man Isaac had on one of his last hunts. Like the monk who is married to the Church, Isaac, the hunter, was in truth and forever married to the wilderness land which he loved yet sought not to possess.

> He could almost see it, tremendous, primeval, looming, musing downward upon this puny evanescent clutter of human sojourn. . . . Because it was his land, although he had never owned a foot of it. He had never wanted to, not even after he saw its ultimate doom, watching it retreat year by year before the onslaught of axe and saw and log-lines and then the dynamite and tractor plows, because it belonged to man. It belonged to all; they had to use it well, humbly with pride. Then suddenly he knew why he had never wanted to own any of it. . . . Because there was just exactly enough of it. *He seemed to see the two of them — himself and the wilderness — coevals* [my emphasis], his own span as a hunter, a woodsman, not contemporary with his first breath but transmitted to him, assumed by him gladly, humbly, with joy and pride, from that old Major de Spain and old Sam Fathers who taught him to hunt, the two spans running out together, not toward oblivion, nothingness, but into a dimension free of both time and space where once more the untreed land warped and wrung to mathematical squares of rank cotton for the frantic old-world people to turn into shells to shoot at one another, would find ample room for both — the names, the faces of the old men he had known and loved and for a little while outlived, moving again among the shade of tall unaxed trees and sightless brakes where the wild strong immortal game ran forever before the tireless belling mortal hounds, falling and rising phoenix-like to the soundless gun.[69]

In the Byzantine rite of matrimony, after the couple has drunk from the common cup and as they are led three times around the lectern in symbolic dance and celebration of their union and journey together for eternity in God's presence, the choir sings several hymns. They express in terse biblical language and by allusion to the whole story of salvation the Orthodox vision of marriage.

> Rejoice, O Isaiah! A Virgin is with child, and shall bear a Son, Emmanuel, both God and man; and Orient is his name; whom magnifying we call the Virgin blessed.
> O Holy martyrs, who fought the good fight and have received your crowns: Entreat ye the Lord that he will have mercy on your souls.
> Glory to thee, O Christ-God, the Apostles' boast, the Martyrs' joy, whose preaching was the consubstantial Trinity.[70]

Through the invocation of the Virgin and her son, Emmanuel, the first stanza (or hymn) recalls the whole theme of the New Creation — celebrated with such magnificent beauty on the Orthodox Feast of Epiphany. Conjugal love is like the virginal purity of Mary, who in her perfect obedience to God gave birth to the "first-born of all creation, . . . the first-born from the dead" (Col. 1:15-18 RSV). The second stanza mentions the holy martyrs, who, by their unselfish witness to the promise of salvation in Jesus Christ, confirmed that their own deaths were a birth into the new life of the Kingdom. The last stanza praises Christ, in whom the faith of all believers rests and by whom also the joy of communion in God is insured.

When natural marriage is elevated to a sacrament of the Church, it becomes a witness to the new creation in Christ. In a sinful world, such a witness inevitably requires *self*-sacrifice, that *self* understood as the ego which in spite of its pretensions to autonomy is captive to sin and death. Marriage is a form of martyrdom. The possessive self-serving ego is put to death and a new self is born, free and in mutual accord and in service to others. Marriage is an image and a proleptic experience of the New Creation in which *eros*, purified by chastity and freed from lust, is sublimated into a selfless desire and active concern for the well-being of the other (i.e., compassion). Likewise, self-sacrifice is translated into a free communion unconstrained by sin or natural necessity. Marriage is made an entrance into the Kingdom by crucifixion (*askesis*). Indicative of this, ancient Christian wedding rings were cast "with two profiles united by a cross."[71] With like significance, in the Byzantine rite of matrimony, before the bride and groom drink from the common cup and dance the dance of Isaiah, they must wear the crowns of martyrdom. Finally a Christian marriage testifies to the fact that the "newness of life" (Rom. 6:4 RSV) is not an individualistic pursuit of salvation. There is an ancient usage no longer followed in the Armenian and Syrian rites for the couple to exchange baptismal crosses.[72] This is a powerful symbol of the fact that the bride and groom surrender their destinies to one another and both together to Christ and the Church. Christian marriage is marriage "in the Lord" because the two who are wed *already* have been united with Christ through baptism. Through baptism they have become imitators and followers of Christ. This priestly vocation is one which baptized Christians bring to marriage. Marriage does not confer it upon them. However, marriage does expand the scope of that priestly service. Marriage commences a relationship and provides an institutional framework in which the individual witness of the two can become a mutual service and take on a social and public dimension prefiguring the Kingdom. Thus, the full Christian meaning of marriage is comprehensible only when a marriage is lived within the context of the whole life of the Church. Like monastic community, marriage is an *institution* with a purpose which transcends the personal goals or purposes of those who enter into it. It is an upbuilding of the Church in service to the Kingdom. Marriage is not only something which happens to the individuals who are wed and the children which they bear by the grace of God. Marriage is something which happens in and to the whole Church.

MARRIAGE AS CHRISTIAN VOCATION

"To have a vocation," writes William J. Everett, "is to have a calling. It is to be called out by a power and purpose beyond ourselves. In this calling out from life-as-usual we find immediate evidence of vocation's tension with nature. It is thrust toward that which is not yet. It is a lure toward the unique new life God intends for us. It is anchored in God's redemptive purpose."[73] Marriage, as we have seen, obtains such a significance in Orthodox liturgy and theology.

Yet social scientists have been telling us for some years now that religious and nonreligious married people alike are losing any sure sense beyond personal attraction and desire for why they are married, and that if they are able to articulate any purposes at all for family these usually are restricted to privatized explanations of it as psychological and physical retreat from the public world of work and politics. This is not a way of saying that Americans are failing to take marriage and family seriously. If anything they take it too seriously, overloading the nuclear family with too great a responsibility for providing persons with a sense of identity and significance in life. The socializing and humanizing functions once shared by church, extended family, local community, ethnic associations, trade unions, schools, and the like, have increasingly fallen upon the nuclear family, as these other institutions and forms of human association have been weakened by a variety of social and economic forces and been replaced by highly rationalized, big and impersonal institutions. Under this moral weight marriage cracks, and the family is incinerated from within by the intense psychological demands placed upon it.

The argument being waged here is not against the family as a place of intimacy and care. For the privatization of the family and the increasing expectations of it as a place of retreat and emotional self-indulgence must not be confused with the intimacy, warmth, and personal nurture appropriate to Christian marriage and family. The privatistic and therapeutic views of marriage and family which have begun to predominate in our society are a grave threat to any Christian or Orthodox belief in marriage as a vocation. If vocation means a "calling out," the view of marriage as "haven from a hostile (or at least indifferent) world" is quite the opposite. This view issues a call to retreat from association with and service to others and purposes which transcend the internal relations, individual ambitions, pleasures, or recreations of family members. The ethical implications of intimacy in Christian marriage and family must be distinguished from the highly individualistic connotations given to privacy in common American currency and law. Privacy has gotten defined as an objective sphere apart from the public. Intimacy connotes no such division of life into two spheres. Rather, it establishes a continuity of human community and purposive activity from the smallest units of human intercourse to the largest. Intimacy generates a supportive network of personal relations and interactions, security, moral instruction, and ritual enactment and celebration of personal, family, and community past. This provides persons with the enabling, necessary sense of identity, worth, and trust to extend themselves, their purposes and activities, into the larger world. Intimacy is expansive, beginning in the primal community of the family and reaching out into the larger spheres of human activity and associa-

tion. Privatism is reflexive, withdrawing from a world in which it cannot find value. Whereas familial intimacy reflects a radical trust in the
goodness and purposiveness of the world, the cult of privacy demon-
strates a gnostic distrust of the world outside of the self. Privacy becomes
the clarion justification for abortion in our society. Intimacy values
human presence and welcomes unknown others into a common world.
The ideology of privacy undercuts all sense of vocation. Intimate life
builds it up.

I have spoken of trust and intimacy as basic requirements of marriage and family understood as vocation. Yet there are indications that
people in our society find it increasingly difficult to trust and experience
intimacy. There seems to be no public setting for such things. The
drive to transform marriage and family into an utterly secluded sphere
of emotional and psychological well-being actually originates from a
frustrated desire to experience trust and intimacy. Marriage and the
family are sought as a sacrosanct enclave for such experience. But in
such a pursuit people make the family an idol. In it they invest their
hope for escape and protection from the threatening, terrifying, bor-
ing time of the "real" world. John Updike portrays this phenomenon
with startling trenchancy in the novel *Couples*. The couples are upwardly mobile suburban people who, drawn out of their otherwise
isolated marriages, huddle together for party, sport, and sex and become, in the words of one of the husbands, "a church," "a magic circle of heads to keep the night out." Freddy Thorner is "frightened
if he doesn't see . . . [the couples] over a weekend." The response of
another of the husbands, Piet Hanema, to this revelation of Freddy's
feelings about the couples is: "That's because he doesn't go to a real
church."[74] Piet attends a "real church." But his evaluation of Freddy's
attribution of churchlike status to the couples is not based in a sure
conviction that the "real church" shelters him any better from the meaninglessness and death which lurk in the world of work and politics and
even now in the recesses of his own bedroom. Certainly neither the
venerable old Congregational church which Piet attends nor the other
churches in Tarbox seem capable of calling the couples back from their
self-idolatry and descent into a new paganism. Perhaps symbolic of
this impotence of the "old religion" to save the inhabitants of Tarbox
from their demonism, the Congregational church burns down at the
end of the story. "The old church proved not only badly gutted but
structurally unsound: a miracle it had not collapsed of itself a decade

ago."[75] In the course of the novel, the couples proceed headlong into a demonic inversion of marriage's values. Unable to find intimacy within their own marriages, the spouses turn to adultery. Deception replaces marital trust and fidelity. Pleasure-seeking uproots mutual love. At the end of the novel, the couples, having devoured each other and dismembered themselves, regroup in different configurations — new "churches" — to continue their pursuit of an always illusive happiness.

The Orthodox Church has failed to transmit satisfactorily the Christian moral significance of marriage to those it weds. Orthodox faithful, no less than their Protestant and Roman Catholic counterparts, if they carry this vision of marriage, do so alongside utterly contradictory, prevalent, and powerfully persuasive secular interpretations of marriage as a convenient or felicitous arrangement for the pursuit of "individual preference, judgment, decision, choice and pleasure."[76] Marriage in our modern secularistic culture is rapidly being transformed from a condominium whose authority derives from purposes which transcend the wishes, needs, interests, or desires of its individual members into an arbitrary, highly subjectivistic, and privatized arrangement for autoerotic satisfaction and therapeutic recreation. "We live in a culture of autoeroticism," writes Christos Yannaras, "a hysteria of erotic thirst beginning and ending with ego, the individual; with the nullification of any relationship and ignorance of the truth of man as a person [as a relational being whose freedom is grounded in a communion of being which transcends self]. Inevitably marriage too is distorted into a rationalistic contract serving utilitarian ends, or preserved as mutual attraction founded on natural eroticism, for ephemeral individual satisfaction."[77]

The authors of *Habits of the Heart* report the following findings based upon their interviews of married couples. These corroborate Yannaras's evaluation:

> On the whole, even the most secure, happily married of our respondents had difficulty when they sought a language in which to articulate their reasons for commitments that went beyond the self. These confusions were particularly clear when they discussed problems of sacrifice and obligation. While they wanted to maintain enduring relationships, they resisted the notion that such relationships might involve obligations that went beyond the partners. Instead they insisted on the "obligation" to communicate

> one's wishes and feelings honestly and attempt to deal with problems in the relationship. They had few ideas of the substantive obligations partners in a relationship might develop [i.e. goals and purposes as a conjugal community made up of two or more and obligations which that community might have to others outside itself and to other institutions or to society]. . . .
>
> Similarly, . . . many . . . were uncomfortable with the idea [of sacrifice]. It was not that they were unwilling to make compromises or sacrifices for their spouses, but they were troubled by the idea of self-denial the term"sacrifice" implied. If you really wanted to do something for the person you loved, they said, it would not be sacrifice. Since the only measure of the good is what is good for the self, something that is really a burden to the self cannot be part of love. Rather, if one is in touch with one's true feeling, one will do something for one's beloved only if one really wants to, and then, by definition, it cannot be a sacrifice.[78]

Alexander Schmemann once observed: "The real sin of marriage today is not adultery or lack of 'adjustment' or 'mental cruelty.' It is the idolization of the family itself, the refusal to understand marriage as directed toward the Kingdom of God. . . . It is not lack of respect for the family that breaks the modern family so easily, making divorce its almost natural shadow. It is the identification of marriage with happiness and the refusal to accept the cross in it."[79] Indeed, the findings of the authors of *Habits of the Heart* indicate that the concepts of sin and salvation rooted in the biblical narrative which lend motive and force to the ascetical struggle within marriage are rapidly becoming incomprehensible to vast numbers of Americans — among them those who weekly populate American churches, Orthodox, Roman Catholic, and Protestant. Under such circumstances the Christian idea of marriage as vocation would appear to be in grave jeopardy.

Clearly, there no longer is a *corpus Christianum* to support the Christian vision of marriage and family as vocation. Equally significant, our society has been undercutting the family's traditional role *as an institution* with social, economic, educational, and political purposes and functions. Robert Nisbet has described this process in *The Quest for Community*.

> In ever enlarging areas of population in modern times, the economic, legal, educational, religious, and recreational functions

of the family have declined or diminished. Politically, membership in the family is superfluous; economically, it is regarded by many as an outright hindrance to success. The family, as someone has put it, is now the accident of the worker rather than his essence. His competitive position may be more favorable without it. Our systems of law and education and all the manifold recreational activities of individuals engaged in their pursuit of happiness have come to rest upon, and to be directed to, the individual, not the family. On all sides we continue to celebrate from the pulpit and rostrum the indispensability to the economy and the State of the family. But, in plain fact, the family is indispensable to neither of these at the present time. The major processes of economy and political administration have become increasingly independent of the symbolism and integrative activities of kinship.[80]

A contemporary Orthodox ethic of marriage and family must necessarily confront the failure thus far of the Orthodox churches to shape a "living" catechesis which takes these developments into serious account. Yet even more troubling is the fact that the Orthodox Church, along with other churches in America, has lent impetus to this impoverishment of the power of the family. A fine example of this is the uncritical adoption by the Orthodox of the Protestant Sunday school model of Christian instruction. One must not forget that the Sunday school system was invented by the Protestant churches in a time when a Protestant Christian culture was presupposed. Further, the schools were born as an integral part of Protestant evangelical and missionary organizations. Sunday schools assume no such evangelical or missiological character in Orthodox parishes, and their curriculums rarely reflect a recognition of the changed cultural status of the Orthodox churches in an advanced secular culture. Furthermore, until recently, Orthodox Sunday schools focused almost exclusively on the child. Given the lack of any other serious adult catechesis, husbands and wives, fathers and mothers, were left without much help from the church to grow in their faith. Thus they were usually incapable of articulating in words or daily living a Christian outlook on marriage and family as Christian vocation. Even as Sunday school instruction has been extended to adults, the benefits have been at the cost of further weakening the family as worshiping and witnessing unit. In imitation of the surrounding culture, the parish increasingly directs its activities to individuals, not to families as primary Christian communities. Families take second place to arbitrary age groupings. The church is compartmentalized into segregated "clubs" whose ecclesiastical importance would seem to outweigh that of the family. And people are brought up with the impression that Christianity is a private individualistic faith in which marriages and families are accidental to Christian witness or *diaconia*.

It is not consistent with the sacramental vision of the Orthodox Church to continue with a model of Christian discipline and *diaconia* which is based upon the values of individualism prevalent in the culture. It is incumbent upon a church which honors marriage as a sacrament of the Kingdom to generate from within its own life values and symbols which provide marriage and family with an institutional identity and purpose. Donna Schaper is right when she states: "Marriage is a covenant involving our deepest selves — our sexuality, fertility, generativity, talent, inadequacy and death. It is our link to past (parents) and future (children). Its very nature is intolerant of superficiality." As she goes on to say, unless these matters of "destiny, nature and purpose," are articulated and lived out communally, within the greater context of God's people *in via* to the Kingdom, "marriage will continue to be the victim of a formerly Christian culture that has lost its identity and therefore is incapable of maintaining its institutions."[81] If the culture has lost this capacity to provide marriage and family with a narrative, symbolic, and value context for being and acting purposively as family, it becomes that much more important that the Church do so. It will not suffice to conclude, as Herbert Anderson does, that "individuation remains the one task allotted to the family that is not done by any other social institution" — this, of course, "qualified by a perspective that is committed to a future." Anderson describes this commitment to the future as "the perpetuation of the species," to be sure not so crudely conceived as merely a biological function but also "for teaching people how to live individually together in order that another generation will be prepared for the ongoing care and nurture of the human species." Anderson would have the family take special responsibility for humanizing an increasingly dehumanized society by providing "the context in which . . . growth toward autonomy might best occur." Anderson is a Christian theologian. Yet he ignores completely the eschatological perspective of Christian faith which enables Christians to go on hoping and finding reason for bringing children into the world in spite of the mortality and desolation of that fallen order. Anderson is correct when, paraphrasing Jose Ortega y Gasset, he says, "People do not live together merely to be together. They live together to do something by themselves or together."[82] But the Christian family cannot be content with envisioning its purpose as that of transmitting values of autonomy, diversity, and the need of community. Such values, whatever their relative merit, cannot stand alone. They require a context, a goal beyond the mere perpetuation of the species or of human culture and civilization. Christian ethics is theocentric ethics. The continued life of the species and its artifacts obtains value only in the knowledge of God's goodness, in his creative and redemptive purpose. Marriage has been made victim of this secular culture precisely because the culture no longer is capable of providing the narrative, symbol, or ritual which places marriage and family under that divine purpose and in service to it.

I will end this essay as I began it. The guiding question for the articulation of an Orthodox ethic of marriage and family is: "What can the Church do to restore a vision of Christian vocation to married and family living?" There has been nothing accidental about the attention I have given in these pages to the Orthodox rites of holy matrimony. The primary elements of the "living" catechesis needed to restore this vision are present already in the liturgy and worship of the Church. Certainly, the vision of marriage as a calling in service to God, Christ's Church, and the Kingdom redound in the rites of matrimony, baptism, and, of course, the Divine Liturgy. But the images, narratives, and symbols which compose this vision need to be taught by the Church in word and action more often than during the rites alone. Baptismal and wedding anniversaries should be celebrated and made the occasions for instruction and service. It is well that churches have begun the practice of premarital counseling. But why should this catechesis and discipline end with the wedding, as it often does? The sacrament of holy matrimony is an entrance into and beginning of the new life lived together in conjugal love. Christian catechesis and discipline ought to deepen and intensify with each year husband and wife live together. As their individual destinies become more intertwined, so should their marriage become identified increasingly with the mission and destiny of the Church. The last prayer of the Byzantine rite speaks directly to this imperative. It says:

May he who by his presence at the marriage feast in Cana of Galilee did declare marriage to be an honourable estate, Christ our true God; through prayers of his all-holy Mother; of the holy, glorious and all laudable Apostles, of the holy, God-crowned Kings and Saints-equal-to-the-Apostles Constantine and Helena; of the holy great martyr Procopius; and of all the Saints, have mercy upon you and save you, foreasmuch as he is good, and loveth mankind. [83]

Thus the final words said to the newly wedded couple and to all those gathered as witnesses to their wedding refer marriage to the apostles, to the martyrs, to St. Procopius, who exhorted spouses to go to martyrdom as to a wedding feast, and to Constantine and Helena, who in their missionary propagation of the faith were equal to the apostles. This prayer alone of the Byzantine rite is a powerful answer to the privatization and disestablishment of family in our society. It provides married people with a transcendent purpose, which society seems no longer capable of giving, for their coming together, remaining together, and raising children. It is a reminder to the Church, as well, that its ethics are not only founded in its evangelical witness but are dependent upon marriages and families equipped with the virtues and vision of the apostles, saints, and martyrs. In this light, the so-called crisis of the family becomes an opportunity for the Orthodox Church to reclaim marriage as an ecclesial entity and in so doing strengthen itself for the testimony it must bear to a despairing post-Christendom world of the hope in Christ's Kingdom.

PART III

Social Ethics

5

The Problem of a Social Ethic:
Diaspora Reflections

IN THIS LATE DECADE of the twentieth century there is nothing radical about saying that Christians throughout the world are becoming a minority in increasingly secular cultures. Many theologians have argued that it is no longer realistic for Christians to see themselves as citizens of Christendom or any kind of Christianized state. The Orthodox theologian John Meyendorff has put the matter this way:

> Today, we are ready to celebrate the burial of Christian empires and states, but have we really abandoned the mistaken aspects of their theology? To ask this question is to imply that the theology of many of our "secularists" is actually the theology of Constantine, Justinian, and Hildebrand, although the means at their disposal are different and, consequently the methods they propose to use are different as well. But the *main* concern is the same. They want to define Christianity in such a way as to solve the problems of this world, to be "relevant" in terms understandable to "secular man," and practically, to use secular means to attain a goal which has been set by others. But then, what about Jesus' answer to Pilate: "My kingdom is not of this world; if my kingdom were of this world, my servants would fight" (John 18:36)? . . .
>
> Christianity has suffered enough because it identified itself with power, with the state, with money, with the establishment. Many of us rightly want to disengage it from these embarrassing allies. In order to win its true freedom *the Church must become itself again and not simply change camps.*[1]

Meyendorff is posing a question which the Orthodox Church, particularly in North America, has only begun to address. Specifically, he
is concerned with the future context in which the Orthodox Church
will need to engage the social, economic, and political structures of
the world. He also has intimated the pressing need for Orthodoxy to
articulate a genuine social ethic.

I wish to argue that such a social ethic will exist only if Orthodox
conscientiously endeavor to come to terms with their recent diaspora[2]
in the West. Though their situation is distinctive, the Orthodox will
not be alone in doing social ethics from a minority perspective.
Theologians of diverse traditions have acknowledged that from this
time into the foreseeable future Christian theology and ethics will need
to take account of this situation. In some of his more recent empirical
studies, the Roman Catholic theologian Karl Rahner has tried to define
just what are the prospects for Christians in light of their minority status:

> Christians cannot expect that any homogeneous society will
> once more emerge which as such can simply be called Christian.
> Those factors in civilization . . . which once produced and sus-
> tained a society of this sort, which was in some "mediaeval" sense
> homogeneously Christian will never return. . . . In so far as it
> might ever be possible to aim at producing a homogeneously
> Christian society in the future the only way in which [it] could
> be pursued would be by using the means of a system which in
> social, political and ideological terms was totalitarian. And this
> is something which the Christian, precisely on principles of free-
> dom of conscience and faith itself, must radically and uncondi-
> tionally reject. . . .
>
> In the concrete this implies that the Church must not
> necessarily hold fast to those positions of power in society which
> in former times she came legitimately to acquire, and which
> perhaps even today cannot be proved to have become unjustified
> in the contemporary scene.[3]

Rahner is not suggesting that Christians disengage themselves from
the world or abandon their "worldly" calling in the Holy Spirit. He
simply is cautioning that when Christians revise their social ethics to
meet the new circumstances they must not remain stuck in a vision
of Christendom.

Similarly, the American Mennonite theologian John Howard

Yoder has written about what will be demanded of Christians in facing the emerging secular order.

> Instead of dreaming about either past or future situations in which Christians did or would constitute the powerful majority in society, we could accept as normal the diaspora situation in which Christians find themselves in most of the world today in which voluntarily committed Christians will increasingly be conscious of standing also in the "post-Christian" North Atlantic world. We should be more relaxed and less compulsive about running the world if we made our peace with our minority situation, seeing this neither as a dirty trick of destiny or as some great new progress but simply as the unveiling of the myth of Christendom which wasn't true even when it was believed.[4]

Thus, both Yoder and Rahner warn that the ever-present temptation to proceed as if the Kingdom hope and the means to its fulfillment are easily translatable into, or correlated with, the goals and power machinations of the secular society is for Christians a particularly dangerous one to which to fall prey in these times. Orthodox ought to heed such admonitions. Their Byzantine past makes them especially susceptible to just the kind of miscalculation of which Yoder and Rahner caution. Yet it would be a mistake also for Orthodox to accept Yoder's conclusion that Christendom is a "myth . . . which wasn't true even when it was believed." In his identification of the minority station from which future Christian, particularly Orthodox, theology must be done, John Meyendorff wisely does not dismiss or condemn out of hand the Byzantine synthesis of church and state. Byzantium was in some real sense, as Rahner says about that medieval phenomenon of a religiously homogeneous society known in East and West alike, a Christian society which contrasts profoundly with the pluralistic, secular societies of North America and Western Europe today. The significance of this fact needs to be taken into full consideration by Orthodox as they shape a contemporary social ethic.

BYZANTINE LEGACY

Byzantium is as much a legacy of twentieth-century diaspora Orthodoxy as of nineteenth-century "old world" Orthodoxy. The success of Orthodox social ethics depends in large measure upon whether the Orthodox remember accurately and interpret truthfully the past which they have brought with them to the West. James T. Johnson has argued that "the task of the religious ethicist . . . consists in faithfully rendering both his own history and that of his community." Johnson observes that Christian and Jewish ethics are inseparable from a historical matrix of values which provides "moral identity," both personal and communal. It also challenges the religious ethicist to ask and attempt to answer the question of what out of that matrix continues to remain normative as living tradition for the religious community.[5] This remembering activity which Johnson identifies as a crucial dimension of religious ethics has been urged by contemporary Orthodox theologians. Their work has corrected many of the West's misunderstandings about the kind of relationship to the empire which the Eastern Church sought and partially achieved. By so doing, Orthodox already have begun to lay the groundwork for a distinctive social ethic in the pursuit of their church mission in this post-Christendom world.

Alexander Schmemann wrote that in Byzantium the Orthodox Church did not seek or obtain, as did the Latin Church, "a juridical agreement, a contract which, while defining the respective rights and obligations of both parties, the Church and the empire, would have preserved their structural distinction from one another."[6] In the East there was not articulated, as there was in the West, a massive dualism of juridical, institutional, and ethical dimensions, whether of the Augustinian two cities, the Gelasian two swords, the Lutheran two realms, or the Enlightenment and post-Enlightenment separation of church and state. The Justinian formulation of the " 'symphony' between 'divine things' and 'human affairs',"[7] between *sacerdotium* and *imperium*, was christological, the union of divine and human realities in a *single* organism, the Christian empire, which is itself the image of the person of Christ who is the "unique source of the . . . civil and ecclesiastical hierarchies."[8] Accordingly the new Christian order was envisioned as fully church and fully state, yet one divine-human subject, one Christian society. The vision was of a realized eschatology and in its persuasion that the Kingdom of God had already taken "flesh" in the terrestrial form of the empire it must be judged utopian. Originally dynamic and eschatological, the vision eventually became an ossified and ahistorical ideology.

The tragic consequences of this ossification are manifold. Nevertheless, the usual description of the Byzantine theocracy as *Caesaro-papist* probably does not apply either. The rubric in its regular usage again assumes that as in the West so in the East there developed a juridical and sociological distinction of church and state as "between two *institutions*, two *powers*, two *governments*."[9] Thus, it is argued that in Byzantium the relationship between the two institutions was one of subordination of church to state. Schmemann states that it is misleading to speak of a subordination of church to state in Byzantium "because for subordination there must be two distinct subjects,"[10] when, in fact, the Byzantine "symphony" turned out to have only one subject, the state, religion being essentially a function of the state. With this in mind many contemporary Orthodox theologians have concluded that the Byzantine synthesis was on balance a great disadvantage to the Church and smothered until at least the thirteenth century the concept of a free church.[11]

The history of the Eastern Church's surrender to the Byzantine state, however, has as much, if not more, significance and instructive value for the Orthodox problem of shaping a social ethic in its dispersion as the actual outcome of the surrender. The original impetus for the Church's reconciliation with the empire was, indeed, christological and rooted ironically in the same eschatology that brought the early Church into conflict with the empire. The point is itself quite important and worthwhile for the Orthodox to remember. It should serve to broaden the vision of a North American Orthodoxy and prepare it for the historical possibility that an Orthodox social ethic consistent with Orthodoxy's original eschatological experience of the Kingdom and vision for the world might be necessarily quite different in shape and content from those social ethics of either its pre-Constantinian or Byzantine past.

During its first four centuries the Church, while going about being that which it is, was confronted by a world organization which claimed universal dominion and salvific power. These claims of the empire were at the source of the early antinomy between the Church and the empire, not—as some have alleged—a world-denying faith of Christians rooted in a radical expectation of the imminent parousia. Schmemann wrote that "a highly 'positive' experience of the Kingdom, not a denial of the world but a certain way of looking at it and experiencing it," placed the early Church in an antagonistic relationship with the empire. The "ultimate content and term of reference" of the early Church's eschatology, he continued, "was not the world, but the Kingdom of God and thus rather than being 'anti-world' it [the Church] was . . . 'pro-Kingdom'."[12] The terms which defined this experience and initially moved the Church into an antagonistic relationship with the empire were not two (church and state) but three (church, world, and Kingdom of God). The Church, understanding itself as the very presence (*mysterion* or sacrament) of the Kingdom of God, could not allow itself to be of service to a worldly organization which claimed to be of divine origin and authority in the person of the emperor and an absolute value and end in itself. The Church, viewed the world as a relative good requiring exorcism of the demonic presence, truly the matter of the sacrament of the Kingdom, but not allowed idolatrous claims to absolute value.

With Constantine's conversion, this same church was addressed by the same worldly organization now expressing an interest — however pale and disingenuous it turned out to be — to adopt the Church's story of salvation and criteria of universality as its own. The Church responded by accepting this invitation to render a "holy service" for the world. It did so by exorcising the world of its demonic powers, by liberating the empire from the thralldom of the "prince of the air" and by making this world "new" before God by the power of the Holy Spirit. In the beginning there existed the possibility that the Church could remain true to itself as the sacrament of the Kingdom, a holy community, God's eschatological vehicle of passage for this world through time into the world to come. But, as John Meyendorff rightly observes, the experiment failed and the blame rests largely with the Church, which endeavored to be not what it is but what it is not. Meyendorff concludes:

> But now that the Constantinian period is over we generally recognize where it was *theologically* wrong: i.e. (1) in thinking that the authority of Christ could be identified with the political *power* of the state, and (2) in considering that the *universality* of the Gospel is definable in political terms.[13]

This judgment probably applies to both Western and Eastern medieval Christianity. But in addressing the peculiar problem of a North American Orthodox social ethic, I need to make one last observation about the different paths Christendom followed in West and East. The Western Church took to heart the Gelasian and Gregorian juridical definitions of it as an institution with power and jurisdiction in this world. Also, it took advantage of the collapse of the political institutions of the Western empire, gaining a victory "in her struggle with the empire. . . . But it was," in Georges Florovsky's words, "a precarious victory. . . . The theocratic claims of the Empire *were* defeated. But in the long run, this only led to the acute 'secularization' of the temporal power in Western Society. A purely 'secular' Society emerged for the first time in Christian history."[14] Renaissance, Enlightenment, and post-Enlightenment modernity thus saw the rise of the autonomous secular state. At first this state was defined as an authority with jurisdiction limited by another authority, the Church. But increasingly this state became the only legitimate power relevant to the whole society. This "triumph" of the state was accompanied by the splintering of Western Christianity itself into numerous competing sects or denominations whose seat of authority was defined by the ascendent state and its civil theologians as restricted to personal conscience and belief.

The Eastern Church did not take — or perhaps have — the opportunity to define itself as an authority or power in the same juridical sense as did its Latin counterpart. Throughout the history of Byzantium the Church held fast to a view of itself as a sacramental organism whose vocation it was to sanctify and transform the imperial world order. In so doing, however, it also forgot — at least in its official theology and role as religion of the state — two fundamental perceptions about its relation to the world and its mission in the world. First, in its efforts to sanctify the social order, the Church forgot its earlier experience of the world both as created good and as a fallen, mortally sick order. The Church, having said *yes* to the invitation to render the empire holy before God, forgot how to say *no* to the imperial claims that Byzantium was the Kingdom of God already realized on earth. Second, the Church permitted itself to be defined as a hierarchy, with the *authority* of spiritual dogmas and the *power* of sacramental graces, at the terrible price of losing sight of its calling as a *free community of faith*, whose very presence in the world is to be both a judgment and a limitation upon the claims of all worldly authorities and powers to being ends in themselves. Thus, for better or for worse, the unity of the Christian commonwealth in the East was not broken as it was in the West. "In spite of all Imperial abuses and failures" and the partial failure of the Church itself to hold fast to its eschatological vocation as sacrament of the Kingdom and prophetic and proleptic witness to it, "the Byzantine Commonwealth retained to the very end its Christian and 'consecrational' character." There was no separation of church and state even at the end. In the words of Georges Florovsky, "Byzantium collapsed as a Christian kingdom, under the burden of its tremendous claims."[15] Byzantium failed as an experiment in Christian politics, but it left no experience or legacy of the secular autonomous state in which there exist a plurality of religious denominations.

THE CONTEXT AND CONDITIONS
OF AN ORTHODOX SOCIAL ETHIC

During the past century there have been two developments which leave the Orthodox Church in a genuine state of crisis. Alexander Schmemann summarized these two developments consummately:

> The first development is the tragically spectacular collapse, one after another, of the old and organic "Orthodox worlds" which only a few decades ago appeared as the self-evident, natural and permanent "home" and environment of the Orthodox Church — and not merely their collapse but also their transformation into the stage for a violent attack launched by an extreme and totalitarian secularism against religion, against the spiritual nature and vocation of man. The second is the rapid and massive growth in the West of the Orthodox diaspora which, however "accidental" it may have been in its origins, signifies the end of the isolation of Orthodoxy in, and its total identification with the "East," and thus the beginning of a new destiny, in the West and within the context of Western culture.[16]

In this situation of decision, the Byzantine legacy can no longer serve as model for the future and yet it must be remembered and understood if the Church is to persist as a genuine *presence* of the Kingdom. Schmemann described graphically the context in which Orthodoxy will have to do social ethics for the forseeable future. Such social ethics necessarily will be that very activity by which the Orthodox Church either interprets or fails to interpret truthfully its diaspora life. In North America the Orthodox Church faces two serious temptations as it struggles to articulate a social ethic consistent with the historical faith. These

are the denominational accommodationist and sectarian countercul-
turalist paths followed by so many of the Christian confessions.

The Danger of Accommodationist Seduction

Together with the mainline American religious denominations,
the Orthodox Church might choose to do service for the "common
faith" of America. The cardinal precept of that faith is that God has
granted all individuals certain inalienable rights which are of *absolute
public concern*, as opposed to all other notions about God or humanity's
nature and transcendent destiny which have a *relative legitimacy* —
only, however, so long as they stay private and do not intrude into
public discussion or seek to influence public policy. For example, the
manner in which the Orthodox Church affirms its traditional opposition to the destruction of fetal life is one possible indication of whether
it will submit itself to this precept and go the accommodationist route.

The Orthodox Church has opposed the present liberal abortion
laws in the United States. It always has considered abortion inconsis-
tent with its vocation as a community whose faith is in an incarnate
God, born of a human mother, who has called that community to
be perfect in his divine-humanity. The easiest and most acceptable
way, however, for the Orthodox Church to make itself a public presence
and therefore a social ethic in our pluralistic, secular society is to argue
against abortion primarily from the standpoint of the individual's rights
to life, liberty, and the pursuit of happiness. Some Orthodox theologians indeed have proceeded to marshal statements from the Greek
fathers to support the case that the fetus is human, is an individual,
and is a person. This is not illegitimate for the Orthodox to do: Orthodoxy's seriousness about grounding moral argument in sound meta-
physics is long-standing. Nevertheless, it would be naive and misguided
for Orthodox theologians and clergy to assume that the larger secular
society is seriously interested in or capable of sustaining discussion at
that level. In fact, by entering the debate in this fashion, the Orthodox
Church will have joined — wittingly or unwittingly, it makes little
difference — a debate which finally turns out to be a "confidence game."
In that game, the argument whether the fetus is a human individual
with the same rights as those of us outside of the womb has already
been lost or is, perhaps, in reality a nonargument because of the hidden governing rule of the game. The rule is that the only criterion

of truth is a procedural one, i.e., how best do we protect the rights of the individual without influencing the character of her life or that of her society, since any attempt at such influence would be an infraction of the individual's rights to privacy and self-determination?[17] This is, after all, the final import of *Roe* v. *Wade*. The Court's decision can rightly be called a sacred document of our "common faith."

By entering the abortion debate in the above described fashion, the Orthodox Church will have moved one significant step closer to becoming an accommodationist denomination with a social ethic of the same stripe. It will have begun reasoning about moral problems in a manner untrue to its own living tradition and merged itself into the mainstream of American secular culture — just another fish in the pluralist waters of liberal democracy. In point of fact, the statements about abortion in the letters of St. Basil or the homilies of St. John Chrysostom were not intended to be metaphysical pronouncements about the beginnings of human life. Nor are they statements about basic human rights in the profoundest sense, leave aside the shallow nominalistic and voluntaristic way in which our society has come to define human rights. They are primarily exhortations directed to a specific community about what kind of a people it is and what behavior is or is not fitting with its identity as the bride of Christ and the sacrament of the Kingdom of trinitarian love open to all life.

Earlier I stated that it would be necessary for the Orthodox Church to remember and understand its Byzantine legacy even if that legacy will no longer serve as a model for an Orthodox social ethic. For that legacy instructs the Church never to forget, as it did in Byzantium and imperial Russia, that it is a community of faith whose very character sets it apart from the world with its passing powers, principalities, and ideologies. There is no easy or consistent correlation of the values and virtues of the Kingdom with those of even so amorphous an ideology as that of liberal democracy. The greatest service the Church can do for any worldly organization is to address that organization as the very presence of the Kingdom in its midst. If the Orthodox Church opposes abortion as the authoritative voice of one philosophy of life among others or as an interest group whose primary ends (i.e., the protection of individual rights) are those of the greater society, it will not be truthful to what it is or what it proclaims itself to be each time the people come together in liturgy. In the long term, the Church will fail to do its divine service as a sign of the Kingdom of God into which all humankind is welcomed, however unlike that Kingdom the present world order is.

It might have been easier to make my point about the dangers of accommodationist seduction through other examples. Certainly, as with many of the mainline American religious denominations, the Orthodox Church—in practice if not officially—has sanctioned uncritically the American economy. This economy would have us become its own liberal—as contrasted with Marxist or socialist—version of autonomous economic human beings, i.e., self-seeking producers in the name of individual fulfillment and self-gratifying consumers in the name of individual enrichment. However, the point I wish to establish is that *even* in its public *opposition* to any single practice or behavior approved by our society the Orthodox Church cannot assume it has avoided the accommodationist errors of its Byzantine past or of other North American churches.

One recent development in American Christianity ought to be especially instructive for the Orthodox as they seek to work out a social ethic which avoids the accommodationist error. It is the rise over the past decade of an activist Protestant "fundamentalism" as the ironic sequel to the socially activist liberal-progressivist church movement of the late 1950s through the early 1970s. Meyendorff's observations cited earlier about the theology of the new "secularists" of the 1960s turning out to be a revised version of the "theology of Constantine, Justinian and Hildebrand" in different circumstances applies also to the theology of the new Christian Right. Although having a very different style and program, the new Christian Right, like the liberal movement which preceded it, has conflated and finally confused the values, virtues, and content of the Kingdom of God with those of our secular order. Whatever the differences in the strategies and goals of these two religious movements, both owe a common debt to Enlightenment American religion, which all too easily associated the content of the Christian faith with the secular precepts of the Republic—those precepts being largely the Enlightenment's full suit of God-given and inalienable individual rights.

Each movement in its own peculiar fashion has expressed a common faith which assumes that the responsibility of a Christian social ethic is to locate and reveal where Christ has been present and at work in this society. To be sure, these two movements have looked in different places for that presence and activity. The liberal progressivists have claimed to locate Christ's presence in the struggles of blacks, minorities, the poor, and the disenfranchised. The Christian Right declares that the true biblical values still inhere in a substantial portion of the working middle class, in the inner sanctuary of the American family, and in the workings of the American free enterprise system. Each movement has sought to align the churches with the social forces it has determined to be the most fit for accomplishing its own version of the Christianization of America. Finally, both movements have spawned social ethics which hold the churches responsible for the historical success of a particular social order. Significantly, the central criterion of that success turns out to be the guarantee of certain rights and freedoms belonging to the individual. Only the matter of *how* those rights and freedom are to be distributed and guaranteed is a bone of contention between the two religious movements.

The accommodationist surrender of the North American churches has taken a variety of forms. Due to its Byzantine past there is a great temptation for the Orthodox Church to forge its own path to surrender. Yet the Orthodox Church carries with it a history which also includes the period of the early church of the catacombs and persecutions, the great captivity under the Ottoman yoke, and the recent era of repression under Soviet rule. This history provides ample experience upon which the Orthodox Church might draw to guide it toward a social ethic which embodies a vision of the Church's relation to the world other than that of a denominational accommodationism.

The Lure of Sectarian Retreat

Not since its first four centuries has the Orthodox Church been situated in a culture so resistant to its transformationist instincts. Unlike its relation to Byzantine culture or its conversion of the Slavic peoples, there are no prospects that the Orthodox Church can make the culture of the North Atlantic world its own. The Orthodox Church could ignore this reality and behave as if the situation were no different than before. Yet it would do so at the great peril of its own internal disillusionment and exhaustion before forces it has not troubled to understand.

If the Orthodox Church manages to steer clear of the accommodationism, there is yet the distinct possibility that, confronted with the situation just described, a church which calls itself universal will retreat into a sectarian spiritualism and a variety of ethnocentric mystiques. Having despaired of persuading a recalcitrant society that it rightly should be the soul of its body, the Orthodox Church might then assume the ghostly presence of a bodiless soul in an otherwise alien society. In other words, it might choose a sectarian counterculturist path. But if it does, that will be a refusal to articulate a real social ethic, even by the internal measure of its own incarnational faith, which has always taken the world itself to be the matter of the sacrament of the Kingdom.

A Catholic "Sectarianism"

In a perceptive article, the Lutheran theologian George Lindbeck describes the character of our pluralistic, secular society and forecasts the future shape of the Church in that society:

> Now a secular culture . . . is one in which there is a plurality of legitimation systems all of which are undermined and weakened by the fact that they are competing with each other in a unified society in which various religious and ideological groups are in close interaction. . . .
> . . . In a pluralistic and secular society, religion and ideology are necessarily banished from the public domain. . . . Questions of high principle and ultimate goals play a smaller and smaller part in the structuring and directing of society's life. A pluralistic secular society is by definition one guided in terms of short-range, rational-pragmatic considerations, on the one hand, and whim and emotion on the other.
> . . . [Such pragmatism] solves practical problems where religion and ideology fail. But what it cannot do is decide about final goals and values. It provides no clues to the nature of true manhood and womanhood, nor can it fill the daily round with a sense of ultimate purpose and meaning. In short, it does not legitimate the human enterprise. Where there is no vision the people perish: and as secularism is the absence of visions, it teeters on the knife-edge between chaos and tyranny.[18]

This milieu is the minority context of the great body of Christians in Western Europe and North America. If, in such a context, the Church truthfully goes about being what it is, it may well look sectarian by "objective" sociological standards. Lindbeck insists, however, that "sectarian" in this sense "does not necessarily imply a divisiveness internal to the Church, but rather points to the intensity and intimacy of the communal life in a minority sharply differentiated from the larger society."[19] Such a sociological "sectarianism" might also be ecumenical or catholic, since it would not necessarily indicate a withdrawal from the world or rejection of it. It could well summon within the Church a much more intense pursuit of its evangelical mission.

The Orthodox Church assumes a rather unique position in the post-Christendom era precisely because it knows — better than perhaps any of the Western confessions — the homelessness and powerlessness which are the earmarks of the new Christian minority status. Its diaspora presence in the West is twofold. It has been expelled from its natural cultures and has arrived in the West at a time in which even that culture is no longer Roman Catholic or Protestant. Nor does it bring with it into the future that dualism of church and state which in the West for so many centuries stood as the bridge between a unified Christendom and a unified secular culture. Thus it is well equipped both to shatter the lingering myth that the Church may lay claim to the private person but not to the public person and to expose the heresy of the new secular monism which, in the name of human liberation and even in the name of Christianity, asks us to reject the transcendent freedom of the Church for a new service to the omnicompetent state.

Lindbeck's thesis about an ecumenical or catholic "sectarianism" has the advantage of visioning a church which, though sharply differentiated from the larger society, is not radically alienated from it. Orthodoxy in North America probably does not face the prospect that an increasingly unified secular society will become virulently anti-Christian. Thus, for the foreseeable future, there will exist opportunities for the Orthodox Church to engage the host culture selectively. The social ethic this presumes, however, would not follow even the dominant patterns of twentieth-century American religious ethics. These patterns have been strikingly similar, whether Protestant or Roman Catholic. This fact is neatly represented by the writings of the two towering figures of twentieth-century American Protestant and Roman Catholic social ethics, Reinhold Niebuhr and John Courtney Murray.[20]

Whatever their differences — and these were significant — both Niebuhr and Murray formulated social ethics for the Christian *individual* in a pluralist society. Both had their eye on how the individual

Christian might affect and shape public policy. Both were persuaded that there were enough religious resources in our culture to effect a strategy of direct individual Christian address of that society toward the influence of public policy. Perhaps, at the time, such a strategy was both justified and prudent. However, the social ethics of Niebuhr and Murray were premised in their respective revisions of the Christendom model. Their revisions banked on the perpetuity of a public consensus less secular and more religious than anything that can be hoped for in the twenty-first century. The appeal to religiously founded principles by which to steer society, though once the confident reserve of Protestant neo-orthodoxy and Roman Catholic neo-Thomism, is now the near exclusive capacity of the Christian Right. The cardinal difference in the Christian Right's apologetic is that, unlike neo-orthodoxy or neo-Thomism, it denies rather than affirms that religious values and secular values can be brought into a constructive or fruitful synthesis. Meanwhile, in the face of secularism, the recent attempts of such religious pluralists and heirs of neo-orthodoxy as Richard John Neuhaus and Martin Marty to continue the argument for a public piety seem not much more than academic exercises in wishful thinking.[21]

The Orthodox Church needs to study carefully the history of the difficult death of the vision of a Christian America. It will have to resist the temptation of offering its own late version of a "neo-Orthodoxy" and instead turn to the fundamentals of its ecclesiology for the inspiration of a social ethic. A truthful interpretation of its new life in North America should render a churchly ethic of presence which concentrates the energies of the faithful in the activity of making the Church itself a fitting bride of Christ and icon of perfection for the world, rather than an instrumentalist ethic of effectiveness which disperses the energies of its people into the whirl of the secular city. In doing this, the Orthodox Church will risk accusations from without of retreat. Nevertheless, it will know that its striving toward the perfection to which Christ calls it constitutes no withdrawal. In the spirit of St. Basil, who translated Christ's love into hospitals and hospices for the sick and weak, the Orthodox Church in its new life within a unified secular culture is required once again to direct its energies toward the creation of new incarnations of Christian *philanthropia*.[21]

Historically, the Church's ability to transform society has depended not upon a power of management over society or political brokerage of its own interests, but rather upon a willingness to exercise its freedom to redeem and re-create a fallen world. This the Church has done in its worship, with the strength of internal discipline and by building from within its unique polity more just and compassionate forms of human relations and services.

THE POLITICS OF ORTHODOXY IN A LIBERAL DEMOCRACY

If Lindbeck's views about the future of the Church in a pluralistic, secular society are correct—and I am persuaded they are—then it is even more imperative for the Church to be clear about its own ecclesial polity and how in its *theoria* and *praxis* that polity can inform, as contrasted with reform, the social, political, and economic life of society. The Church's task is not to reform society. Reform is a function of the politics of the state, though the Church will hope that needed reform results from its witness to the state.

The Conciliar, Trinitarian Form of Orthodox Polity

The Church is a council "in the deepest meaning of the word," wrote Alexander Schmemann, "because she is primarily the revelation of the blessed Trinity, of God and of divine life as essentially a perfect council." He continued: "The Church is Trinitarian in both 'form' and 'content' because she is the restoration of man and his life as an image of God, who is Trinity. She is an image of the Trinity and the gift of Trinitarian life because life is redeemed and restored in her as essentially *conciliar*."[23] In Orthodox theology the true criteria of justice inhere in the trinitarian life of God to which all humankind is restored by Christ. These are *living* criteria which must be discerned through active faith and are not reducible to any mental schemata or system of rules or principles. The essential elements of this conciliar life are: (1) "unity in a communion of relationship," (2) "specificity and uniqueness of persons," and (3) "ordering of the common life."[24] The unity of the trinitarian life is a relationship of distinct and unique Persons whose identity is deepened by the perfectly reciprocal and communicative love which binds them together.

The two transcendent regulative principles of this communion are equality and freedom. The equality of such a communion, however, escapes being an impersonal equality of interchangeable participants because it does not exclude a hierarchy. Imaging the trinitarian life of Father, Son and Holy Spirit, the conciliar life of the Church is hierarchical. Yet this hierarchy is not one of subordination (i.e., submission to an impersonal order).[25] Rather, it is one of obedience founded in a free, loving, and perfectly communicative relationship among unique persons, equal in the fullness of their humanity, yet due a freely offered obedience according to the special gifts which they bring to the common life. The freedom in this communion does not subvert the unity because this freedom is the expression of a perfectly obedient yet uncoerced will. Neither does the unity destroy the specificity of persons or suppress their creative energies, because this unity is not achieved by an externally imposed will. Rather, it is the externalization of the coinhering mutual love of those who freely join into relation with one another.

It is not possible here to enumerate all the ways in which the Orthodox Church falls short of this trinitarian life and does not fulfill its self-imposed promise at the close of each eucharistic gathering to bring that very same life to the rest of the world. The Church, rooted in penitent faith, knows that in this fallen world perfect equality and perfect freedom are impossible and, indeed, that these two principles of justice are in a dialectical, sometimes even conflictual, relationship. Out of a contrite heart, the Church knows that as a community of sinners it is no less afflicted by the old Adam's impulses to anarchy and the lust for power than the world which it, as the holy people of God, is called to serve humbly. And it knows that the measure of its success in meeting that task is not the achievement of some perfectly just society along the path of history.

The Witness of the Orthodox Church to the State

The Church's failure to fulfill the trinitarian conciliar life even within its *own* polity should not become an excuse for not doing social ethics. Stanley Hauerwas has expressed this matter eloquently:

> "Social Ethics" is not what the church does after it has got its theological convictions straight and its house in order. In contrast, our theological conviction and corresponding community *are* a social ethic, for they provide the necessary context for us to understand the world in which we live. The church serves the

world first by providing categories of interpretation that offer the means for us to understand ourselves truthfully, e.g., as a sinful yet redeemed people.[26]

It is not the Church's business to make social policy, let alone prescribe what is the best form of government. For Christians the meaning and value of a particular state or political regime is relative to the Kingdom of God and not to one or another political theory or ideology. From this perspective our world is fallen and in need of the redemption which is only found in the Church. In the words of St. Paul:

> For the creation waits with eager longing for the revealing of the sons of God; for the creation was subjected to futility, not by its own will but by the will of him who subjected it in hope; because the creation itself will be set free from its bondage to decay and obtain the glorious liberty of the children of God. (Rom. 8:19–21 RSV)

Thus it comes as no surprise to the Church that every political system is experienced as oppressive, unfree, and unjust to one degree or another and that the poor and powerless suffer the most.

Even as the Orthodox Church falls short of the conciliar life which is the Kingdom constitution of its polity, its political responsibility is to expose the *lie* of every political system and ideology that with it all things are right. It does not matter where the Church is situated or what the form of the political system is, the Orthodox Church's social ethic begins with an exorcism of the social order. Every time the Orthodox Church performs the rite of baptism it begins anew its social ethic. For through the baptismal exorcisms the Church exposes evil as a real, personal, and cosmic power which holds the world in thralldom. Evil holds such power through the lie that this world is an end in itself and by keeping the world in ignorance of the fact that it (for example, the water and oil) is the very matter of the sacrament of the Kingdom.

The lie of every state that it is an end in itself needs to be exposed over and over, and the truth that it can be of service to the Kingdom of God needs to be revealed repeatedly. The language of the Kingdom should not be confused with that by which all states legitimate the rule of a few over the many. All worldly dominion involves the servile submission of some to the will of others. As such, all political systems stand under the judgment of the one Lord, Jesus Christ, whose Kingdom is one of "personal love which exacts from the freedom of His creatures a total conversion towards Him, a freely accomplished union."[27] It is this very same Ruler, who, we are told, "disarmed the principalities and powers and made public example of them, triumphing over them" (Col. 2:15 RSV).

By this measure the Orthodox Church will act no differently in a liberal democracy than in any other political system. Of all forms of government, Yoder has written,

> democracy is the least oppressive since it provides the strongest language of justification and therefore of critique which the subjects may use to mitigate its oppressiveness. But it does not make of democracy, and especially it does not make of most regimes which today claim to be democracies, a fundamentally new kind of sociological structure.[28]

Yoder's observation is a reminder to the Orthodox that even in their enjoyment of the benefits of a "free society," which contrasts so sharply with their subjugation under the Ottoman yoke and their present captivity within Communist societies, they should not forget how to say no to those claims to final truth and universal significance which are made by all states, including democracies. Orthodox social ethics, however, cannot be founded solely upon a "negative theology" of the state. Christian social ethics must also include a "positive theology" of the state. States, as Scripture and Tradition teach, will always exist in a fallen and sinful world. The state is, as Augustine and Luther taught, a "prophylactic" against personal and collective evil. However, the state, which is itself "ordered" by the divine *oikonomia*, also serves a positive good toward the improvement of humankind's earthly existence. It is not required that the Orthodox Church expound, confirm, or defend a theory of legitimation for democracy or any other form of government. Rather, Orthodox social ethics should be a discerning activity by which the Church strives to find effective ways of prompting the state to establish just relations within society and among political communities.

Thus, insofar as a liberal democracy claims to found its legitimacy in the consent of the governed arrived at through the free and open discussion of the people's concerns, the very presence of the Orthodox Church *should* make a difference in how honestly that claim is made and how conscientiously it is pursued. This will be accomplished if the Church itself conscientiously and publicly strives to perfect its own conciliar life. Unlike the situation in totalitarian states, the Orthodox Church in America has the distinct opportunity to expose its life fully and publicly to the rest of society and actually to engage that society with the conciliar action which is the sign and sacrament of the Kingdom. This also will be a kenotic activity, inasmuch as the Church inevitably will expose its flaws and failures to all. In this way, the Orthodox Church will be offering itself as an alternative model within the midst of a liberal democracy by which that society's own claims to being free and open might be judged. This is possible not because the Orthodox Church is an ideal democracy but, rather, because those qualities of equality and freedom claimed by liberal democracies to be the character of their social relations are given their full content and meaning through the Christian story of salvation and the *leitourgia* of the faithful by which the Kingdom is made present.

The sort of social engagement which is most consistent with the Orthodox Church's conciliar polity is dialogical. An easy and poor substitute for genuine dialogue is the style of official church declaration adopted by the mainline American churches and so often trumpeted by their spokespersons in a rather self-congratulatory manner as proof of the Church's prophetic witness to the state. Perhaps there is room for such official declarations as a form of social criticism, but actions speak louder than words. The 1983 Pastoral Letter by the National Conference of Catholic Bishops, *The Challenge of Peace: God's Promise and our Response,*[29] went far toward surpassing this declaratory style, attempting to blend policy recommendations to the greater political community with words of pastoral counsel to the faithful. The results were not entirely successful. The great strength of the letter, however, is not in its final form or in its content, with which others both within the Roman Catholic Church and outside it may disagree, but rather in the method of its composition. Not only did the bishops courageously bring the conciliar life of the Church to important segments of our society — members of academia, of the military and medical professions, and former and present government officials — but they also extended the dialogue to both Roman Catholic laity and the general public by publishing drafts of the Pastoral Letter for discussion, debate, and criticism.

Lest there be any misunderstanding about this matter, I would hasten to add that the dialogical action of the Church should not be initiated always or even most of the time by the hierarchy. It should be the outreach of the conciliar life of the people of God in eucharistic assembly. The political responsibility of the Orthodox Christian begins in the *local parish, not in the local precinct.*

Truth, Justice and the Church

"Justice is itself the great standing policy of civil society,"[30] wrote Edmund Burke. There is an overwhelming need for the kind of presence and action of the Church in our society as I have described, precisely because in our society justice has been emptied of nearly all content and meaning by our secular morality and law. Justice has been so construed in our everyday decisions, in our courts, and in government policy that it no longer obtains the quality of relations between persons in community. Rather, it has been redefined as the possession of individuals whose alleged right to autonomy and self-determination outweighs the claims to exist of all other values that might be held in common and might hold *us* in common.

Americans have become confused about what constitutes justice in their relations with the life of the fetus, in the punishment of criminals, in proscribing the uses of pornography, in the relations of the sexes, in the relations within the family, in this nation's relations with other nations (friend and foe) and in the use and nonuse of violence and warfare. While there is no one single cause for this, surely one important reason is that we have gone far toward rendering justice contentless, merely a procedural matter, a strategy of preventing autonomous entities — whether persons, corporations, or nations — from imposing someone's values on someone else. We have as a society lost the ability to say, *"That is true for us."*

The Church remains a community which is able to say: *"That is true for us."* And so wherever it continues to be that which it is, it becomes increasingly an anomaly and source of embarrassment for many. But it is also the Church's destiny and mission that its very presence expose the shortcomings of every social order by measure of the Kingdom and by that same measure provide the *truth* which shall make all things new.

A SOCIAL ETHIC FOR WHOM?

My efforts in this essay have been limited to demonstrating how a diaspora reflection toward the articulation of an Orthodox social ethic might begin and what shape that ethic might take. Furthermore, I make no special truth claims for my position beyond Orthodoxy in North America. The competency and responsibility for working out Orthodox social ethics in other places, whether in Western or Eastern Europe, Russia, or the Middle East, belong to the Orthodox there situated. I maintain a strong contextual concern which, I believe, also is consistent with Orthodox tradition.

But does such a social ethic have a relation, relevance, or responsibility to other churches in North America? In ecumenical discussions the Orthodox Church has stated repeatedly that it "does not expect that other Christians be converted to Orthodoxy in its historical and cultural reality of the past and present."[31] This principle applies also to the working out of social ethics. The kind of Orthodox social ethic here described is conditioned partly by what the Orthodox Church has been and partly by where it is presently. I agree with James T. Johnson that a historical-cultural remembering activity is vital to Christian ethics. Much of what I have said has been of that nature. But, clearly, there is much in the history of Christian confessions which is particular and not universally shared. We should expect, therefore, that the various churches in America often will respond differently to the challenges presented by our secular society. They even will define those challenges differently. Thus, I am *not* making universal truth claims about what Christian social ethics should be for all the American churches. This ought not suggest, however, that Orthodox are quick to despair of church unity, nor does the Orthodox Church profess a thoroughgoing relativism regarding what is true for Christians or what is held to be true among the Christian churches.

While I am not prescribing a social ethic for all the American churches, as an Orthodox I hope that if the Orthodox Church conducts itself as indicated here its action will encourage like conduct by other churches. This hope is premised in the conviction stated by Nikos Nissiotis, that what "the churches *actually do as churches* constitutes the authentic expression of their undivided unity."[32] This conviction about what constitutes a genuine expression of the universal Church is founded in a trinitarian and christological faith which is itself the common inheritance of all Christians. Unity, as Nissiotis states, "is not something subsequently given to the Church from a source outside the Church after that Church has come into existence from other causes. It is the *sine qua non* of the very existence of the Church implanted by the Holy Spirit among men."[33] The unity of the Church is not a state achieved by agreement "between the different conceptions" of unity held by the various churches. Rather unity is an "obligation to remain in that condition in which we are recreated by the Spirit as One in the One Undivided Church."[34] Such unity "derives from the inseparable union between the three persons of the Holy Trinity given to us as an historical event on the day of Pentecost."[35] It is equally derived from the Incarnation by which the Second Person of the Trinity is revealed as He in whom all creation inheres and is redeemed as his very body. Unity is not something achieved "only through consideration of *'what'* we believe this Church unity to be . . . but also through *'how'* we exist as Christians."[36] It is not the business of the Orthodox Church, therefore, to prescribe for other churches in America what their social ethics should be. It *is* the obligation — indeed, the mission — of the Orthodox Church to conduct itself in a manner fitting as the bride of Christ and the sign of trinitarian life for all other churches to see and, hopefully, to which to respond in kind.

6

Orthodoxy and the American Order:

Symphonia, Civil Religion or What?

"Is it that God has at last removed his blessing from the U.S.A. and what we feel now is just the clank of the old historical machinery, the sudden jerking ahead of the roller coaster cars as the chain catches hold and carries us back into history with its ordinary catastrophes, carries us out and up toward the brink from that felicitous and privileged siding where even unbelievers admitted that if it was not God who blessed the U.S.A., then at least some great good luck had befallen us, and that now the blessing or the luck is over, the machinery clanks, the chain catches hold, and the cars jerk forward?"

Walker Percy, *Love in the Ruins*

THE OVERWHELMING AMERICAN religious phenomenon of the last decade has been the rise of a militant Christian Right. In this activist fundamentalist movement we have seen the reaction of an indigenously American, evangelical Christianity to the collapse of that religious canopy over the culture which until very recent times retained the frame and fabric of Protestant Christianity. Similarly, the issue of church-state relations debated during the 1984 presidential contest was not the invention of Ronald Reagan's rhetoric. He was voicing the concern of a substantial portion of his constituency that somehow religious language and practice are being "outlawed" from the public realm. Walter Mondale's accusation that the President was threatening Americans with a new form of religious theocracy and justification for religious intolerance was no answer to the suspicion held even by many of his own supporters that, whatever the evident dangers in Reagan's assertions about the relation of religion to public morality, the restoration of a civic piety or public philosophy is needed. Thus, recently, voices from within mainline Protestantism also have lamented the increasingly rapid divestiture of religion from the public square. Consistent with their "custodial" outlook toward the American culture and liberal democracy, Martin Marty and Richard John Neuhaus[1] have acknowledged the religious significance of the new religious right and have mounted their own call to arms of the great "middle" body of Christian churches in America to a reinvigorated public presence and culture-formative role. Not entirely unlike their fundamentalist kinfolk, Marty and Neuhaus seek to forge a new moral consensus. They differ with the religious right in their persuasion that this consensus can be forged by the churches in cooperation with secular people who also value a civic piety or public philosophy.

Whatever the diversity of visions lately projected of the relation between religion and morality or church and state, the background is a final cultural disestablishment of Christianity. In this essay I sort out the salient religious and cultural forces belonging to the American "Christendom" and those contributing to its collapse, with a view toward the special challenges these forces present to Orthodoxy as it seeks to make sense of its presence in North America and to define its mission. The prescribed mode of engagement with the culture consistent with Orthodox ecclesiology is shown to contrast significantly with the social ethics of both fundamentalist and mainline churches.

THE ORTHODOX PROBLEM

The American order presents Orthodoxy with a constellation of values and institutions largely unfamiliar to the Orthodox Church before its recent diaspora in the West. The Orthodox Church was not an active participant in the development of modernity. It did not go through a Renaissance, Reformation, and Enlightenment, of which the primary American religious realities—the separation arrangement and that concrete manifestation of religious freedom, denominationalism—are products. Thus, the Western and modern trends toward the definition of church and state as two autonomous juridical entities does not belong to the vast stretch of Orthodox history. Furthermore, an expanding religious pluralism within, somewhat paradoxically, an also increas-

ingly secular society does not correspond with past Orthodox experience
of the world, the Orthodox Church's historic definition of its relationship to the world, or its expectations for the world. Even in its later
existence under the Ottoman yoke, Orthodoxy in its various national
and ethnic divisions was organized within a system of religious administration, the *millet* system, which respected in a peculiarly Ottoman fashion the Constantinian arrangement of church-state relations.
Nor did the plurality of religions within the Ottoman Empire raise
the issue of religious freedom in such a fashion as to put in question
Ottoman Islamic hegemony. Meanwhile, the Orthodox Church in
Russia aligned itself with the state, citing the Byzantine example as
warrant for its behavior, even if the actual arrangement was uniquely
Russian and not Byzantine. One thing was sure: Orthodoxy was the
undisputed religion of the Russian theocratic state. Thus American
separationism, religious pluralism, and denominationalism were bound
to be a puzzlement for Orthodoxy. Richard John Neuhaus identifies
the Orthodox problem when he observes that Orthodoxy in America
is "uncertain about whether it is *the church* in America, an American
denomination, or the Eastern Orthodox Church in Exile."[2] Indeed,
the Orthodox Church has not gotten very far in testing publicly its
catholic ecclesiology against the background of American separationism
and denominationalism.

But Orthodoxy's difficulties in interpreting and working creatively
with American separationism and denominationalism are not restricted
to that legacy of self-understanding and world relations which it brought
with it to the West. There are difficulties whose sources have specifically
to do with the radical changes which the historic American relationship between religion and culture is undergoing presently. For it does
appear, as I have suggested above, that the Enlightenment solution
to the breakdown of a united Christendom which established in America a legal separation of church and state finally has borne the fruit
of a highly secular society. It is a society which insists increasingly that
religious values and beliefs, as explicitly just that—i.e., religious—
claim no rightful place in public morality or role in public policy. This,
in turn, has exposed in stark relief the neutering effects of denominationalism upon Christianity and Judaism in America. The relativiza-
tion of religious conviction and reduction of the biblical religion to a
pale shadow of its historic presence as prophetic and salvific faith and
action in the world are inescapable phenomena of American culture.

On the positive side, however, Orthodoxy brings theological, liturgical, and ethical resources to this culture which, when added together, make a sum different from that of Western Christianity, Roman Catholic and Protestant. These can be exploited by the Orthodox. Orthodoxy has come to America with no appreciable historical stake in the Enlightenment doctrine of the separation of church and state. In fact, it bears an ecclesiology which exposes the metaphysical shallowness of that doctrine, especially in its latter-day interpretation, which radically delimits the mission of the Church in the world. This matter requires further exploration. But suffice it to say for the moment that the juridical terms in which the doctrine of the separation of church and state seeks to capture the Church's presence is, from the point of view of Orthodox ecclesiology, no description of the Church's true essence. According to such an ecclesiology, that essence is not juridical (or legal) but antinomical and eschatological. And contrary to the privatistic and functionalistic terms in which the separation doctrine defines the Church's mission—a definition which denominationalism promotes—the field of the Church's mission is nothing less than the whole fabric of human life, not just individuals, but the social, economic,and political relations, the institutions and values of human community. The irony in the final collapse of the American "Christendom" which the Orthodox Church must grasp is that while the secularism which breeds off such a divestiture raises a grave challenge to the salvific mission of the Church, the Church, having been released finally from all custodial obligations toward the culture, is now free, as it has not been for more than a millennium, to shake the foundations and through its own worship and community bring a criteriological vision and judgment to the "earthly" city.

A CASE IN POINT

Orthodox theologians in America have said little about the appropriate strategy for the Orthodox Church in its relations with the culture and the American democratic order. One exception to this rule is the Greek theologian Stanley Harakas. Harakas's analysis and normative recommendations, however, are not ones which I finally favor. He is not able to let go of Orthodoxy's Constantinian legacy; nor does he appreciate sufficiently the dangers of cultural accommodationism which a persistence in such a model of social ethics entails. His reformulation of the Orthodox theory of *symphonia* misses the chance to forge out of the present situation a church with a renewed sense of evangelical witness. Nevertheless, a review and critique of Harakas's position sets my constructive proposal in concrete reference to a contemporary Orthodox point of view, one which is representative of a substantial body of Orthodox sentiment.

Harakas's views are most fully elaborated in an article entitled "Orthodox Church-State Theory and American Democracy."[3] His goal in that essay is to work out some lines of correspondence or correlation between certain elements of the historic Orthodox theory of *symphonia* on church-state relations and, as he readily agrees, the quite different, even contradictory, theory of church-state relations embodied in the American system of separation. Harakas cites the Greek Orthodox theologian John Karmiris as saying that " 'in principle, the Orthodox reject both the system of Church control over the State and the system of State control over the Church, as well as the system of separation.' " The theory of *symphonia* envisions a " 'system of harmony and mutuality (*symphonia* and *synallelia*) [between church and state] which is based on the sufficiency and independence of the two co-existing and cooperating principles and powers [within one common society], without the subjugation of either the State to the Church or the Church to the State.' " This harmony is premised on the belief, continues Harakas, that "both Church and State are creatures of one Lord." Both have been brought into existence to serve particular purposes within any given social order, the Church "to initiate the Kingdom of God and to prepare for its eschatological realization" and the state "to serve the worldly needs of humanity, providing order, peace, justice and external harmony."[4] Obviously, states Harakas, American social, legal, and political realities do not reflect such a vision or disposition toward the ordering of human values and institutions.

> *Symphonia* calls for a close relationship of Church and State in which the State, in the person of the Emperor, was perceived to be protector of the Church, aided the Church in its work, embodied its canons and doctrine in Imperial law and intervened on the Church's behalf to deal with heresy and schism. For the Empire, the Church functioned as its soul and spirit, destined to provide inner unity and divine blessing for the State. The sys-

tem of *symphonia* meant a close and intimate relation of Church and State.

In contrast, the system of separation of Church and State as developed in the United States removed religious considerations from State concern and competency. This policy, strictly adhered to, has consistently widened the formal or appearance of formal relationships between religion and the State. . . . Both in spirit and form, it must be clearly admitted that the two systems of thought, considered as wholes, are diametrically opposed to each other.[5]

It may be, as Harakas notes, that the theory of *symphonia* is not inherently wedded to any specific political order, such as monarchy. But it is, in its inspiration and history, bound almost inextricably to the vision of a Christendom. Likewise, Harakas is unable to disengage himself from that vision, however much he seeks to modify it through his efforts to reinterpret "certain elements" of the *symphonia* theory and apply them in what he calls a "deontological, that is, ethical mode"[6] to the social and legal reality of separation in America. Harakas realizes that the identification of the Christian faith with the culture and the Church's influence upon the political processes cannot be very explicit under the separation arrangement and in view of the pluralism and secularity of the contemporary American order. This does not dissuade him, however, from insisting that another modified form of identification, different from that in the Orthodox Byzantine or Russian past, is not only possible but desirable. After all, reasons Harakas, the Orthodox Church, under the separation arrangement and consistent with the theory of *symphonia*, enjoys institutional autonomy and the freedom to preach and teach the Orthodox faith. This means that even though there is no Patriarchal presence which can mediate the Christian faith to the state through the emperor, there remains the opportunity for the Orthodox Church through the free citizens and Orthodox laity to "whisper" in the ear of the state. Since *demos* replaces Patriarch and emperor within a liberal democracy, *demos* if "churched" can presumably influence and shape the values of the society toward a Christian vision of life.[7] The means available to the Orthodox Church (and all other churches, presumably) are: (1) raising Christian social consciousness, and (2) at times assuming the posture of an interest group.

The Church, both as institution and as the people of God, must learn the methods appropriate to the time, age and place in which it finds itself. In the United States great moral issues are decided as often as not by letter campaigns, official and unofficial lobbying and petition. Part of the method by which the Orthodox Church can proclaim the Gospel in a democracy is by participating in the law-making procedure with the methods described above. The two major approaches which are appropriate to the Church are to prepare sharpened Christian consciences in the laity and to mobolize that consciousness in appropriate efforts at influencing legislation.[8]

Harakas's model of engagement is not so much pragmatic finally as it is functionalist. While it is perfectly clear from his extensive other writings that Harakas does not normally want to view religion's value in terms of its social utility, when reasoning about the relation of religion to public morality his argument comes out to be just about that. Religion, he tells us, is important to public life because it provides the moral ligaments which hold it together and give it strength for the purposes of justice and civic order pursued in the secular realm. "The State," he says, "needs the Church to help keep up the common morality, even though [under the American arrangement of separation] it cannot directly appeal to the Church for its legal judgment and sanctions."[9] Without the public influence of religion, a common morality to which the state must appeal for legitimation of its legislation and policies would not exist. Orthodoxy, therefore, is called upon to play a public role in the formation of the civic piety of the American people akin to the role it played in Byzantium, where, to be sure, the theory of *symphonia*, accepted as normative by both church and state, made that work easier. Harakas is realist enough to recognize that Orthodoxy's situation within a pervasive American religious pluralism and denominationalism leaves it with no prospect of being the primary, leave aside sole, religious force shaping the civic piety of the American people. Still, Orthodoxy, he proposes, must make its peace with the American pluralism. The Orthodox Church should make "its own identity with the nation . . . sufficiently broad and deep so that the concerns of the Church transcend its own membership and seek the welfare of the whole people."[10]

Worrisome in Harakas's proposal is not so much the goal of the common good which he envisions as the process of acculturation and accommodation for the Church which he incidentally invites. There could be no complaint with Harakas's prescription were it merely a call for Orthodox to overcome their habitual ethnocentrism and exercise a more faithful witness to the whole national community of the catholic truth of salvation sustained in the ongoing life and communion of the people of God. But Harakas robs the historical moment of any prospect of a renewed redemptive tension between the values and purposes of the Kingdom of God eschatologically present in the Church and the fallen order and values of the earthly city. This is the truly significant challenge presented to the Orthodox Church here in America—to reinvigorate the antinomy of church and world order which the New Testament writers and early Church understood as necessary for the gospel of salvation to ring true and powerful. Instead, Harakas would have the Orthodox Church assume its place beside the other mainline churches in America as contributor to and custodian of a common American faith and identity. The Orthodox Church should "learn to speak to the nation as a whole, to concern itself with the common problems of the people of this country," he says, and in so doing perhaps "become in some measure the 'soul' of the nation." Harakas identifies the purposes to which the Church should commit itself as the pursuit of "justice, fairness, spiritual values, the struggle against social and personal evil, human dignity, mutual love, the protection of personal freedom and rights, as well as the promotion of the sense of responsible citizenship."[11] Harakas hastily conflates the goals of the state with the objectives and purpose of Christian mission. This is not surprising since, as we have observed above, his tendency is to hypostatize *demos* and, on the level of Christian practice, merge the Christian laity into *demos'* ruling action upon a democratic order.

CONSTANTINIANISM AND NEO-CONSTANTINIANISM: THE HISTORIC PROTESTANT ACCOMMODATION

There is a sense in which Harakas has merely picked up where the Constantinian and Justinian synthesis of church and state left off. His efforts to account and compensate for the radical disjunction between the theocratic Byzantine past, with its unified Christian society,

and the secular American present, with its legal and sociological separation of church and state, land him in the same pit of cultural accommodation into which the mainline Protestant churches in America thrust
themselves earlier in this century. If, as some have argued, the Church
in the Byzantine synthesis forfeited its spiritual freedom and eschatological identity as the proleptic presence of the new order of Christ's
Kingdom in the world and became instead a legitimating organ of
theocratic absolutism,[12] so, in this century, the American mainline
churches have rendered themselves handmaids of the new liberal democratic order. Under the original Constantinianism, the state, in theory
at least, defined itself to be subject to religion. Constantine and Justinian were undoubtedly anxious about their standing before God. They,
however, did not hesitate either to make the state's purpose (e.g., its
security and dominion) the goals of the Church's functions. In other
words, the Byzantine princes used the Church as an organ of sacral
legitimation. Against just this trend in Byzantium monasticism raised
its voice of prophetic criticism and on occasion sent into the midst of
the imperial court a confessor who, sometimes at the cost of his own
life, called back the Church to its evangelical faith and reminded it
that the presence of Christ's Kingdom was only in the Church and
not embodied in the empire.

The neo-Constantinianism of the contemporary American Christian churches amounts to the surrender of their evangelical witness.
That surrender is compounded by a long history of compromise and
accommodation of the Protestant churches to liberalism and nationalism. Under the American arrangement of separation and under
the influence of a pervasive secularism, which by its very nature dismisses
the reality of God's active presence in this world, those who rule worry
not—certainly not in any conscientious public way—how they stand
before God, though, as yet, most do not hesitate to use God's name
to sanctify their own politics or the self-interest of the nation. The
churches accept this utilitarian definition of their nature and purpose.
In America the parade of church leaders is unceasing who, seeking to
influence the actors in the worldly exercise of dominion, assume for
themselves the mindset of those who rule by the sword rather than
by the power of the Cross.

The background of this situation is the Great Accommodation
of the mainline Protestant churches, which reached its apogee in the
Social Gospel movement of the late nineteenth and early twentieth

century. The leaders of that movement, the Washington Gladdens, Walter Rauschenbusches and Josiah Strongs, set out to Christianize the social order. Specifically, this meant challenging laissez-faire capitalism with a new vision of social and economic justice reflecting what they took to be the ethical essence of the Christian gospel. They saw themselves as issuing a prophetic call to the nation to live by the values of the Kingdom, which they readily associated with egalitarian justice, and heralding the manifest destiny of the American nation, which they viewed as the bearer of Christianity and democracy to the rest of the world. Nor was the mediating theology of a Rauschenbusch, which yet retained an evangelical core and nearness to St. Paul and the Hebrew prophets, sustained by the Social Gospel movement as a whole. The Protestant liberalism which seeped into much of mainline Christianity through the Social Gospel lost any sure sense of the Church as fundamentally in tension with civilization. The antinomy of church and world was gradually reduced to a pragmatic political and social struggle against the corporate evil of laissez-faire capitalism. The liberal theology, having lost "the sense of the broken relation between God and man, between the present and the coming Kingdom,"[13] submitted the Church as an agency, God-blessed to be sure, in service to the culture. The Church's soteriological mission was redefined in terms of the best aspirations of American liberal reform. Indeed, church, nation, and civilization were effectively equated one with another in the persuasion that American culture had absorbed already much of the spirit and ethical content of Christianity and that this was the almost inevitable evolutionary course of world civilization. As the religious historian Robert T. Handy has observed of the liberal movement, "The nation itself as bearer of civilization was elevated as an agency of the subjugation of the world to Christ! The mission of Christian faith was virtually being identified with the national destiny, with the progress of Civilization."[14]

Protestant fundamentalism has been interpreted as a traditionalist response to this Christian liberalism and cultural accommodationism of mainline American Protestantism. But in our day the fundamentalist countermovement with its newly acquired activist spirit shows no less a penchant to identify itself with the culture than did the Social Gospel. For the Social Gospel the medium of this accommodation was a progressivist ideology; for the contemporary religious right and kindred Protestant challengers to the mainline ascendency it is a latter-day ideology of economic and social conservatism. This conservative accommodation comes in a variety of styles, usually populist in appeal, whether Jim Bakker's consumerist religion for the blue collar, elderly, and socially marginalized classes; Jerry Falwell's religion of militant middle-class Americanism; or Robert Schuller's religion of self-help and positive thinking for the upwardly mobile white-collar professional.

Such religion is 100 percent American. It wholeheartedly sacralizes the American economic and political system. It acknowledges no antinomy between Christian faith and the American Way. If such religion has a complaint with American culture, it is that the society has drifted away from a past ideal embodiment of Christianity. The antinomy of church and world is often replaced with an almost Manichaean dualism, whether it be capitalism against communism, or born-again Christians against secular humanists and other subverters of the American Christendom. The vital eschatological tension between Christ's calling to a life of spiritual freedom and perfection and the violence of the fallen powers and principalities of this world is frequently replaced by a thoroughly fatalistic and flat-footed apocalypticism.

THE NAKED PUBLIC SQUARE: ANOTHER WRONG TURN

In his recent book *The Naked Public Square*, Richard John Neuhaus rails against what he interprets as the prevalent extreme secularist interpretations being given of late to the historic principle of separation of church and state. As every student of American culture knows, the separation principle is embedded in the American Constitution and has been inherited from the medieval debate over the relative powers of the imperial and sacerdotal authorities. The impetus in recent years of American legal and political thinking on church-state questions, says Neuhaus, has been to define religion as an activity and persuasion appropriate to the sphere of private behavior, but severely suspect when it seeks to influence the public—political—realm. The examples Neuhaus offers are, for example, the Supreme Court ban on prayer in public schools and the attempt to abstract the question of the legality of abortion from all religious and moral reasoning in the *Roe* v. *Wade* decision. The banner under which such arguments are made is that the ideal stance of government toward religion is total neutrality. This thinking, argues Neuhaus, proceeds under the erroneous assumption that liberal democracy is safest when protected from the influence of religious beliefs and values and that, likewise, religion is most truly itself when religious values and practices are disentangled totally from the public square and the political process.[15] This reasoning, he says, ignores the fact that the American culture has been greatly shaped by Protestant Christianity in particular and biblical theism in general. Likewise, in its defiance of the Tillichian insight that religion is the heart of culture and culture is the form of religion, it would deprive our liberal democracy of the historically evolved symbols of transcendence rooted in Judeo-Christian faith which have grounded our public values and legitimated American institutions. In other words, insists Neuhaus, this process of voiding the public square of religious values and symbols is also a grave threat to our free institutions, robbing them of a higher reference and source of legitimation and prescribed limit.

Neuhaus stands as a rather unambiguous example of a Protestant mainline theologian and churchman who in some fundamental sense refuses to let go of the idea of an American Christendom. One chapter of his book is titled, quite sympathetically, "Christendom Reconsidered." Indeed, as critical as Neuhaus is of the strategy and many of the goals of the new religious right, his fascination with the movement is largely explained by the sympathy he has with the movement's frustration over the lost grip of Protestant religion on the culture as a formative force and source and measure of public values.

Neuhaus makes a serious cultural miscalculation when he appeals to the religious spirit of the American people and strategizes in consensualist language on the basis of such a proposed religiosity about the new culture-formative role of American Christianity. For while three quarters of Americans might describe themselves as religious, there is little other evidence to indicate that such religiosity always includes the content or conviction of biblical faith. The trend in America toward the secularization of religion identified by Will Herberg nearly three decades ago has increased, not decreased. It is more, not less, true today than in the 1950s that "Americans who so overwhelmingly affirm their belief in God and their membership in historic churches" also affirm in a "majority. . . , without any sense of incongruousness, that their religion has little to do with their politics or business affairs, except to provide an additional sanction and drive"[16] to pursue such autonomous secular goals. Contrary to what Neuhaus might wish to think and what Harvey Cox also seems to want to believe in his recent book, *Religion in the Secular City*,[17] the rapid secularization of American life which was much talked about in the sixties continues to advance. The new fundamentalism is not, as these authors suggest, some revelation of the persistence (or harbinger of the renewal) of biblical religion in the culture. Indeed, I would be more inclined to argue that the rise of this reactionary religion is a symptom of the truly advanced pace of secularization in our society. Further, it is very improbable that such a secular culture is going to be receptive to anything but the most compromising efforts by the Church to demonstrate some mutual immanence of Christianity and culture as Neuhaus and Cox each in his own way proposes should be done.[18]

Neuhaus's proposal that the churches ought to concentrate on nurturing a new public piety turns out to be just another twist in the Protestant mainline accommodationism and no new departure. The functionalistic ecclesiology seen in Harakas's revision of the old Constantinianism is just as present in Neuhaus's revision of the new Constantinianism. In contrast to this functionalism which judges religion's value primarily in terms of its culture-formative role, Orthodox ecclesiology insists that what God requires primarily of the Church in all times and all places is that it attend to its salvific mission in the world. This cannot be equated simply with culture formation or maintenance. "The Church," wrote Alexander Schmemann, "is never more present to the world and more 'useful' to it than when she is totally free from it, free from it not only 'externally,' i.e., independent from its structures and powers, but also and primarily internally, i.e., free from her own spiritual surrender to its values and treasures."[19] This is good advice for Christians in the so-called postmodern age now being heralded by some contemporary theologians.

ANOTHER PERSPECTIVE ON SEPARATION OF CHURCH AND STATE

It is more than twenty-five years since the publication of John Courtney Murray's *We Hold These Truths*, his seminal Roman Catholic interpretation of the relation of religion to the American order. Murray's primary purpose in the book was to demonstrate how the Roman Catholic tradition of natural law could sharpen and clarify a public philosophy adequate to guide America through perilous times both at home and in international politics. My interest in *We Hold These Truths* is Murray's smartly nuanced argument for why the Roman Catholic Church in America should accept the legal principle and historic American prejudice in favor of separation of church and state.[20]

Murray argued for this accommodation while rejecting all efforts to make a theology of separation or to elevate it to a religious doctrine valid wherever the Church is present. Thus he rightly distanced himself from free church Protestants and latter-day secularists who, for vastly different reasons, wish to claim that such an arrangement is universally correct and applicable. Murray preferred to rest his case in favor of separation on the prudential judgment that historically it has secured in America a public peace among potentially warring religious parties which no other conceivable arrangement could have procured. Thus, argued Murray, the "no establishment" and "free exercise" clauses of the First Amendment need not be viewed as sectarian propositions unsuited to a catholic faith or as universally valid principles. Rather, they could be affirmed provisionally as necessary conclusions of practical reasons reflecting on the history of the plurality of religious and nonreligious community in America, as well as the force of individualism and the impulse to self-government and volunteerism in American life. Further, the "free exercise" and "no establishment" clauses of the First Amendment, he argued, do obtain historically a relative ethical warrant, since they promote the human need and desire for a temporal peace and social concord. And, no less important, these "articles of peace" have secured a genuine freedom for the churches in America. The clear distinction between church and state in the Constitution which circumscribes the powers of government has wisely limited those powers, as Murray said, "to the pursuit of certain enumerated secular purposes (to say that the purposes are secular is not to deny that many are also moral; so for instance the establishment of justice, peace, the promotion of the general welfare, etc.). Thus made autonomous in its own sphere, government . . . [is] denied all competence in the field of religion."[21] I submit that with all of the above observations and conclusions Orthodox can agree and that in such they ought to seek guidance.

But there is a point in Murray's analysis beyond which Orthodox cannot go. In his discussion of the American separation of church and state, Murray defined the Church as "the armature of man's spiritual freedom and as a structural principle of a free society."[22] Following in this fashion, he described the relation of the Church to the whole realm of secular life as fulfilling two specific purposes. First, persons find in the Church a spiritual freedom and corporate identity as the people of God which transcends the claims of the public and political powers. And second, the Church is an institution in which a moral consensus can be mobilized effectively and brought to bear upon the state in order to temper and humanize state power. Thus Murray's analysis gave to the separation theory a moral substance which tilts against the contemporary tendency for its complete secularization into a church-antagonistic wall of separation doctrine. His overriding concern seems to have been to secure in theory the role of the Church as a mediating institution between the state and the democratic public, guarding against state absolutism. Murray did not claim to be saying anything new here. He deliberately sought to show that the separationist distinction between church and state can serve the spiritual freedom and destiny of humankind and need not be so interpreted as to support the modern secularist penchant for an autonomous state free of all external constraints, including the Church, upon its behavior.

The Orthodox disagreement with Murray's analysis would not be on this level of moral and practical argument but would have to do specifically with the ecclesiology, largely implicit, which is behind his public theology. As a true heir of the old Constantinianism, Murray, the neo-Thomist — like his Protestant neo-orthodox counterpart and contemporary, Reinhold Niebuhr — made his ecclesiology the support of a theory of the best possible political order for a pluralistic society. His embrace of the separation arrangement serves the greater political strategy of reconstructing the American Christendom, albeit in republican terms, under the guidance of a natural reason shared by Christian and non-Christian alike.[23] Here it is that the error of Murray's strategy emerges. Trenchantly, Franklin Littell has observed that "every discussion of religious liberty which begins with the political objective ends in confusion. The political benefits of religious liberty, and they are very great, are *derivative*: they are the legitimate result, the proper fruit, of a right understanding of the role and mission of the church in human history."[24] The confusion of which Littell is speaking is that in such theologies as those of Murray and Niebuhr the *sine qua non* of the Church gets defined willy-nilly as the pursuit of that political good in which the state is guided by Christian virtues and principles. In Murray's case, to be sure, these include natural virtues and principles which are available to reason.

This sort of reinterpretation of the Church's evangelical mission and subordination of it to the purposes of Christianizing the state is an inheritance of Latin as well as Byzantine Christendom. It is not by any means accidental that those in America who have been most alert to such wrong turns in Christian social ethics are representatives of free church Protestantism, such as Franklin Littell. Yet I would like to argue for the moment that this process by which Christian social ethics historically became a strategy of political rule rather than a missiological action upon the world took a specific turn in the West which has made the Orthodox presence in the West and specifically in America highly problematic. The Church in the Byzantine East allowed itself to become a sacramental functionary of the Byzantine state; but it did not, as in the Latin West, define itself in juridical terms as a power and authority in relation and/or juxtaposition to the state. The latter was the strong sense of the Church which John Courtney Murray carried in his head as he wrote on church-state relations. And thus for Murray the arguments about religious freedom and church-state relations pivot on juridical questionings about the delimitation of these two institutions and their respective spheres of power and authority. Murray, therefore, could take immediate advantage of the legal logic of the constitutional principle of separation, in a way Orthodox cannot, in order to argue his case that the purposes of the Church are capable not only of being comprehended in terms of law but of being translated by reason into postulates applicable to a proper definition and delimitation of the state's purposes. This, Murray believed, is what makes religious freedom possible and a free society its necessary correlative. It is a highly attractive theory.

A RETURN TO CHRISTIAN SOCIAL ETHICS AS MISSION

When the question of church-state relations is posed in the above fashion, the sacramental nature and eschatological mission of the Church almost invariably gets lost beneath a strategy to secure and preserve the best possible temporal arrangement of competing or co-operative spiritual and secular powers. Lost is the true incarnational vision of a unified creation under one Lord. The substitution of a juridical interpretation of the relation of church and state (or secular order) for an eschatological understanding of the Church's relationship to the world is the beginning of Western secularism. In the East the Church was reduced to a spiritual organ of the Byzantine state and the eschatological freedom of the Church confined ultimately to liturgy and monastic vocation. The church-world relationship of eschatological tension between the "old" and the "new" creation was subordinated tragically to a vision of an ecumenical Christian society. Nevertheless, to whatever extent the evangelical mission of the Church in the East was gradually subordinated and put into the service of the imperial ambitions of the Byzantine state, the Orthodox Church remained in its own self-conception and liturgical practice a sacramental and eschatological presence of the Kingdom in a world which, though fallen, was theonomous and the very matter of the Spirit's sanctifying action. A secularistic disjunction of church and world and church and state into two autonomous realms was not known in the East. Such a secularism and metaphysical dualism, however, was gestated from within the Latin Church itself through its theology and its exercise of an ethic of power vis-à-vis the state. The Latin Church came to see itself very much as an institution in which power and authority reside and freedom, even political freedom, is a correlative of obedience to that power and that authority. Under the weight of this juridical ecclesiology, the eschatology of the Latin Church became individualistic, static, and futuristic, the Kingdom of God being defined largely as a *state* of beatitude or a vision of God "beyond" this world. This loss of a sense of the *mysterion* and of the Church as the antinomical presence of God's Kingdom in the world contributed to the severance in Roman Catholicism of the ontological connection between the Church, as sacramental and eschatological presence of the Kingdom, and the world. Thus the experience of the Church as the subject of antinomy in the world, for the sake of the world, was replaced in the West by a variety of metaphysical dualisms in which, depending upon the specific spirituality or ethic, some lesser or greater degree of tension, competition, or cooperation between church and secular order is posited. Viewed in this light, the Gelasian theory of the two swords, Luther's notion of the two realms, and the American principle of separation of church and state all have more in common with one another than any one of the three has in common with the Orthodox vision of church and world.

Here is the source of the difficulty for the Orthodox Church in America when it seeks to map out a strategy of engagement with the American culture and to interpret the claims which American democratic institutions and laws make about the nature of the public realm and the role of the churches in it. For while the Orthodox Church might on prudential and pragmatic grounds live with the American separation arrangement, it remains impossible for it to develop a social ethic which treats that arrangement as consistent with the truth in its own ecclesiology and soteriology, as Protestants and Roman Catholics have been able to do. Orthodoxy in America, if it is truthful to its catholic faith, cannot view the separation arrangement as normative for the life of the Church or indicative of the real relationship of church and world. Orthodoxy cannot accept the discontinuity of nature and grace which all latter-day notions of the separation arrangement presuppose almost as a metaphysical postulate. Contrary to the dualism of the separation arrangement, Orthodoxy must insist that the Church in its very essence contains the world and expresses its very fulfillment and destiny in eucharistic worship. There is no separation, tension, or competition between church and world experienced as two autonomous institutions, rather there is the experience of an antinomy between church and *world* (a far more inclusive — not juridical — term than *state*) when the Church gathered in sacramental action exposes the world in its true nature and purpose as God's good creation and matter out of which his Kingdom is brought into existence. For it is only in and through this divine truth about the world revealed in the life of the Church that the world itself is confronted with the magnitude of its sin and the dark deception of its violent and deadly ways.

The theological data of the Christian faith, known in its first order in the very person of the Incarnate Lord and in its second and third orders through Scripture and worship, indicates that the Church is the world as redeemed and reconciled, eschatologically stripped of the sin which sets the powers and principalities of this world against the reign of God. If there is any sort of Christian dualism, it is ethical — not ontological, as American separationism implies and modern secularism presupposes.[25] The world of nature and the world of grace are not discontinuous because it was through and by the Word that "all things were made" (John 1:3 RSV) and "in him all things hold together" (Col. 1:17 RSV). Not even sin, however great its disruptive force, can change this. For as seen in Christ's life, death, and Resurrection, the creative and redeeming action of God is even more powerful than the Evil One. It is in an ethical, not ontological, sense that the Gospel of John speaks of the world as the enemy of Christ and his Church. Christ is in the world, "the light has come into the world" (John 3:19 RSV). His Spirit is present and sanctifying within the Church but also within the world, insofar as the Church eucharistically contains the whole world. The antimony of church and world, the judgment which the Church brings into the world, exists because the wicked have chosen darkness and rejected the light, not because God has set himself against the world or because the world is somehow separated from his grace. "For God so loved the world that he gave his only Son" (John 3:16 RSV). The children of light are as strangers and sojourners in this world, but not in any sociological sense. This world belongs as much to them as it does to the children of darkness. Indeed, it is even more theirs, insofar as they know it as God's field of redemption and love. It is their eschatological faith in a transfigured world, freed of the rule of the principalities and powers of the fallen order, that makes it impossible for Christians to call this present world order "home." For they are able to see and experience the world as it is intended by God and can be content neither with the darkness in which it takes pleasure nor with its rejection of the light which would reveal its true nature and fulfillment.

This is no mere Christian version of utopia. A living truth is at stake, a truth not reducible merely to a set of rational postulates or legal arrangements. This Christian truth is an action in God's behalf upon the world for the sake of the world. "But he who does what is true comes to the light, that it may be clearly seen that his deeds have been wrought in God" (John 3:21 RSV). The people of God gather in liturgical response to his call in order that they in their lives reveal his very presence in the world and the reconciling love through which he draws back that darkened and fragmented world into the light and wholeness of his Kingdom.

"Our way of thinking," wrote Irenaeus, "harmonizes with the Eucharist, and the Eucharist in its turn confirms our way of thinking."[26] Christian truth is rooted in the praxis of worship. And that praxis exists for no other reason than to make known God's judgment and reconciling presence in the world. Eucharistic worship does not suppose the Church as a structure of power. Through worship Christians come to know themselves as agapic (powerless but charismatic) mission to the world. It is not the business of the Church to impose a new, presumably more just, ethic of power on the world. Rather, it is the calling of the people of God to demonstrate his love for the world through their obedient service to his Kingdom. There is no objection in this ecclesiology to the state exercising a temporal governance over human community relatively free of a meddling church. This is a function which the Church readily grants to the state. The trouble is that the separation doctrine perpetrates the secular notion that the world really does not need the Church or God. It denies that there is a serious connection between religious practice and belief and the conduct or destiny of worldly affairs or even worldly justice. In other words it denies the primary experience of Christian worship, that in and through the Church God heals the ruptured relationship between his creation and himself, reconciling all in Jesus Christ (2 Cor. 5:17–21 RSV). There is something inherently contradictory about Orthodox Christians coming together in worship to declare that they have experienced such a thing and promising that they will behave consistently with that truth and then going out into the world to take their directives from a legal arrangement which declares that none of this is really so.

CIVIL RELIGION OR CHRISTIAN WITNESS

John Howard Yoder has argued that "by transforming the separation of church and state from the original notion of the Anabaptists, Friends, and Baptists, which had been rooted in the incommensurability of two orders, into the pragmatic fair-play notion of the Bill of Rights — namely, that no sect should have an unfair advantage and that the matter of establishment should be left to the several states — room was created for a new and more powerful version of the fusion of civil and religious covenants"[27] in America. The argument which Yoder makes from these critical observations is most intriguing and, I think, correct, not because the free church version of separation was right — it exhibits one version of that dualism alluded to above which is at the source of Western secularism — but because he trenchantly exposes the powerful impetus in the ideology of separation toward a civil religion and the commensurate spiritual impoverishment of the American churches. Similarly, David Little has hit the nail on the head when he argues that the secular warrants for separation are based in a positivistic description of religious belief as volatile enthusiasm and ephemeral opinion and in a utilitarian toleration of such phenomena as private matters of no relevance or use in public and civil life.[28] Under the rules of such an ideology all claims by a church that it is more than a local manifestation of the people of God—i.e., that it is catholic and universal and that the truth it promotes is a public truth for the good of all—will be judged as in defiance of the established rules of fair play.

Such an ideology presents a special problem for churches such as the Roman Catholic, Episcopal, or Orthodox, for whom mission in and to the world is inseparable from a catholic ecclesiology. But this ideology also has the power to persuade these churches and other American churches historically accustomed to an establishment status to accept the invitation forthcoming from the civil authorities to sanctify the civil covenant in a "new version of the ancient status of 'establishment'."[29] Forthwith the catholic and evangelical aspirations of the American churches are transmuted into loyalties to the national purpose and redefined as spiritual service to the nation. Of course, the agreement is one which places no obligation upon the civil authority to regard the Church as in any sense an equal. This new form of Constantinianism is also thoroughly Erastian. Yet the churches behave as if it is not and gladly seek in this relationship compensation for the particularity of denominationalism, with the self-assurance that by entering into it they are fulfilling their mission to the world.

Already, Orthodoxy, deprived of its traditional influence on its native cultures, has demonstrated a powerful propensity to substitute the civil religion for its loss. Unfortunately, when Stanley Harakas speaks of the Orthodox Church serving the highest values and goals of the nation, one detects in such a conscious reformulation of the *symphonia* theory the invitation—surely not intended by the author, but nevertheless real—for a new form of surrender of the Church's free identity and mission to a historic social order. This kind of plea is particularly dangerous for a church such as the Orthodox which has identified itself so completely in the past with ethnic and nationalistic aspirations, whether Greek, Russian, Armenian, or Serbian. To impress upon such a church an "obligation" to serve the American order as the source and inspiration for a common morality, as Harakas does, is to invite Americanized Orthodox of present and future generations who have abandoned the old ethnic and nationalistic goals to a new uncritical identification of their faith with the American Way, just as their parents and grandparents equated their Orthodox faith with Hellenism or Armenianism.

It is not enough, however, simply to reject the civil religion while acknowledging that for some it is a good which binds together the nation and provides it with a sense of purpose and a source of transcendent judgment, or that for others it is a mixed blessing and curse, providing all that the former say it does but also presenting the threat of idolatry on all levels of American life, public and private. To assume such a tactic is to miss the opportunity to do what is actually required of any Christian theologian who would seek to radically redefine the Church's mode of engagement with the American culture. Civil religion is not the issue, though it is certainly symptomatic of the problem with which this inquiry has been concerned. The problem is that the American churches by and large have forgotten the meaning and content of a truly catholic ecclesiology and mission and have substituted in its place one which images the Church in terms of the divided world which God wishes to redeem and make whole through the Church's action upon it. Taken in this light, it doesn't matter much whether American denominationalism is understood as the inevitable adjustment to the secular doctrine of separation or as the reason why it had come to be. No church which understands itself through an ecclesiology like that of the Orthodox Church will remain truthful to its own nature and purpose if it accepts that nomenclature as self-definitive. But worse still, once a church makes its vestments from the cloth of the world's own dividedness, it renders itself incapable of being the presence of the Kingdom to the world.

The deadly force of denominationalism is not the objective sociological reality of a plurality of churches within a single culture or society. The Church is prepared by the story of Creation, Fall and salvation which it carries forth into the world to make sense of this tragic condition and even find hope in it. No, the real threat of denominationalism is that as theory, history, or description it supplants that story as the normative account of the Church's relation to the world. This is not merely a threat. Nearly thirty years ago in *Protestant — Catholic — Jew*, Will Herberg described this as accomplished in the minds of most Americans. "In America," he wrote, "religious pluralism is thus not merely a historical and political fact; it is, in the mind of Americans, the primordial condition of things, an essential aspect of the American Way of Life, and therefore in itself an aspect of religious belief. Americans, in other words, believe that the plurality of religious groups is a proper and legitimate condition."[30] Yet this pluralism which Americans take as belonging to the very essence of Christianity or religion in general is not the pluralism of the trinitarian Kingdom. It is not a pluralism which participates in the unity of God, unless the nation be taken as God! Indeed, when the Christian churches accept the neo-Constantinian role of sacralizing the American order within the separation arrangement and under the overarching symbolism of the American civil religion, all talk of a transcendent source of criticism above the nation tends to become just that — talk. If the measure of my students in an urban Roman Catholic college is any indication of what Americans — even those who identify with a church — think, then when Americans think *nation* and *church*, as Herberg detected even in the 1950s, they already define *church* as a constitutive element of *nation*, not as transcending it.

THE STRUGGLE FOR CATHOLICITY IN A DENOMINATIONAL SOCIETY

Orthodox ecclesiology is able to acknowledge, account for, and address denominationalism as one instance of the fragmentariness of a fallen creation. The Church is in and is a part of this broken world. The Church, like the one whom it follows, does not escape all its disintegrative forces; rather it endures those forces for the sake of the world. Sectarianism is impermissible on christological grounds.

Following the lead of Ernst Troeltsch, H. Richard Niebuhr, in *The Social Sources of Denominationalism*, tried to make some positive sense out of the sectarian impetus and denominational character of American Christianity. Sects, he argued, have served the purpose throughout history of "recalling Christendom to its mission." The real "evil of denominationalism," he went on to say, "lies in the conditions which make the rise of sects desirable and necessary: in the failure of the churches to transcend the social conditions which fashion them into caste organizations, to sublimate their loyalties to standards and institutions only remotely relevant if not contrary to the Christian ideal, to resist the temptation of making their own self-preservation and extension the primary object of their endeavor."[31] Niebuhr's account in many ways remains an apt description of the sources of sectarianism and denominationalism in America. Certainly his charge against the mainline churches in America that they have not been able to remain both catholic and evangelical was well taken. His argument about the good of sectarian movements is also persuasive. However, on the other side of the ledger, even as sectarian and free church varieties of Protestantism have served a purpose comparable to the monasticism of early and medieval Christianity, they have not been the equivalent thereof. The successful persistence of these Protestant countermovements in an "against the world" ethic is also a measure of their failure to be a catholic presence of the Kingdom *in* the world. Monasticism—particularly Eastern monasticism, which did not become clericized as did Western monasticism—was able to criticize the Church as institution from *within* the Church for the sake of the purity and unity of the Church.

Sectarian and denominational Protestantism represents a breakdown of an essential internal antinomy within the Church. For the Church to be mission in and to the world there must exist within its *unified* life the antinomy of flesh and spirit, institution and event, world and Kingdom which the Church itself introduces into the world as the eschatological presence of the Kingdom. The absence of this antinomy within a *unified* life of the Church and its externalization into many competing main church bodies and sects is the very essence of American denominationalism.

Niebuhr rightly viewed this as an ultimately intolerable situation which threatens the catholicity and evangelical mission of the Church. The Church's very *sine qua non* is jeopardized. But Niebuhr's solution lapsed into a romanticized vision of a pneumatic church known through its loving acts. Interestingly, Niebuhr took up the Franciscan movement as an example of the real presence of this agapic fellowship with its purifying and regenerating effects upon the Church. Niebuhr failed to take sufficient notice, however, of the fact that the Franciscan movement remained associated with the catholic body of the Church and did not break off as a separate sect. The great creative good which this powerful, largely lay, movement achieved for the Church had to do most especially with the fact that it kept the antinomy of flesh and spirit, institution and event, and world and Kingdom located within a unified Church. In the case of the Franciscans the spirit remained incarnate. The same cannot be said of the Society of Friends, which Niebuhr also mentions as an example of the true church within the Church. This does not deny the good which Niebuhr says the Friends

have done within the culture.[32] Yet perhaps the theological relocation of the primary field of Christian antinomy — neo-orthodoxy called
it dialectic or tension — from within the Church itself to the culture
is the clearest proof of how far American Protestantism has gone in
forgetting the other more truly catholic alternative. Little wonder also
that Protestant neo-orthodoxy turned from ecclesiology to a theology
of culture.

But, as I have argued throughout, the most alluring temptation
for Orthodoxy is to shape its ecclesiology in America into an instrument of a new cultural and political accommodationism. Due to the
peculiar circumstances of the American social reality, such an accommodation would be far more damaging to the Orthodox Church and
its mission to the world than anything that happened in the Byzantine or Russian past. The catholicity of the Orthodox Church is threatened here in ways unknown to it in its past; and these largely have
to do with the explosive pluralism, reductive relativism, and seduc-
tive secularism of the American order. In view of this, the single greatest
challenge which the denominational society presents to Orthodoxy is
that of coming to terms with its own particularity. Here, perhaps, Orthodoxy has a positive lesson to learn from the representatives of the
American free church Protestant tradition. By attending to and prac-
ticing their particularity as discrete disciplined communities of faith,
they have exercised a freedom vis-à-vis the culture which only the
monastic communities of an earlier era obtained elsewhere. While learning this lesson, however, Orthodoxy must remember also that the
primary focus of the church-world antinomy is the Church itself. This
catholic insight is jeopardized not only by the American social reality
but because, by and large, the Orthodox have arrived in it without
the monks. I am not certain the old monasticism is as dead as some
have argued. But even if this is so, the situation in some sense merely
reverts back to that before the advent of monasticism in the fourth
century. As has been the case always, the future of the Church and
its mission rests finally in the hands of the laity. The apostolic, catholic,
and evangelical faith is not the possession of priests and bishops; it
is the possession of the whole people of God. The retention by the
Orthodox Church of its catholicity and the achievement of a truly
evangelical presence in America may well be determined by whether
or not it gives birth to a lay movement which reaffirms the truths of

the faith, the call to holiness, and the vision of Christ's Kingdom which monasticism has represented.

Until some kind of a monastic presence in its old or a new, as yet undefined, shape arises from within the life of the Church, the Orthodox Church in America ought to be learning how to be catholic while acknowledging that sociologically it is only one among many churches here in America. This understanding ought to foster within the internal life of the Church a renewed emphasis upon the catholicity of the Church experienced and expressed eucharistically rather than judged by the external standards of the civil religion or any political ideology. The Church knows that even within the particularity of the local community, in the eucharistic gathering under the presidency of the bishop, Christ is totally present; and those gathered have a taste of the unity of life and peace which nations promise but are unable to deliver. A people with just this knowledge and the conviction to give expression to it wherever they go, in word and in deed, by loving acts and by entering into just relations with others, by timely rebuke of economic and political evils, and by pioneering new forms of human association and human service, may not always seem of much consequence from the world's point of view. This, however, should be no discouragement. For by being such a people, the Church "is a sign that God, not the nations," not politics, not economics, not science, not business or technology, "rules this world."[33] By being such a presence in the world, the Church provides the vision and lived experience through which those within the Church, and even those outside it, can discern in human history and the journey of the American nation something more than the mere clank of machinery, the chain catching hold, the cars jerking forward. I do not think that Christ expects any more of his people than this. The rest he has willingly taken upon himself to accomplish in his own time.

7

The Americanization of Orthodoxy:
Crisis and Challenge

ALL OF THE ORTHODOX CHURCHES in America have stories to tell of dispersion. And any serious attempt by Orthodox Americans to address the new station of their national churches in the unfamiliar context of a pluralistic, secular society, whose Christian roots are not even Orthodox, has to begin with a truthful telling of these stories. This is no less the case for Armenian Orthodox than for Greek, Roumanian, or Syrian Orthodox. Yet, perhaps, the case of the Armenian diaspora, and the success or failure of the Armenian Church to make sense of it, can serve as a special case study. This I propose because of the intensity of the Armenian experience due to the genocide of 1915–23. For if there is such a thing as "a tragically spectacular collapse"[1] of an Orthodox world which sent an Orthodox people into a worldwide diaspora and set the pattern for other such dispersions of the twentieth century, it is the Turkish genocide of the Armenians during the First World War.

In this final chapter, I intend to reflect theologically from out of the Armenian experience and to expand the discussion into an analysis of some of the problems facing the Orthodox churches in America. Orthodoxy in America is at a critical moment. Until now the Orthodox churches have been immigrant churches retaining in bold relief the stamp of their national origins. The time has come, however, when to persist as such risks not only estranging vast numbers of American-born Orthodox but closing off all future opportunities for effectively witnessing to the Orthodox faith in this American society. None of these churches, however much they may wish to, can persist here as the kind of national churches which they were in their indigenous cultures. If they continue to behave as if they can re-create their historical Orthodox homes in America, the likelihood is that they in time simply will exhaust themselves before social forces which were never adequately understood. The challenges these churches must answer not only in order to survive but in order to meet the spiritual needs of their people are unlike any that Orthodoxy has encountered in the past. Their mission requires a greater witness to the apostolic faith *without the expectation* that, as in Byzantium or the conversion of the Slavic peoples, Orthodoxy can make this secular and pluralistic culture of North America its own, yet *with the conviction* that the faith they live is filled with truth and of ultimate concern to all who would look and listen.

THE ARMENIAN CHURCH IN DIASPORA

Armenians in the diaspora will often respond to those inquiring of their national origin and religious faith that Armenia was the first nation to adopt Christianity as a state religion. The date of that national conversion is 314 (some put it as far back as 301), coming one year after the Edict of Milan (313), which granted official toleration of Christianity within the Roman Empire. It precedes by nearly seventy years Theodosius's promulgation of Christianity as the official religion of the empire. This Christian nation survived until the modern era, but not without a series of tragedies and setbacks which culminated in the genocide and great dispersion of the First World War. Indeed, diaspora has been a recurrent experience of the Armenian nation. In the tenth century the Armenians were driven out of greater Armenia by the Seljuk Turk invaders. A massive migration followed the fall of Ani, the great medieval city-fortress and capital of Armenia. Many of the nobility took refuge to the south and founded the independent kingdom of Cilicia. In 1375 that kingdom succumbed to the Memlouks. Armenians fled as far as Poland, Roumania, Bulgaria, and Hungary. Another migration occurred in 1451 with the fall of Constantinople. The sultans sought to counterbalance the Greek presence by moving thousands of Armenians—whose skills in commerce and the crafts were valued by the new Turkic rulers—to the city from Armenia and Cilicia. At this time an Armenian patriarchate was also established in Constantinople. During the sixteenth century the

Turkish-Persian wars broke out, and at the turn of the seventeenth century Armenia was invaded by the Persians. Those Armenians who could escape the conquerors emigrated to the Balkan countries and Eastern Europe to join those of earlier immigrations. Many who were not able to flee were deported in 1605 to the Persian capital of Isfahan, eventually founding nearby the Armenian city of New Julfa.

These national hardships did not destroy the distinctively Christian national ethos of the Armenian people. Indeed, they evoked heroic stances in defense of the historic faith. Armenians persist in looking to this history as proof and encouragement that they as a people and church can overcome the devastation to the national and religious life wrought by the genocide and great dispersion of this century. Nevertheless, there also has been self-delusion in this sort of thinking which has prevented the Armenian Church from meeting the formidable challenges to its religious life posed by the new American host culture and society. Such thinking, in its self-delusion, has been symptomatic of the Armenian Church's refusal to come to terms with what actually happened in 1915. The Armenocide was not only the slaughter of one and one half million Armenians, fully one-half of the Armenians in the historic homeland, but the very death of the Armenian Christian world. The Christian nation which St. Gregory the Illuminator founded in the fourth century had been slowly strangled by the Ottoman Yoke and was finally crucified and put to death by the Young Turk.

In this century most of the national Orthodox churches have suffered Golgothas similar to that of the Armenian Church, though, again, perhaps none were quite so devastating to the national life. As in the Armenian case, these churches also have experienced a virtual resurrection. Armenians are familiar with homilies and Easter sermons on the resurrection of their nation and church. Yet, so very often these sermons trumpet a triumphalism which encourages Armenians to behave as if the old Armenian world had never died and is yet present wherever they gather together as church. Like the disciples, who after the Crucifixion of their Lord could not believe what had happened and when encountered by Jesus in his resurrected glorified body did not recognize him, Armenians also have not yet perceived the Armenian Church in its resurrected body. The diaspora resurrection of the Armenian Church is in the form of a spiritual body. This new life spells the end of the Armenian Church's long isolation from the other Christian churches for the sake of the nation's survival. Yet, the Church behaves as if it is still under the Ottoman *millet* system.[2] In other words, the Church continues to deny the collapse of the temporal order to which it once gave birth and for so long assumed primary responsibility. For Armenians in the American diaspora the Church became that refuge in which they could pursue the illusion of a golden age, which they also believed the Church was somehow capable of restoring. The Church existed in order to make the "old world" present and not the Kingdom of God. Cut off from the traditional religious life and with little available means of recalling the actual substance of the historical piety and practice, Armenians in the American diaspora constructed an ersatz religiosity which amounted to a fantastic and futile endeavor to sacralize an extreme ethnocentrism and secular nationalism.

Contributing to this spiritual malaise, there arose a jurisdictional dispute during the 1930s which finally divided the Armenian Church in America into two dioceses, one under the Catholicos of the See of Holy Etchmiadzin in Soviet Armenia and the other under the Catholicos of the Holy See of Cilicia in Antelias, Lebanon. The rift continues to this day, although in recent years bilateral talks and negotiations between representatives of the two dioceses have inched toward unification. Nevertheless, the politics of the rift and the very processes presumably directed toward its settlement also reveal the extent to which the Armenian Church has undergone a secularization which has vitiated the spiritual life of its people, even threatening the continued presence of the Armenian Church in America. Thus, for some, the question of Church unity remains a function of Cold War politics: "What will happen without the leverage of the 'free' See of Cilicia in the Church here in America?" "Could the Armenian Church become a servile pawn of Soviet politics mediated by the Catholicos in Etchmiadzin?" These sorts of questions were raised, in fact, by members of the National Representative Assembly of the Prelacy of the Armenian Apostolic Church in America during May 1984. Aside from what grounds such political questions obtain in the real world of today, they raise the spectre of a church whose whole reason for existing has become, in the minds of many of its leaders, to wage a political war over the Armenian nation's destiny — whether it will be free or Soviet, limited to the present boundaries or expanded into eastern Turkey. Where real politics end and fantasy begins is sometimes difficult to discern within the Armenian national diaspora life. What is certain is that the secularization within the Armenian Church threatens to render its presence all

but meaningless to those American-born Armenians of a third and
fourth generation who hunger for the bread of life and no longer would
have the Church be that place in which the old world of the past is
projected into the future as the hope upon which hinges the meaning
of one's personal existence or Armenian identity. For these American-
born Armenians such a hope is a dream alien to the world in which
they live out their daily lives. And an institution whose purpose it is
to enact such a world is both strange and irrelevant.

Typical of what I have in mind are the proceedings and discussions of the 1984 National Representative Assembly of the Prelacy of
the Armenian Apostolic Church in America. This is the diocese in which
I was raised. For members of both Armenian dioceses the issue of unity
has become compelling, because it is believed that unity might clear
the way for greater and more intense efforts to address the massive
attrition of the second and third generations and now the children of
these American-born Armenians, descendents of the great immigration during and after the First World War. For, in spite of the recent
and large new immigration of Armenians from the Middle East, which
has given a new breadth of life to a declining church,[3] the fact remains
that the underlying causes for the loss of the great body of third generation American-born Armenians have not been answered, have deprived
the Church of a much needed lay leadership, and promises to work
the same effect in the future upon the second and third generations
of the new immigration.

Yet the debate over unity that unfolded at the National Representative Assembly demonstrated the degree to which the Armenian
Church's reason for being has been misunderstood by its own people.
Never once in all the debate was it argued: "Unity must be achieved
because the people of God, who are called to holiness, must never
do such violence to the body of their Lord." Nor did even one member
say in so many words: "We cannot go on dividing our Lord's garments
and crucifying him on a cross of ungodly political controversies." Instead, one heard: "We must have unity in order to save ourselves."
By this was meant "save our ethnic identity." The Church, however,
does not exist in order to save anyone's ethnicity. If Armenians continue to view their church as the means to such an end, they will not
only fail to achieve unity in America; they also will fail to retain the
great numbers of American-born Armenians now and in the future.
Not all the blame lies with the laity. Lay ignorance of what the Church

is and why it exists is largely the tragic legacy of the Ottoman captivity, the genocide, and the great diaspora. There is also a failure of the hierarchy and clergy which has endeavored fruitlessly to sacralize a nationalism and ethnocentricism which itself threatens to consume the Church. The question which the leadership of the Armenian Church, lay and clerical alike, has not asked itself, but which must eventually be raised is: "How much sense can the Church's relentless efforts to link the Armenian nation (inevitably interpreted politically by its people) with the Christian faith mean in any concrete or personal way to third and fourth generation Armenian-Americans who live in a culture which is not Armenian and soon will be, if it is not already, not even nominally Christian?" The loss of vast numbers of my generation of American-born Armenians was not due to any failure by the Armenian Church to be Armenian or national enough. Rather, this happened because the Church sacrificed its evangelical mission and catholic teaching on the altar of a secular nationalism which was not by any stretch of the imagination the faith of the fathers and did little to meet the spiritual needs of a generation born in America and already twice removed from the Ottoman past.

THE SECULARIZATION OF ORTHODOXY IN AMERICA

I tell this sad story because it could well stand as a symbol for much of what has gone wrong with Orthodoxy in America. Ukranians, Greeks, and Russians of the second and third generations relate similar versions of this tale. In each case, a national church uprooted from its natural soil has continued to behave as if that uprooting never happened, or at least as if the new soil into which it had been transplanted was no different than the soil from which it was removed. It is a peculiar historical irony that churches which once were so attentive to the cultural context in which they evangelized would be so utterly inattentive in a later time to the new cultural context into which they were thrust by historical forces beyond their control. One can agree with John Meyendorff's assessment: "There is a fully legitimate degree to which the Church can identify itself with national ethos and tradition and assume some responsibility for the society in which it exists." But it is also true, as Meyendorff argues, that in the nineteenth century there was a clear reversal in the scale of values even within the Orthodox national cultures. "The 'nation' and its interests began to be considered as ends in themselves, and instead of guiding their nations to Christ, most Orthodox churches accepted *de facto* control by secular national interests."[4] That situation has persisted to one degree or another in most, if not all, of the Orthodox churches in America, except that here such secular national aspirations have had to adjust to American pluralism and redefine themselves as ethnic alongside other legitimate ethnic aspirations. Also, in order for such an ethnicity to gain acceptance in the American culture, it must undergo a transformation which is, in spite of what the most hard-core nationalist in the church might imagine, a gradual acculturation. Ethnic churches are churches in the process of Americanization even as they persist in calling up memories of past national glories or submit themselves as instruments of one ethnic nationalism or another. The sad irony in all this is that a national Orthodox church in America, when used as an instrument of ethnic self-preservation, finally is unable to meet the expectations of those who would have it so. The forces of assimilation in the surrounding culture are simply too great. The people who retreat weekly into the church which they have made their ethnic enclave are bringing into that church willy-nilly the very American character from which they would have the church shelter them.

The potential tragedy in this process is not that the Greek, Russian, and Armenian churches are becoming more American, but that they are becoming so uncritically and at great cost to the Orthodox faith. The secularization process which Meyendorff refers to as actually having begun in the indigenous cultures continues in America, only in a far more convoluted and subtle manner. For the Church, having been made into an instrument of ethnic or national aspirations, substitutes a secular religion of ethnicity for the catholic faith. Thus, it becomes doubly unattractive to American-born Greeks, Russians, or Armenians, who find the Church increasingly alien as well as unable to meet their spiritual needs.

More needs to be said about the secularity of this religion of ethnicity which so often prevails in Orthodox parishes and in the personal lives of Orthodox Americans. For our purposes, secularism can be defined quite simply as the loss or absence of the experience of God. The secular religion of ethnicity is characterized by a lack of seriousness about worship and holiness but great seriousness about survival and success in the world. In this instance, survival and success are sought through the perpetuation of an ethnic culture such that it and those adhering to it are accepted and respected within the greater society. The Church gets defined as the instrument of this worldly activity, and the measure of the Church's value is a worldly calculus of its utility or usefulness in achieving these goals. Likewise, the Church becomes the custodian of a folk culture of culinary arts, dance, and ancient religious rituals and artifacts, the primary value of the latter being their beauty or distinctiveness as Greek or Russian whose religious meaning is reserved for the "experts." Recently, a dedicated lay woman and leader in the Armenian Church remarked to me, "We worry about losing our culture, our food, our music . . . but no one ever asks whether we are losing our faith." She summed up quite well the secularization of the Orthodox churches in America.

By becoming thus secularized the Orthodox churches stand also to become Americanized in the worst possible fashion, one which poses a deadly threat to their catholic faith. The ethnicity which Orthodox Americans call upon their church to guard, protect, and promote is quite compatible with a whole constellation of secular values belonging to the American Way which get referred to God for religious sanction. It does not matter whether the values receive religious sanction in the Russian Orthodox Church or the Southern Baptist Church. For example, the obsession with survival, which in many Orthodox parishes becomes the primary motive to action, quickly opens the door to the translation of the parish from a body of believers who come together to worship the living Lord to a community of survivors whose primary responsibility is to themselves as a group dedicated to the preservation of its ethnic identity. In order to accomplish this end, the last conceivable means of doing so would seem to be the liturgy. Time and energy is best spent organizing bake sales, dances, and bingo games and providing a variety of educational and recreational activities for young and old. The liturgy itself becomes one instrument with which to legitimize the other more important activities that must take place.

The question demands asking and answering: "How in essence does this Greek or Armenian parish differ from the Girl Scouts, the local garden club, Republican club, or health spa?" Its proposed end might be different, i.e., preserving and fostering the ethnic heritage, but are its instrumental values and organization any different? And, in fact, is success in preserving one's "Greekness" or "Armenianness" in a pluralistic society such as ours really different in essence from being a good Democrat, a dedicated Shriner, or a Boy Scout? By no means should my remarks be construed as a complete prejudice against all forms of ethnic or cultural association relative to Christian faith. America is a multicommunal society. And this is, on balance, a social good. Christian belief is a human faith, and there is no such thing as a non-cultural Christianity. People, by virtue of their very humanity, have need of some familiar cultural environment within and through which to express and enact their faith. But my point has been made. The catholic and universal Church must be something more, something greater, than that ethnic church to which many Orthodox parishes in America have been reduced. The Orthodox parish, in order to be the Church, must serve a spiritual end which challenges and does not mimic the world's values of survival, success, and self- or group-glorification.

THE FUTURE OF ORTHODOXY IN AMERICA

In America, the Orthodox Church faces a two-horned challenge at the close of the twentieth century. First, it must find ways of retaining the third and fourth generations of the early immigrations, using their talents and meeting their spiritual needs. Second, it must learn both the discernment and the vigilance necessary to resist the secular impetus of the American Way as that ethos impinges increasingly upon the Church's life. I cannot here answer just how all these challenges should be met. Indeed that task lies well beyond my purview and competence. But, through the example of the crisis of the Armenian Church in America, I have endeavored to introduce and to explore some of the prickly facets of this two-horned problem as it affects one church.

With respect, however, to the first horn of the problem one final caveat must be added. The successful retention and / or retrieval of the third and fourth generations is not without its own attendant problems. For, once the Orthodox churches are in the hands of these thoroughly Americanized Orthodox and the churches have passed beyond the stage of immigrant church, the second horn of the challenge to Orthodoxy will come into full play. These Americanized Orthodox will bring with them into the Church a full array of secular values and dispositions which in an American, rather than specifically ethnic, fashion work toward reducing the Church to an instrument of secular agendas. This prospect warrants some discussion and serves as a way of closing.

Some thirty years ago, the late Will Herberg published his now classic study of religion and ethnicity in America, *Protestant-Catholic-Jew*. In it he argued that there is an ethnic skeleton to American religion. He also observed that with the added flesh of successive generations the ethnic skeleton becomes less pronounced and visible. American religion takes on the tripartite composition of three great religious communities which stand in unity and tension with one another and with the American culture. From the title of the book it is clear that Herberg did not include Orthodoxy among the three. This was not because Herberg was unaware of the presence of the Orthodox Church. Rather, Herberg judged that, as of the mid or late 1950s, Orthodoxy had not yet come of age in America. It remained an immigrant or ethnic church, inward looking, not yet having had rise within it a third generation of American-born Greeks, Russians, or Syrians.[5] Unlike their fathers and mothers, the sons and daughters of immigrants, members of this third generation are not perplexed by a double identity of being somehow foreigners — though once removed — and also Americans. The third generation, observed Herberg, is comfortably American. It partakes of the American life without a sense of inferiority, without an acute uneasiness with its past ethnic background, or a need to ground that ethnic identity in constant ritual reenactment of that past. This generation, as Herberg explained, is not without its own need to place itself in American society. Indeed, it seeks a religious means of establishing a distinctive identity within American society. But it does not desire to do so in the explicitly ethnic modes of its parents or grandparents. Herberg's analysis remains powerfully descriptive of American religion, even in the 1980s. It certainly tells us something about the present state of Orthodoxy. If Orthodoxy was in adolescence as an American religion thirty years ago, it has grown to maturity since that time. The third generation has come of age. Yet does this mean that Orthodoxy should now make its rightful claim to being the "fourth major faith" of American religion and gratefully join the other three in their common communion before the altar of the American Way? I do not think Herberg would have argued such a thing. One compelling message of Herberg's book was that the American Way, however respectful of religion and religious freedom, is also a highly secularized creed whose impetus is to reduce the biblical faith to one function and department

of itself, thus transforming that faith into something it is not in its
historic expressions. He wrote:

> In this kind of religion there is no sense of transcendence, no
> sense of the nothingness of man and his works before a holy God;
> in this kind of religion the values of life, and life itself, are not
> submitted to Almighty God to judge, to shatter, and to recon-
> struct; on the contrary, life, and the values of life, are given an
> ultimate sanction by being identified with the divine. In this kind
> of religion it is not man who serves God, but God who is mobil-
> ized and made to serve man and his purposes — whether these
> purposes be economic prosperity, free enterprise, social reform,
> democracy, happiness, security, or "peace of mind." God is con-
> ceived as man's "omnipotent servant," faith is a sure-fire device
> to get what we want.[6]

Previously, I referred to the secularization already undergone by
the Orthodox churches in America. It may well be that in the future,
Orthodox Christians who have become fully Americanized will follow
the lead of other churches in America and use their religion to justify
the whole range of secular values and activities of the American Way
to which Herberg makes reference. For example, until the present,
Orthodox have looked with considerable skepticism upon the social
activism of mainline Protestants and Roman Catholics. Herberg's analysis provides solid ground upon which to raise serious questions about
the manner in which these churches have submitted themselves as instruments of this or that political ideology or cause. However, as I
already pointed out, the Orthodox have been busy making their own
faith serve ethnic and national movements, the net effect of which
is idolization of the group or its culture. Past and present Orthodox
habit indicates that an Americanized Orthodoxy of the future, having abandoned the nationalistic programs of the earlier days, might
well proceed to endorse uncritically the American Way.

In an article written some twenty years ago, Alexander Schmemann reflected on just these challenges to Orthodoxy in America. In
it he warned of the great temptation for Orthodoxy to become simply
the "fourth major faith." He said that if an Orthodoxy in America
were to take that path, much of what makes the Orthodox Church
distinct and faithful to the apostolic witness would be lost.[7] There is
much that is good in the American culture; but there is also much

which is, in fact, utterly corrosive of and antithetical to Christian belief and practice. American culture's pervasive hedonism, materialism, and instrumentalism seek to persuade that this world is an end in itself and that all meaning and purpose are determined by whatever pleasure, power, and wealth one can "get out of life." Orthodoxy cannot assume — as its Byzantine past would dispose it to do — that there is an easy correlation between its faith and the culture. On both the personal and corporate levels Orthodoxy must come to terms with a historic situation in which there is no *symphonia* with the prevailing culture. Being a faithful and conscientious Orthodox means that one's values and actions will often conflict or be in tension with the prevailing mores of one's community and neighbors. This requires a courage that itself needs the support of the parish and ultimately the full body of Orthodox believers in America.

Finally, if my analysis concerning the present state of the Orthodox churches in America even approximates accuracy, the work ahead which would keep Orthodoxy on a straight path will be difficult. It amounts to nothing less than the rehabilitation of an apostolic and evangelical life in the midst of an increasingly secular society. The first object to keep in mind is that the striving must be to deepen the Christian character of Orthodox and not "to keep the 'American Orthodox' as Russian or as Greek as possible" or to make the " 'Russian' or 'Greek Orthodox' as American as possible."[8] If there is one fundamental failure of the Orthodox churches in America, it is their inability, or perhaps lack of interest, to produce an educated laity. I do not mean education in the strictly formal sense, either, though to be sure there is desperate need for Orthodox laity with degrees in theology, divinity, and religious education. Rather, I have in mind a church in which there is an ongoing and living catechesis. Knowing that one is Orthodox is not enough. One must have *good reasons* for being Christian and Orthodox. The inability of Orthodox Christians to answer satisfactorily for themselves or for the friendly religious or secular inquirer what difference it makes to be an Orthodox Christian is a terrible judgment upon the Orthodox Church in America. It prevents the Church from being an effective mission to the world.

Such instruction in Christian character and conviction starts with worship. For example, the primary text for Orthodox ethics is the baptismal rite. The call for liturgical revival cannot be dismissed as the esoteric interest of aesthetic savants addicted to ancient ritual and music.

This call is rooted in the recognition that it is in worship and prayer, in the *lex orandi*, that Christian discipline and character have their beginnings and are constantly deepened and enriched. Thus, the living ongoing catechesis which I am advocating must begin with a liturgical revival. But it has to extend beyond the sanctuary also. That which takes place below in the social hall or adjacently in the classrooms must reflect the spirit of the *lex orandi* and embody it in religious community and active engagement with society.

Lamentably, the Orthodox parish has taken on a life largely autonomous of and unrelated to the life of worship and prayer. This fact is neatly symbolized by the familiar scene in many Orthodox parishes on any given Sunday of the members of the parish council huddled in an anteroom counting change rather than gathered with the faithful in the sanctuary. The Orthodox parish needs to be transformed from a Sunday version of "business as usual" into a leavening agency of discipleship and Christian mission. How to make the parish serious once again about mission deserves an answer which is yet forthcoming. But when this comes it will not be from any single individual or group of people. It will arise from the earnest endeavors of those Orthodox everywhere who, aware of the momentous challenges facing their church, have striven in all possible ways within their church communities to "aim at righteousness, godliness, faith, love, steadfastness, gentleness" and to "fight the good fight of faith; take hold of the eternal life to which [they] made the good confession in the presence of many witnesses" (1 Tim. 6:11–12 RSV).

Notes

INTRODUCTION

1. A partial list of Orthodox in North America who have written on such matters must include: John L. Boojamra, Demetrios Constantelos, Georges Florovsky, Stanley S. Harakas, Thomas Hopko, John Meyendorff, Alexander Schmemann, and Alexander F. C. Webster. But of these only Harakas and Webster would describe themselves as ethicists. Most of these authors have published books, some of which are relevant to ethics. Articles by these authors have appeared most frequently in such periodicals as: the *Greek Orthodox Theological Review, Diakonia, St. Vladimir's Theological Quarterly*, and the *Journal of Ecumenical Studies*. For a more comprehensive account of contemporary Orthodox ethicists, particularly a description of the work of Greek writers, see Stanley S. Harakas, *Toward Transfigured Life: The Theoria of Eastern Orthodox Ethics* (Minneapolis: Light & Life Publishing Co., 1983). In chapter 1 Harakas identifies the three major schools of Greek Orthodox thought, Athenian, Constantinopolitan and Thessalonian. Throughout the book he reports the ethics done within these schools.

2. Harakas, *Transfigured Life*, pp. 1–2.

3. For a comprehensive account of this relationship between Protestant and Roman Catholic ethics see James M. Gustafson, *Protestant and Roman Catholic Ethics: Prospects for Rapprochement* (Chicago: University of Chicago Press, 1978).

4. David Kelsey, "Method, Theological" in *The Westminster Dictionary of Christian Theology*, ed. Alan Richardson and John Bowdin (Philadelphia: Westminster Press, 1983), pp. 363–67.

5. Alexander Schmemann, *Church, World, Mission* (Crestwood, N.Y.: St. Vladimir's Seminary Press, 1979), p. 8.

1. THE SHAPE OF ORTHODOX ETHICS

1. Nicholas Cabasilas, *The Life in Christ*, trans. Carmino J. DeCatanzaro (Crestwood, N.Y.: St. Vladimir's Seminary Press, 1974), p. 228 (bk. 7).

2. Ibid., p. 211.

3. Ibid., pp. 210–11.

4. Ibid., pp. 190–91.

5. Maximus the Confessor, "Contemplative and Active Texts," ed. and trans. E. Kadloubovsky and G. E. Palmer, in *Early Fathers of the Philokalia* (London: Faber & Faber, 1954), p. 368.

6. Quoted in Victor Gollancz, *Man and God* (Boston: Houghton & Mifflin Co., 1951), p. 50.

7. Conscience is, as well, the "inner court" through which God convicts the sinner of deviation from the good. But even if human beings did not stand condemned by the measure of the Law, conscience would still remain in them as that positive power of discerning the good and appropriating it into their lives. Conscience belongs to the original image of God in humankind. See Stanley S. Harakas, "The Centrality of Conscience in Eastern Orthodox Ethics," *Greek Orthodox Theological Review* 23 (Summer 1978): 131–44, for a discussion of conscience by a contemporary Orthodox writer.

8. I should mention at this juncture that the Greek fathers and Orthodox writers have made an important distinction between Christ, who is the Image of God, and humanity, which is made according to the image of God. Thus it can be said that the divine image in human beings is a copy of the Image of God, Christ. Or, Christ is by generation and by nature (essence) the very Image of God the Father, and humanity is God's image by imitation (as the artist's painting or sculpture is an imitation of nature). See Gerhardt B. Ladner, "The Concept of the Image in the Greek Fathers and the Byzantine Iconoclastic Controversy," *Dumbarton Oaks Papers* 7 (Washington, D.C.: Dumbarton Oaks Center for Byzantine Studies, 1953), pp. 3–34.

9. John of Damascus, *Exposition of the Orthodox Faith*, in *A Selected Library of Nicene and Post-Nicene Fathers of the Christian Church*, vol. 9 (Grand Rapids, Mich.: Wm. B. Eerdmans Publishing Co. 1957), p. 31 (bk. 2, chap. 12).

10. Cabasilas, *Life in Christ*, p. 126 (bk. 4).

11. Ibid., p. 49 (bk. 1).

12. Ibid.

13. Ibid., p. 191 (bk. 6).

14. Gregory of Sinai, "Texts on Commandments and Dogmas," ed. and trans. E. Kadloubovsky and G. E. H. Palmer, in *Writings from the Philokalia on Prayer of the Heart* (London: Faber & Faber, 1951), p. 53.

15. Maximus the Confessor, *The Four Centuries on Charity*, in *St. Maximus the Confessor*, trans. Polycarp Sherwood, in *Ancient Christian Writers*, vol. 22 (New York/Ramsey, N.J.: Newman Press, 1955), p. 138 (century 1.12).

16. Vladimir Lossky, *The Mystical Theology of the Eastern Church* (Cambridge: James Clarke & Co. 1957), p. 81.

17. Cabasilas, *Life in Christ*, p. 122 (bk. 4).

18. The Greek fathers and Byzantine theologians handed on a rich language and a host of possibilities for making a distinction between personality and individuality. When, for example, the Cappadocians and Maximus the Confessor insist that in speaking of the Trinity it must be said that three equals one and one equals three, these theologians have provided the significant means by which to argue that persons cannot be added together to make a sum, and that, similarly, they are not reducible to parts of a whole. While the Greek fathers and Byzantine writers did not work out the full anthropological implications of the theological language of personality, it is clear that they refused to define the Persons of the Trinity as numerical individuals of a divine species, since the divine nature is absolutely simple and indivisible.

The Chalcedonian and post-Chalcedonian Byzantine Christology says that the person of the Incarnation is clearly the Logos, the very Son of God, consubstantial with the Father. Mary is the God-bearer (*Theotokos*). But Jesus Christ is also consubstantial with his mother. Thus, Christ is a human individual (able to be counted in the census); but it would be error to say that he is an individual god. More than implicit here is the possibility, indeed the requirement, to distinguish between person(ality) and individual(ity), although the two obviously are not incommensurate.

We might want to say on the basis of the above that the individual is constituted of all the determinate qualities of the particular nature (adding up to something perhaps unique and distinct from others of that nature, but not necessarily amounting to that which is personality). In this sense the individual, however distinct and discrete, is, nevertheless conditioned physically, psychologically, and socially according to its nature and external environment, while personality is indeterminate. "Personhood is freedom in relation to nature." See Vladimir Lossky, *Orthodox Theology: An Introduction*, trans. Ian and Ihita Kesarcodi-Watson (Crestwood, N.Y.: St. Vladimir's Seminary Press, 1978), p. 42. Perhaps this helps explain why the biological, psychological, and social sciences can readily identify and account for that which is determinate and conditioned in the human individual and the human species but have difficulty accounting for or explaining away the freedom of the human person.

19. Here I have in mind specifically the doctrine of the "two wills" declared by the Sixth Ecumenical Council held at Constantinople that, since Christ is true man as well as true God, he must have both a human and a divine will. This doctrinal statement corresponds with the doctrine of the Trinity, in which it is affirmed that there are three hypostases but only one divine nature, and that there is only a single will and a single action which can be

attributed to the Godhead. Thus in the doctrine of the Trinity it is clear that will is an attribute of nature and not of hypostasis. As a note, I should add that the Armenian Church, together with the several other Oriental Orthodox Churches has never accepted the doctrine of "two wills" nor agreed to the precise formulation of the doctrine of the "two natures" arrived at by the Council of Chalcedon. See Karekin Sarkissian, *The Council of Chalcedon and the Armenian Church* (London: SPCK, 1965).

20. Quoted by Lossky, *Mystical Theology*, p. 126.

21. See Vladimir Solovyev, *God, Man and the Church*, trans. Donald Atwater (Cambridge: James Clarke & Co., 1937), p. 26.

22. John Meyendorff, *Byzantine Theology* (New York: Fordham University Press, 1974), p. 215.

23. Ernst Benz, *The Eastern Orthodox Church*, trans. Richard and Clara Winston (Garden City, N.Y.: Doubleday & Co., 1963), p. 151.

24. Basil of Caesarea, *The Long Rules*, in *St. Basil: The Ascetical Works*, trans. M. Monica Wagner, in *The Fathers of the Church*, vol. 9 (New York: Fathers of the Church, 1950), p. 233 (q. 2).

25. For discussion of the role of natural law theory in Orthodox theology and ethics, see Stanley S. Harakas, "The Natural Law Teaching of the Eastern Orthodox Church," *Greek Orthodox Theological Review* 9 (Winter 1963–64): 215–24; "Orthodox Perspectives on Natural Law," in *Selected Papers, Eighth Annual Meeting* (Newton Center, Mass: American Society of Christian Ethics, 1977), pp. 41–56; and *Toward Transfigured Life: The Theoria of Orthodox Ethics* (Minneapolis, Minn.: Light & Life Publishing Co., 1983), esp. chap. 6.

26. Meyendorff, *Byzantine Theology*, p. 89.

27. Gregory of Sinai, "Texts," p. 40.

28. Ibid., p. 41.

29. In this section I consider the subject matter which is often identified as belonging to social ethics. So far as I know, Orthodox writers generally have not made a formal distinction between personal ethics and social ethics. The moral life is not split in two realms. Nor are there two moralities. Yet, Orthodoxy has recognized that the use and arbitration of power in social and political relations is greater in magnitude and usually more complex than in personal and family relations, and that there are particular virtues which are proper to political and social relations.

30. Alexander Schmemann, *Church, World and Mission* (Crestwood, N.Y.: St. Vladimir's Seminary Press, 1979), pp. 76–77.

31. Ibid., p. 149.

32. I am borrowing the rubric used by H. Richard Niebuhr in *Christ and Culture* (New York: Harper & Row, 1951) to describe the fifth type of Christian social ethic which he identifies in that book.

33. Georges Florovsky, *The Collected Works of Georges Florovsky*, vol.

2, *Christianity and Culture* (Belmont, Mass: Nordland Publishing Co., 1974). p. 99.

34. Ibid., p. 128.

35. Ibid., p. 133.

36. Basil, *Long Rules*, pp. 239–240 (q. 3).

37. For a recent discussion of this theme by an Orthodox theologian see Emilianos Timiadis, "Restoration and Liberation in and by the Community," *Greek Orthodox Theological Review* 19, no. 2 (Autumn 1974): 131–57.

38. Lossky, *Orthodox Theology*, p. 15.

2. LOVE IN ORTHODOX ETHICS

1. Ernst Benz, *The Eastern Orthodox Church* (New York: Doubleday & Co. 1963), pp. 150–51.

2. Sergius Bulgakov, *The Orthodox Church* (Maitland, Fla.: Three Hierarchs Seminary Press, 1935), p. 179.

3. Dumitru Staniloae, *Theology and the Church* (Crestwood, N.Y.: St. Vladimir's Seminary Press, 1980), p. 89.

4. Vladimir Lossky points out, the term "Father cause" was used by the Greek fathers only in an analogical way. "In our experience, the cause is superior to the effect. In God, on the contrary, the cause as fulfillment of personal love cannot produce inferior effects: it wishes them to be equal in dignity, and is therefore also the cause and effect of their equality. Besides, in God, there is no extraposition of cause and effect" (*Orthodox Theology: An Introduction* [Crestwood, N.Y.: St. Vladimir's Seminary Press, 1978], p. 47.

5. Ibid., p. 44.

6. Ibid., p. 47.

7. Staniloae, *Theology*, p. 79.

8. Gregory of Nyssa, "On the Difference between *ousia* and hypostasis 1–4," in *Documents in Early Christian Thought*, ed. Maurice Wiles and Mark Santor (Cambridge: At the University Press, 1975), p. 34. Although included among the letters of Basil, this work is now generally attributed to Gregory of Nyssa.

9. In this section I depend very much on the analysis of Staniloae, *Theology*, pp. 92–108.

10. Ibid., p. 93. Some further explanation probably is in order regarding what I have just said about the imperfection or egocentricity of a love shared between only two. The argument is both a structural statement about created humanity and a description of the fallen human condition.

First, Orthodox theology does not conceive of the human person apart from his or her presence within a community of love, however broken that community might be or however distorted its love. The norm for such a community is the trinitarian fullness of the Godhead itself. Such a pleromic reciprocity or community is not possible without three. Contemporary social theory would tend to support this view that genuine society is a relation of three or more agents.

Second, to speak of an erotic self-contained mutuality of two, as I do in the following sentence, is already to presuppose the Fall and the endemic egoism which afflicts all human relationships. The perfect society of the three remains a goal of human striving not yet obtained but all the while made possible through the *graced* life in Christ and in the Church. The following discussion of the relation of the two parents toward the child and vice versa is a normative statement about the possibilities opened to human beings by nature and through God's grace in marriage and in the family. Yet marriage itself is fallen and in need of redemption. Contrary to idealistic and romantic views of marriage, the possibilities it provides for trinitarian love will be lost and regained over and over again.

11. *The Blessing of Marriage or the Canon of the Rite of Holy Matrimony according to the Usage of the Armenian Apostolic Orthodox Church* (New York: Armenian Church Publication, 1953), p. 54.

12. Staniloae, *Theology*, pp. 95–96.

13. Alexander Schmemann, *For the Life of the World* (Crestwood, N.Y.: St Vladimir's Seminary Press, 1973), p. 89.

14. Vladimir Lossky, *The Mystical Theology of the Eastern Church* (Cambridge: James Clarke & Co., 1957), p. 60.

15. Staniloae, *Theology*, p. 89.

16. Ibid., p. 80.

17. John of Damascus, *Exposition of the Orthodox Faith*, in *A Select Library of Nicene and Post-Nicene Fathers of the Christian Church*, Second Series, vol. 9 (Grand Rapids, Mich.: Wm. B. Eerdmans Publishing Co., 1957), pp. 10–11 (bk. 1, chap. 8).

18. Ibid., p. 10.

19. Gregory of Nyssa, *The Great Catechism*, in *A Select Library of Nicene and Post-Nicene Fathers of the Christian Church*, Second Series, vol. 5 (Grand Rapids, Mich.: Wm. B. Eerdmans Publishing Co., 1979), p. 479 (chap. 5).

20. George A. Tavard, *A Way of Love* (Maryknoll, N.Y.: Orbis Books, 1977), p. 68.

21. Maximus the Confessor, "Contemplative and Active Texts," in *Early Fathers of the Philokalia*, ed. E. Kadloubovsky and G. E. Palmer (London: Faber & Faber, 1954), p. 365.

22. Lossky, *Orthodox Theology*, p. 42.

23. Gregory of Nyssa, *On the Making of Man*, in *A Select Library of Nicene and Post-Nicene Fathers of the Christian Church*, Second Series, vol. 5 (Grand Rapids, Mich.: Wm. B. Eerdmans Publishing Co., 1979), p. 405 (16.11).

24. Schmemann, *Life of the World*, p. 35.

25. Staniloae, *Theology*, p. 195.

26. *Divine Liturgy of the Armenian Apostolic Orthodox Church* (New York: Delphic Press, 1950), pp. 61–63.

27. Gilbert Meilaender, *Friendship: A Study in Theological Ethics* (Notre Dame, Ind.: University of Notre Dame Press, 1981), p. 33. Meilaender adopts Anders Nygren's distinction between *agape* as true Christian love and *caritas* which combines *eros* with *agape's* pure selflessness. He does not endorse, however, Nygren's negative judgment of *caritas* as corruptive of the Christian ideal. Meilaender's position is that while *caritas'* vision and seeking of relation and reciprocity is in tension with *agape*, such reciprocity or mutuality is, paradoxically, the transcendent fulfillment of *agape*. Orthodoxy makes no such distinction between *agape* and *caritas*. They are regarded as one in the same divine love, the incarnate form of which is perfected in Jesus Christ.

28. Ibid., p. 34.

29. I am much indebted to George A. Tavard's discussion of the parable of the good Samaritan in *Love*, pp. 36–39.

30. Origen, *Commentary on the Gospel According to Matthew*, in *Ante-Nicene Christian Library*, Original Supplement to the American Edition, vol. 9 (New York: Charles Scribner's Sons, 1903), p. 498 (bk. 14.7).

31. In making several statements of this kind, I am not denying the usefulness of such a distinction as a tool of ethical analysis; I am saying that this distinction cannot be the axis upon which turns an ethic such as the one I have been describing, which is kerygmatic, sacramental, missionary, and eschatological.

32. "The friends of Christ love all sincerely, but are not loved by all; the friends of the world neither love all nor are loved by all. The friends of Christ preserve the bond of charity until the end; the friends of the world until they are in conflict with one another for the things of the world." Maximus the Confessor, *The Four Centuries on Charity*, in *St. Maximus the Confessor*, trans. Polycarp Sherwood, in *Ancient Christian Writers*, vol. 22 (New York/Ramsey, N.J.: Newman Press, 1955), p. 208 (century 4:98).

33. Martin C. D'Arcy, *The Mind and the Heart of Love* (New York: Meridian, 1954).

34. Augustine, *City of God* (New York: Modern Library, Random House, 1950), p. 347 (bk. 11, chap. 2).

35. Flannery O'Connor, *Three by Flannery O'Connor* (New York: New American Library, 1983), p. 192.

36. Ibid., p. 230.

37. Ibid., p. 193.

38. Fyodor Dostoevsky, *The Brothers Karamazov* (New York: Bantam Books, 1970), p. 276.

39. Ibid., pp. 294–95.

40. Ibid., pp. 284–85.

41. O'Connor, *Three*, p. 192.

42. "At his high school he was the expert on testing. All his professional decisions were prefabricated and did not involve his participation. He was not deceived that this was a whole life or a full life, he only knew that it was the way his life had to be lived if it were going to have any dignity at all." Ibid., p. 193.

43. Nicholas Cabasilas, *The Life in Christ* (Crestwood, N.Y. St. Vladimir's Seminary Press, 1974), pp. 96-97 (bk. 2).

44. Maximus the Confessor, *Four Centuries*, p. 138 (century 1.10).

45. John Chrysostom, *Homilies on the Gospel of Saint Matthew*, in *A Select Library of Nicene and Post-Nicene Fathers of the Christian Church*, vol. 10 (Grand Rapids, Mich.: Wm. B. Eerdmans Publishing Co., 1956), p. 111. (homily 16.2).

46. Cabasilas, *Life in Christ*, p. 188 (bk. 7).

47. John of Damascus, *An Exact Exposition of the Orthodox Faith*, in *St. John of Damascus: Writings*, in *The Fathers of the Church*, vol. 37 (New York: Fathers of the Church, 1958), p. 303 (bk. 3, chap. 14).

48. Gregory of Nyssa, *Great Catechism*, p. 452.

49. Gregory of Sinai, "Texts on Commandments and Dogmas," in *Writings from the Philokalia on Prayer of the Heart*, ed. E. Kadloubovsky and G. E. H. Palmer (London: Faber & Faber, 1951), p. 53.

50. *Divine Liturgy (Armenian)*, p. 79.

51. Gregory of Sinai, "Texts," p. 53.

52. St. Basil and St. Theodore of Studium, the two great figures of Eastern monasticism, thought of Christian morality as one, arguing that the single standard of Christian morality applicable to all Christians is perfected by the monk. They also insisted that the asceticism of the monastic life is continuous with the life of every believer. John Chrysostom makes no bones about there being one standard which applies to all believers. Addressing married people, he writes: "And if these beatitudes were spoken to solitaries only, and the secular person cannot fulfill them, yet He [Christ] permitted marriage, then He has destroyed all men. For if it be not possible, with marriage, to perform the duties of solitaries all things have perished and are destroyed, and the functions of virtue of shut up in a strait." *Homilies on the Epistle to the Hebrews*, in *A Select Library of Nicene and Post-Nicene Fathers*, vol. 14 (Christian Literature Co. 1890), p. 402 (homily 7.2). Nicholas

Cabasilas strikes a more circumspect note, though in the same spirit. "No one would claim that the same virtues are needed by those who govern the state and those who live as private citizens, or by those who have no further vow to God after the baptismal washing and those who live the monastic life and have taken the vows of virginity and poverty and thus own neither property nor their own selves. But the debt which . . . is common to all who are called by the name of Christ, must also be paid by all. . . . Among Christians no one is unaware that he is under obligation to undertake the whole task. All alike, when they joined Him in the beginning, vowed to follow Him through all things, and it was after they had thus bound themselves by those covenants they underwent the sacral rites of Baptism. . . . Since the Savior's commands are thus binding on all the faithful and are capable of fulfillment by those who are willing, they are most necessary." Cabasilas, *Life in Christ*, p. 160 (bk. 7).

53. Stanley Hauerwas, *A Community of Character* (Notre Dame, Ind: University of Notre Dame Press, 1981), p. 70.

54. Maximus the Confessor, *Four Centuries*, p. 181 (century 3:47).

55. Symeon the New Theologian, *St. Symeon the New Theologian: The Discourses* in *The Classics of Western Spirituality* (Ramsey, N.J.: Paulist Press, 1980), p. 237.

56. Symeon the New Theologian, "Practical and Theological Precepts," in *Early Fathers of the Philokalia*, ed. E. Kadloubovsky and G.E. Palmer (London: Faber & Faber, 1954), p. 122.

57. Georges Florovsky, *The Collected Works of Georges Florovsky*, vol. 1: *Bible, Church and Tradition: An Eastern Orthodox View* (Belmont, Mass.: Nordland Publishing Co., 1972), p. 43.

58. Vladimir Lossky, *In the Image and Likeness of God* (Crestwood, N.Y.: St. Vladimir's Seminary Press, 1974), p. 152.

3. SEEING WORSHIP AS ETHICS

1. Stanley S. Harakas, *Toward Transfigured Life: The Theoria of Eastern Orthodox Ethics* (Minneapolis, Minn.: Light & Life Publishing Co., 1983), pp. 1-2. There is ample testimony among the fathers as to the appropriateness of, indeed necessity for, such a distinction. Athanasius observed that the apostle Paul "deemed it necessary, in the first place, to make known the word concerning Christ, and the mystery regarding Him; and then afterwards to point to the correction of habits, so that when they had learned to know the Lord, they might earnestly desire to do those things, which He commanded." Athanasius, "*Festal Letters*," in *St. Athanasius' Selected Works and Letters*, in *A Select Library of Nicene and Post-Nicene Fathers of the Christian Church*,

vol. 9 (Grand Rapids, Mich: Wm. B. Eerdmans Publishing Co., 1957), p. 533 (letter 13).

2. I point to the way in which this separation has affected Orthodoxy beginning on pp. 65–66 and again on pp. 67–68.

3. Paul Ramsey, "Liturgy and Ethics," *Journal of Religious Ethics* 7, no. 2 (Fall 1979): 166, n. 5.

4. Alexander Schmemann, "Debate on the Liturgy: Liturgical Theology, Theology of Liturgy, and Liturgical Reform," *St. Vladimir's Theological Quarterly*, 13, no. 4 (1969): 218.

5. Ramsey, "Liturgy and Ethics," p. 145.

6. Stanley Hauerwas, *The Peaceable Kingdom* (Notre Dame, Ind.: University of Notre Dame Press, 1983), pp. 51, 52, 53, 54.

7. Ramsey, "Liturgy and Ethics," p. 150.

8. I have used Emilianos Timiadis's translation of this passage as it appears in his "Restoration and Liberation in and by the Community," *Greek Orthodox Theological Review* 19, no. 2 (Autumn 1974): 54. See also John Chrysostom, *Homilies on the Gospel of St. Matthew*, in *A Select Library of Nicene and Post-Nicene Fathers of the Christian Church*, vol. 10 (Grand Rapids, Mich.: Wm. B. Eerdmans Publishing Co., 1956), pp. 434–35 (homily 71).

9. I am not trying to solve the broad issue of Christian ethics vs. philosophical ethics here. I am reminded, however, of John of Damascus's definition: "Philosophy is the making of oneself like God." John of Damascus, *St. John of Damascus: Writings (The Fount of Knowledge)*, trans. Frederic H. Chase, Jr., in *The Fathers of the Church: A New Translation* (New York: Fathers of the Church, 1958), p. 11.

10. This formulation is based upon the arguments presented by my colleague James J. Buckley, "Lex Orandi, Lex Agendi: Prayer, Action and Sacramentologies," Unpublished, esp. pp. 1, 25–26.

11. See John Meyendorff for a discussion of the meaning of baptism in the Orthodox tradition, particularly as that meaning contrasts with the Western tradition since Augustine. John Meyendorff, *Byzantine Theology* (New York: Fordham University Press, 1974), pp. 145–46.

12. A Monk of the Eastern Church, *Orthodox Spirituality* (Crestwood, N.Y.: St. Vladimir's Seminary Press, 1978), p. 42.

13. Alexander Schmemann, *Of Water and Spirit* (Crestwood, N.Y.: St. Vladimir's Seminary Press, 1974), p. 112.

14. Walter Rauschenbusch, *A Theology for the Social Gospel* (Nashville, Tenn.: Abingdon Press, 1978), p. 201.

15. Ibid., p. 200.

16. Garabed Kochakian, ed., *The Sacraments: Symbols of Our Faith* (New York: Diocese of the Armenian Church, 1983), p. 23.

17. Isabel Florence Hapgood, ed. and trans., *Service Book of the Holy Orthodox-Catholic Apostolic Church* (Englewood, N.J.: Antiochian Orthodox Christian Archdiocese, 1975), p. 271.

18. Kochakian, *Sacraments*, pp. 18–19.

19. Rauschenbusch, *Social Gospel*, p. 201.

20. Hapgood, *Service Book*, pp. 278–79.

21. Flannery O'Connor, "The Fiction Writer and His Countryside," in *Mystery and Manners*, ed. Sally and Robert Fitzgerald (New York: Farrar, Straus & Giroux, 1969), p. 35. The passage is from Cyril's "Procatechesis" to "The Catechetical Lectures," in *Cyril of Jerusalem, Gregory Nazianzen*, in *A Select Library of Nicene and Post-Nicene Fathers of the Christian Church*, vol. 7 (Grand Rapids, Mich.: Wm. B. Eerdmans Publishing Co., 1978), p. 5.

22. Hapgood, *Service Book*, pp. 271–72.

23. Schmemann, *Water and Spirit*, p. 25.

24. Karl Barth, *Church Dogmatics*, ed. and trans. G. W. Bromiley and T. F. Torrance (Edinburgh: T & T Clark, 1975), p. 698 (1.2).

25. This homily is collected, along with other fourth-century homilies on baptism, in Edward Yarnold, S. J., *The Awe-Inspiring Rites of Initiation* (Middlegreen, Slough: St. Paul Publications, 1971), p. 166 (baptismal homily 2.22).

26. Thanks especially to Maximus the Confessor, Orthodoxy makes a distinction between a natural will and a gnomic will. The natural will belongs to all human beings insofar as they all share a common nature. When the human being follows this "natural will, which presupposes life in God, God's cooperation and communion, he is truly free." But, as John Meyendorff explains, "man also possesses another potential, determined not by his nature, but by each human person, or hypostasis, the freedom of choice, of revolt, of movement against nature, and therefore, of self destruction." This personal freedom was exercised in a choice for evil by Adam and Eve with the enduring consequence for humanity of "separation from God, from true knowledge, from all the assurance secured by 'natural' existence. It implies hesitation, wandering, and suffering; this is the gnomic will (*gnome*, opinion), a function of the hypostatic, or personal life, not of nature." Meyendorff, *Byzantine Theology*, p. 38.

27. Kochakian, *Sacraments*, p. 28. In his "Address on Religious Instruction" (usually rendered "Catechetical Oration") Gregory of Nyssa discusses this matter of what baptism actually effects in the person and her character.

> We have, I think, to consider what follows baptism. It is a point which many of those who approach its grace neglect, deluding themselves and being born in appearance only and not in reality. For the change our life undergoes through rebirth would not be a change were we to con-

> tinue in our present state. . . . It is patent to everyone that we receive the saving birth for the purpose of renewing and changing our nature. Yet baptism produces no essential change in human nature. Neither reason nor understanding, nor capacity for knowledge, nor anything else that marks human nature, undergoes a change. For the change would certainly be for the worse, were any of these characteristics of our nature to be altered. If, then, these facilities are not changed, and yet the birth from above does in some way refashion man, we must inquire what that change is which the grace of rebirth brings about.

Gregory refers to the washing which makes us clean. But it is possible that this washing will have only affected the body and not the soul. If "anger . . . covetous passion or unbridled and shameful thoughts and pride, envy, and arrogance," characterize a person even after baptism, then "I will say without shrinking that in such a case the water is only water, and the gift of the Holy Spirit is nowhere evident in action." Growth into holiness is a synergistic action. We become sons and daughters of the Father through his gracious adoption and our earnest imitation of him and his Son.

> Now the child born of someone certainly shares his parent's nature. If, then, you have received God and become his child, let your way of life testify to the God within you: make it clear who your Father is! The marks by which we recognize God are the very ones by which a son of his must show his relation to him: "he opens his hand and fills everything living with joy" [Ps. 145:16]; "he overlooks iniquity" [Mic. 7:18 (LXX)]; "he relents of his evil purpose" [Joel 2:13]; "the Lord is kind to all, and is not angry with us every day [Ps. 145:9; 7:12 (LXX)]; "God is straightforward and there is no unrighteousness in him" [Ps. 92:15] — and the similar sayings scattered through Scripture for our instruction. If you are like this, you have genuinely become a child of God. But if you persist in displaying the marks of evil, it is useless to prattle to yourself about the birth from above.

Clearly, for Gregory of Nyssa the only proper use of divine adoption is as the opportunity and occasion for personal growth into divine similitude. Deification (*theosis*) belongs to Christian ethics. Gregory of Nyssa, "An Address on Religious Instruction," in *Christology of the Later Fathers*, ed. Edward Rochie Hardy and Cyril C. Richardson, in *Library of Christian Classics* (Philadelphia: Westminster Press, 1954), pp. 323–25.

28. Yarnold, *Awe-Inspiring Rites*, p. 167 (baptismal homily 2.23).

29. Ibid., p. 170 (homily 2.29).

30. Kochakian, *Sacraments*, p. 23.

31. Ibid., p. 29.

32. Gregory of Nyssa addressed this matter:

The manner of our salvation, owes its efficacy less to instruction by teaching than to what He who entered into fellowship with man actually did. In him life became a reality, so that by means of the flesh which he assumed and thereby deified salvation might come to all that was akin to it. Hence it was necessary to devise some way by which, in the baptismal procedure, there might be an affinity and likeness between disciple and master. We must therefore note what characterized the Author of our life, in order that (as the apostle says [Heb. 2:10]) those who follow may pattern themselves after the Pioneer of our salvation. Gregory of Nyssa, "Religious Instruction," p. 314).

33. George Khodre, "The Church as the Privileged Witness of God," in *Martyria/Mission*: The Witness of the Orthodox Churches Today, ed. Ion Bria (Geneva: World Council of Churches, 1980), p. 34.

34. William J. Everett, "Liturgy and Ethics: A Response to Saliers and Ramsey," *Journal of Religious Ethics* 7, no. 2 (Fall 1979): 209. See also two additional articles by Everett, "Liturgy and American Society: An Invocation for Ethical Analysis," *Anglican Theological Review* 56, no. 1 (January 1974): 16–34, and "Ecclesiology and Political Authority: A Dialogue with Hannah Arendt," *Encounter* [36, no. 1 (Winter 1975): 26–36. I also note an unpublished manuscript, "Towards God's Perfect Public," presented at the twentieth annual meeting of the Society of Christian Ethics, Washington, D.C., January 16, 1982. One difference between Everett's position and my own that calls for comment derives from our very different ecclesiologies. At the center of Orthodox ecclesiology is the eucharistic communion. The eucharist is a manifestation of the Church's unity, wholeness, and catholicity. Thus it is during and within this activity above all others that the Church *proclaims* (publicizes) most fully the truth of salvation in Jesus Christ. When Everett, who speaks out of a free church Protestant tradition, writes of the publicization of God's republic, he has in mind, "preaching, scripture reading . . . , prayer and song" (Everett, private letter to author). Also, I am not inclined, as Everett is, to replace Kingdom language with republic language. Everett argues that the term *Kingdom of God* is too rooted in the familial and reinforces certain ethnic and cultic behavior within the Christian churches. He prefers the term *republic* because in our age it is the dominant and most powerful symbol of the public realm. I prefer the term *Kingdom of God* because of its ability (in my view a quality *republic* lacks) to express the transcendence or eschatological character of God's reign.

35. Everett, "Liturgy and Ethics," p. 210.
36. Ibid., p. 209.
37. Ibid., pp. 207, 208, 209.

38. *Divine Liturgy of the Armenian Apostolic Orthodox Church* (New York: Delphic Press, 1950), p. 65.

39. Stanley Hauerwas, *Truthfulness and Tragedy* (Notre Dame, Ind.: University of Notre Dame Press, 1977), pp. 142–43.

40. Ralph A. Keifer, "Christian Initiation: The State of the Question," in *Made, Not Born*, (Notre Dame, Ind.: University of Notre Dame Press, 1976), p. 147.

41. *Divine Liturgy (Armenian)*, p. 65.

42. Everett, "Liturgy and Ethics," p. 208.

43. Timiadis, "Restoration and Liberation," p. 151.

44. Geoffrey Wainwright, *Doxology* (New York: Oxford University Press, 1980), p. 426.

45. National Conference of Catholic Bishops, *The Challenge of Peace: God's Promise and Our Response* (Washington, D.C.: U.S. Catholic Conference, Office of Publishing and Promotion Services, 1983), p. 90. It is disappointing and symptomatic of the separation of Christian ethical reflection from worship, however, that the bishops relegated their all too brief discussion of the Mass to the final "pastoral" section of the document directed specifically to Roman Catholic lay and religious. Would it not have been appropriate for the bishops to have explored the implications of the worshiping life of the Church—which is, after all, the primal activity of the Body of Christ in the world—as a *primary* source of the ethics of war and peace? There are more encouraging signs in the third draft of the Bishops' pastoral letter on the economy. For example, Chapter 5 of that document invokes the liturgical sources of the ethic fairly forcefully. But, as in its predecessor, this discussion is reserved for the close of the letter. An exploration of the virtues and values inhering within and effected by prayer and worship could have added force and depth to the important Chapter 2 of the letter, "The Christian Vision of Economic Life." National Conference of Catholic Bishops, *Economic Justice for All: Catholic Social Teaching and the U.S. Economy* (Washington, D.C.: U.S. Catholic Conference, 1986).

46. Thomas Hopko, *All the Fullness of God* (Crestwood, N.Y.: St. Vladimir's Seminary Press, 1982), p. 172.

47. *Divine Liturgy (Armenian)*, pp. 189–91.

48. See pp. 62–64.

49. *Divine Liturgy (Armenian)*, p. 105.

4. AN ETHIC OF MARRIAGE AND FAMILY

1. In the following discussion the terms *marriage* and *family* are used rather interchangeably. I am aware that from a broader sociological perspec-

tive this is problematic. But I do not wish to speak in such a voice. I also recognize that in recent years a variety of forms of family have been identified and that definitions of family have multiplied. The theologian John L. Boojamra has developed a definition which is consistent with the Orthodox Church's teaching. It reflects the central premise of this essay, which is that within the Orthodox tradition marriage and family have a distinctive ecclesiological character and purpose. Boojamra's definition is not intended as a purely descriptive account of the form(s) marriage and family take in this society or any other. Rather, it states a norm of marriage and family. Family, writes Boojamra, may be defined as "any group of people, related by blood or will, living together in an intentionally permanent relationship, with or without children, whose bond has been sealed by a commitment to maintain community which is at once intimate and nurturing" (John L. Boojamra, "Theological and Pedagogical Perspectives on the Family as Educator," *Greek Orthodox Theological Review* 29 no. 1 [Spring 1984]: 4-5). The last element of this definition is particularly important. The family group is bonded together under a seal of commitment to permanence. This bond of permanent relationship is defined as sacramental marriage between male and female performed by the Church. Thus, marriage is not only characterized by permanence, intimacy, and heterosexuality; it is also a community of persons which is sacred and important to the life and mission of the Church, this being declared through a public liturgical blessing.

2. Robert Bellah, et al., *Habits of the Heart* (Berkeley and Los Angeles: University of California Press, 1985), p. 112.

3. Brigitte Berger and Peter Berger, *The War Over the Family* (Garden City, N.Y.: University of California Press, 1983), and Christopher Lasch, *Haven in a Heartless World* (New York: Basic Books, 1977).

4. Berger and Berger, *Family*, p. 110.

5. Ibid., p. 112.

6. Ibid., p. 172.

7. Ibid., p. 132.

8. Ibid.

9. Such hyperindividualism belongs to Bellah's second definition of individualism as "a belief that the individual has a primary reality, whereas society is a second order, derived or artificial construct." Bellah calls this "ontological individualism" (Bellah, et al., *Habits*, p. 334). Narcissists, as Christopher Lasch has described them, aggressively seek self-gratification as a right owed to them by society. They avoid social commitments, whether of family or political vocation, viewing these as a threat to their personal freedom—leaving them subject to objective demands or responsibilities and the pain of being judged by others on the basis of them. Narcissism is closely related to the "ontological individualism" identified by Bellah. It entails an

"ideology of nonbinding commitments and open-ended relationships—an ideology that registers so faithfully the psychic needs of the late twentieth century—condemns all expectations, standards, and codes of conduct as 'unrealistic' " (Lasch, *Haven*, p. 140).

10. Berger and Berger, *Family*, p. 3.

11. Stanley S. Harakas, *Contemporary Moral Issues* (Minneapolis, Minn.: Light & Life Publishing Co., 1982), pp. 100, 101. Harakas's concern with what might be described as a natural social responsibility of marriage is not one I wish to dismiss out of hand. One might even want to relate such a natural social responsibility to the sacramentality of marriage in a far more explicit fashion than anything I imply in this essay or that Harakas has done. But it has not been my interest here to develop the notion of such a natural social responsibility. I am not inclined to think this is the best strategy to pursue in light of how the tradition itself interprets marriage, nor do I think it is the wisest thing to do given the present distraught state of secular and Christian marriage within this society. Even granting that such a social responsibility exists, it necessarily will be clarified, indeed transformed, through the Christian understanding and practice of marriage as a vocation in Christ in service to the Church. Fr. Harakas has told me that the article cited was originally prepared to serve as a position paper for the greater public to be issued by the Greek Orthodox Archdiocese of North and South America, which explains in part why it is cast as it is.

12. Ibid., p. 100.

13. Ibid., p. 104

14. Bellah, et al., *Habits*, p. 93.

15. John Chrysostom, "Homilies on Ephesians," in *A Select Library of Nicene and Post-Nicene Fathers of the Christian Church*, First Series, vol. 12 (Grand Rapids, Mich.: Wm. B. Eerdmans Publishing Co., 1956), p. 148 (homily 20).

16. Clement of Alexandria, "On Marriage" (*Stromateis* 3), trans. John Ernest Leonard Oulton and Henry Chadwick, in *Alexandrian Christianity, The Library of Christian Classics*, vol. 3 (London: SCM Press, 1954), p. 71 (bk. 3, chap. 10).

17. Perhaps I ought to explain exactly why this biblical passage is invoked here. First, I am not intending to use it as some kind of proof text that marriage is really sacramental. The matter obviously is not quite that simple. My warrant for invoking Ephesians 5:32 is that it appears centrally in the Orthodox rites of matrimony as determined by tradition. Here it takes its place within a narrative setting, the "story" of marriage being told multivocally through a typological hermeneutic. In the Byzantine rite, for example, Ephesians 5:32 is read during the royal procession when the bride and groom are crowned and declared king and queen of a new creation, a new "kingdom,"

a type of the Church. Thus marriage participates in a divine mystery, the fullness of which is revealed in Christ and the Church. The reading of the story of the marriage at Cana (John 2) follows almost immediately thereafter to reinforce this. For according to the Johannine theology the miracle of the wine is the first sign of the in-breaking Kingdom of God. It seems almost obvious from what one finds in the rite that a theological interpretation going on in the rite itself endows these passages with sacramental meaning even beyond any such meaning they might obtain in the Gospel or Pauline contexts.

18. Theodore Mackin, S.J., *What Is Marriage* (Ramsey, N.J.: Paulist Press, 1982), p. 328.

19. Boojamra, "Theological and Pedagogical," p. 7.

20. Basil, *The Long Rules*, in *St. Basil: The Ascetical Works*, trans. M. Monica Wagner, *The Fathers of the Church*, vol. 9 (New York: Fathers of the Church, 1950), p. 248.

21. Paul Evdokimov, "The Theology of Marriage," in *Marriage and Christian Tradition*, trans. Sr. Agnes Cunningham, S.S.C.M. (Techny, Ill.: Divine Word Publications, 1968), p. 89. See also Evdokimov's more exhaustive study, *The Sacrament of Love*, (Crestwood, N.Y.: St. Vladimir's Seminary Press, 1985).

22. John Chrysostom, "Homilies on Ephesians," p. 143 (homily 20).

23. Basil, *On the Hexaemeron*, in *Saint Basil: Exegetic Homilies*, trans. Sr. Agnes Way, C.D.P., *The Fathers of the Church*, vol. 46 (Washington, D.C.: Catholic University Press of America, 1963), p. 114 (homily 7).

24. John Chrysostom sums all this up in the following: "They come to be made into one body. See the mystery of love! If the two do not become one, they cannot increase; they can increase only by decreasing! How great is the strength of unity! God's ingenuity in the beginning divided one flesh into two; but He wanted to show that it remained one even after its division, so He made it impossible for either half to procreate without the other. Now do you see how great a mystery marriage is? From one man, Adam, he made Eve; then He reunited these two into one, so that their children would be produced from a single source. Likewise, husband and wife are not two, but one; if he is the head and she is the body, how can they be two? She was made from his side; so they are two halves of one organism." (John Chrysostom, *St. John Chrysostom on Marriage and Family Life*, trans. Catherine P. Roth and David Anderson [Crestwood, N.Y.: St. Vladimir's Seminary Press, 1986], p. 75 [homily 12 on Colossians 4:18]. Also available as "Homilies on Colossians," in *A Select Library of Nicene and Post-Nicene Fathers of the Christian Church*, First Series, Vol. 12 [Grand Rapids, Mich.: Wm. B. Eerdmans Publishing Co., 1956], p. 318 [homily 20].)

25. Christos Yannaras, *The Freedom of Morality*, trans. Elizabeth Briere (Crestwood, N.Y.: St. Vladimir's Seminary Press, 1984), p. 162.

26. Evdokimov, "Theology of Marriage," pp. 71–72.

27. Ibid., p. 74.

28. Basil, *Long Rules*, p. 248.

29. *The Blessing of Marriage or The Canon of the Rite of Holy Matrimony according to the Usage of the Armenian Apostolic Orthodox Church* (New York: Armenian Church Publications, 1953), p. 54.

30. *Rite of Holy Matrimony (Armenian)*, p. 55.

31. Quoted by Kenneth Stevenson, *Nuptial Blessing* (New York: Oxford University Press, 1983), pp. 111–12.

32. Donna Schaper, "Marriage: The Impossible Commitment," in *Moral Issues and Christian Response*, ed. Paul T. Jersild and Dale A. Johnson (New York: Holt, Rinehart & Winston, 1983), p. 103.

33. Ibid.

34. Isabel Florence Hapgood, ed. and trans., *Service Book of the Holy Orthodox-Catholic Apostolic Church* (Englewood, N.J.: Antiochian Orthodox Christian Archdiocese, 1975), p. 297.

35. Stevenson, *Nuptial*, p. 112.

36. *Rite of Holy Matrimony (Armenian)*, p. 56.

37. There is no uniform code or set of rules among the Orthodox churches governing divorce. But generally several criteria for judging a marriage to be dissolved have evolved. These include the following: adultery, apostasy, desertion or absence for more than five years, certain serious physical illnesses (which, for example, might prevent physical union and consummation of the marriage), incurable psychological illnesses, extreme cruelty, or abuse (these are measures of incompatibility). All of these, as I indicate further on in this section, are considered instances in which, as Paul Evdokimov has said, there is a "death of the very matter of the sacrament (love)" or in which the ends of marriage are utterly frustrated. See Evdokimov, *Sacrament of Love*, p. 184.

38. William J. Everett, *Blessed Be the Bond* (Philadelphia: Fortress Press, 1985), p. 19.

39. See page 87.

40. Theodore Stylianopoulos, "Toward a Theology of Marriage in the Orthodox Church." *Greek Orthodox Theological Review*, 22, no. 1 (Fall 1977): 270.

41. Hapgood, *Service Book,* p. 296.

42. Stylianopoulos, "Theology of Marriage," p. 270.

43. See John Meyendorff, *Marriage: An Orthodox Perspective* (Crestwood, N.Y.: St. Vladimir's Seminary Press, 1984), esp. pp. 44–47, 54–58, for discussions of remarriage and divorce respectively; also Demetrios J. Constantelos, *Marriage, Sexuality and Celibacy: A Greek Orthodox Perspective* (Minneapolis, Minn.: Life & Light Publishing Co., 1975); Evdokimov,

Sacrament of Love, esp. chap. 6; Lewis J. Patvos, "The Orthodox Position on Divorce," *Diakonia* 5, no. 11 (1970); 4–15; and Elia Melia, "Divorce in the Orthodox Church," *Diakonia* 10, no. 3 (1975): 280–82.

44. Leonard Boff, "The Sacrament of Marriage," in *The Future of Marriage*, ed. William Bassett and Peter Huizing, *Concilium*, New Series, vol. 8, no. 7 (New York: Herder & Herder, 1973), p. 32.

45. *Rite of Holy Matrimony (Armenian)*, p. 63.

46. For an insightful reading of the Byzantine rites of matrimony and second marriage from which I have drawn in these remarks, see Paul Ramsey, "Liturgy and Ethics," *Journal of Religious Ethics*, 7, no. 2 (Fall 1979), esp. pp. 153–60.

47. Hapgood, *Service Book*, pp. 292–93.

48. Hapgood, *Service Book*, p. 304.

49. Ibid.

50. Ibid., p. 305.

51. See page 92.

52. Hapgood, *Service Book*, p. 296.

53. Ibid., p. 305.

54. Ramsey, "Liturgy and Ethics," p. 155.

55. I have not found articulated either within the canons governing divorce and remarriage or among Orthodox interpreters explicit theological warrants or exhaustively worked out explanations for why the Church thinks the way it does about remarriage and why a penitential character is appropriate for the Order of Second Marriage, even in cases where the death of a spouse and not divorce is the background of such a marriage. Much, however, is implied. And we are not without guidance. I will venture two theological reasons for the penitential character of the rite. They are speculative and I, not the tradition, take final responsibility for them. First, the vows of fidelity and chastity through which persons enter into marriage are not of a kind simply erased by the death of a spouse. They continue to have a spiritual claim upon a person even after the loss of the partner. Left single by death, the surviving spouse remains united by an undying love with the deceased partner in God. For such a person, remaining single is the most consistent way of continuing to conform to the character of life (the very character of God who has revealed himself in his steadfast love for his creatures in life and death) to which he was called by Christ through marriage. In singleness such a person continues to honor the covenant of everlasting love to which each married person has committed himself in imitation of God's covenant with Israel. This logic helps account for harsh statements by several church fathers, synods, and canons about remarriage and even their analogy of such marriages to bigamy. This also helps explain the removal from the Order of Second Marriage of prayers and vows of fidelity and chastity.

The second reason is connected with the first. A rite of remarriage is an appropriate moment in a person's life and in the life of the whole community to do penance even when the marriage follows upon the death, not divorce, of a spouse, precisely because the remarriage is a reminder of that death and of the state of sin and death in which we all have been placed since Adam's transgression (Rom. 5:12). The penitential character of the rite makes good sense given the nature and meaning of marriage itself as described above. It makes added sense if we do not restrict ourselves to individualistic and voluntaristic notions of sin but think in terms of corporate sin which is not necessarily voluntary and attaches to all of us.

56. I do not want to leave the impression that the tradition is settled on this matter. In contrast to the Roman Catholic Church, within Orthodoxy a certain ambivalence pertaining to it was allowed to stand. This ambivalence is present even within the writings of singular authors such as Clement of Alexandria, who is cited in the text which follows. Here I quote at length Paul Evdokimov's way of describing the issue. My own interpretation as developed in the following pages is strongly sympathetic with that of Evdokimov. See *Sacrament of Love*, pp. 65–66:

> There is no reason, except a pedagogic one . . . , to call one path or the other the preeminent Christianity, since what is valid for all of Christendom is thereby valid for each of the two states. The East has never made the distinction between the "precepts" and the "evangelical counsels." The Gospel in its totality is addressed to each person; everyone in his own situation is called to the *absolute* of the Gospel. Trying to prove the superiority of one state over the other is therefore useless: it is an abstract, because impersonal, process. The renunciation at work in both cases is as good as the positive content that the human being brings to it: the intensity of the love of God.
>
> St. Paul's pastoral sense seeks the fulfillment of an undivided service. The nuptial community, which is the "domestic church," and the monastic community shed light upon each other and help one another in this same service. Church doctrine has never lost sight of this balance. Councils and synods have defended it against the assaults of Manichaeism and extreme spirituality.

Evdokimov mentions some interesting examples of how in practice within the *ordo* and tradition marriage and celibacy actually do "shed light upon each other and help one another in . . . [the] same service." (Ibid., p. 66.)

> In marriage the nature of man is changed sacramentally, as it is, though in another mode, in the one who becomes a monk. The deepest

inner relationship unites the two. The promises exchanged by the betrothed introduce them in a certain manner into a special monasticism, because here too there is a dying to the past and a rebirth into a new life. Moreover, the rite of entrance into the monastic order makes use of nuptial symbolism (the terms "betrothed" and "spouse"), while the ancient marriage rite included the monastic tonsure, signifying the common surrender of the two wills to God. Thus marriage includes within itself the monastic state, and that is why the latter is not a sacrament. The two converge as complementary aspects of the same virginal reality of the human spirit. The ancient Russian tradition viewed the time of engagement as a monastic novitiate. After the marriage ceremony, a retreat in a monastery was prescribed for the newly married to prepare for entrance into their "nuptial priesthood." (Ibid., p. 68).

57. Dmitri Dudko, *Our Hope* (Crestwood, N.Y.: St. Vladimir's Seminary Press, 1975), p. 57.

58. Clement of Alexandria, "On Spiritual Perfection" (*Stromateis* 7), trans. John Ernest Leonard Oulton and Henry Chadwick, in *Alexandrian Christianity*, *The Library of Christian Classics*, vol. 3 (London: SCM Press, 1954) p. 138.

59. John Chrysostom, "Homilies on the Hebrews, in *A Select Library of the Nicene and Post-Nicene Fathers of the Christian Church* (New York: Christian Literature Co., 1890), p. 402 (homily 7).

60. Hapgood, *Service Book*, p. 294.

61. *Rite of Holy Matrimony (Armenian)*, p. 56.

62. William Faulkner, *Go Down Moses* (New York: Vintage Books, 1970), p. 257.

63. Ibid., p. 311.

64. Ibid., pp. 312, 314.

65. Ibid., p. 295.

66. Ibid., p. 313.

67. Ibid., pp. 314–15.

68. Ibid., p. 352.

69. Ibid., pp. 353–54.

70. Hapgood, *Service Book*, p. 300.

71. Evdokimov, "Theology of Marriage," p. 101.

72. Ibid., p. 98.

73. Everett, *Blessed Bond*, p. 111.

74. John Updike, *Couples* (New York: Alfred A. Knopf, 1968), p. 7.

75. Ibid., p. 457.

76. Yannaras, *Morality*, p. 170.

77. Ibid.

78. Bellah, et al., *Habits*, p. 109.

79. Alexander Schmemann, *For the Life of the World* (Crestwood, N.Y.: St. Vladimir's Seminary Press, 1973), p. 90.

80. Robert A. Nisbet, *The Quest for Community* (New York: Oxford University Press, 1969), p. 60.

81. Schaper, "Marriage," p. 104.

82. Herbert Anderson, "The Family Under Stress: A Crisis of Purpose," in *Moral Issues and Christian Response*, ed. Paul T. Jersild and Dale A. Johnson (New York: Holt, Rinehart & Winston, 1983), p. 124.

83. Hapgood, *Service Book*, p. 301.

5. THE PROBLEM OF A SOCIAL ETHIC

1. John Meyendorff, *Living Tradition* (Crestwood, N.Y.: St. Vladimir's Seminary Press, 1978), p. 143.

2. I employ the rubric *diaspora* with hesitancy. Several Orthodox theologians have cautioned against its use. Thomas Hopko argues that it is "a notoriously unchristian term which betrays in its very utterance how far we are in practice from what, by God's grace, we still somehow retain in theory." *All the Fullness of God* (Crestwood, N.Y.: St. Vladimir's Seminary Press, 1982), p. 186. Hopko surely is calling to mind the evangelical commission bestowed upon the Church by Christ to "go therefore and make disciples of all nations, baptizing them in the name of the Father and of the Son and of the Holy Spirit, teaching them to observe all that I have commanded you; and lo, I am with you always, to the close of the age" (Matt. 28:19–20 RSV). Indeed, the only acceptable theological use of the term *diaspora* would be to have it mean the very missionary and eschatological character of the Church as temporal pilgrimage and proleptic sign of the promised Kingdom of God. But this clearly is not how the term has been used most often by Orthodox. Rather, as John Meyendorff has pointed out, *diaspora* has been employed to set up a deceiving contrast between a so-called normative Orthodox existence in "Orthodox countries" and an entirely abnormal and peripheral existence of the Church in "foreign" places. This, Meyendorff argues, is an ahistorical and unrealistic description of Orthodoxy in the contemporary world, since there are no longer any "Orthodox Christian societies in the traditional and accepted sense of the word." *Catholicity and the Church* (Crestwood, N.Y.: St. Vladimir's Seminary Press, 1983), p. 104. I am in complete agreement with such admonitions. Yet *diaspora* retains a valid sociological use. It identifies the recent, often forced, dispersion of historic Orthodox communities from indigenous lands. For by and large Orthodoxy did not come to America as Christian mission, but in the form of immigrant communities

of various national and ethnic identities. And in varying degrees those communities, even as they identify themselves as religious and church, continue to think of themselves as dispersed out of a homeland. This indeed has severely inhibited the development of a sense of Christian mission among Orthodox in America. I take Hopko's and Meyendorff's warnings against an uncritical use of *diaspora* in theological contexts as directed toward a correction of that unfortunate unbiblical state of mind. But employed sociologically the term takes realistic account of the fact that Orthodox Christians in America continue to think of themselves and behave as displaced or even exiled ethnic religious communities. *Diaspora* may then describe a transitional phase of acculturation and ecclesiological adjustment through which much of Orthodoxy in North America is still passing.

3. Kark Rahner, *Theological Investigations*, vol. 12, *Confrontations*, trans. David Bourke (New York: Seabury Press, 1974), pp. 204–205.

4. John Howard Yoder, *The Priestly Kingdom* (Notre Dame, Ind.: University of Notre Dame Press, 1984), p. 158.

5. James T. Johnson, "On Keeping Faith: The Uses of History for Religious Ethics," *Journal of Religious Ethics* 7 (Spring 1979): 115.

6. Alexander Schmemann, *Church, World, Mission* (Crestwood, N.Y.: St. Vladimir's Seminary Press, 1979), p. 69.

7. John Meyendorff, *Byzantine Theology* (New York: Fordham University Press, 1976), p. 213.

8. Ibid., pp. 213–24.

9. Schmemann, *Church*, p. 34.

10. Alexander Schmemann, *The Historical Road of Eastern Orthodoxy* (Crestwood, N.Y.: St. Vladimir's Seminary Pres, 1972), p. 152.

11. See, for example, John L. Boojamra, "Constantine and Justinian," in *Orthodox Synthesis*, ed. Joseph J. Allen (Crestwood, N.Y.: St. Vladimir's Seminary Press, 1981), pp. 189–209.

12. Schmemann, *Church*, p. 28.

13. Meyendorff, *Living Tradition*, p. 143.

14. Georges Florovsky, *The Collected Works of Georges Florovsky*, vol. 2, *Christianity and Culture* (Belmont, Mass.: Nordland Publishing Co., 1974), pp. 82–83.

15. Ibid., p. 83.

16. Schmemann, *Church*, p. 8.

17. Francis Canavan has written a series of probing articles in which he presents a fairly devastating critique of the present state of American pluralism. The term "confidence game" is his. Francis Canavan, "The Dilemma of Liberal Pluralism," *The Human Life Review* 5, no. 3 (Summer 1979), esp. pp. 7–9; "Simple-Minded Separationism," *Human Life Review* 3, no. 4 (Fall 1977): 36–46; "Our Pluralistic Society," *Communio* 9, no. 4 (Winter 1982):

355–67. See also Stanley Hauerwas, *A Community of Character* (Notre Dame: University of Notre Dame Press, 1981), pp. 215–19.

18. George Lindbeck, "Ecumenism and the Future of Belief," *Una Sancta* 25, no. 3 (1968): 10–11.

19. Ibid., p. 12.

20. See particularly Reinhold Niebuhr, *The Children of Light and the Children of Darkness* (New York: Charles Scribner's Sons, 1944); and John Courtney Murray, *We Hold These Truths* (New York: Sheed & Ward, 1960).

21. See Richard John Neuhaus, *Time Toward Home: The American Experiment as Revelation* (New York: Seabury Press, 1975), and *The Naked Public Square: Religion and Democracy in America* (Grand Rapids, Mich.: Wm. B. Eerdmans Publishing Co., 1984); and Martin Marty, *The Public Church* (New York: Crossroad Press, 1981).

22. See Demetrios Contantelos, *Byzantine Philanthropy and Social Welfare*, pts. 1 and 2, Rutgers Byzantine Series 4 (New Brunswick, N.J.: Rutgers University Press, 1968).

23. Schmemann, *Church*, pp. 163, 164.

24. "Consultation on 'The Church's Struggle for Justice,' " in *The Orthodox Church in the Ecumenical Movement*, ed. Constantine G. Patelos (Geneva: World Council of Churches, 1978), p. 119. Much of what I have to say in this section is inspired by this document.

25. Schmemann, *Church*, p. 165.

26. Hauerwas, *Community*, p. 109.

27. Vladimir Lossky, *In the Image and Likeness of God* (Crestwood, N.Y.: St. Vladimir's Seminary Press, 1974), p. 214.

28. Yoder, *Priestly Kingdom*, pp. 158–59.

29. National Conference of Catholic Bishops, *The Challenge of Peace: God's Promise and Our Response* (Washington, D.C.: U.S. Catholic Conference, Official Publishing and Promotion Services, 1983).

30. Edmund Burke, The Works of the Right Honorable Edmund Burke, vol. 3, *Reflections on the Revolution in France* (Boston: Little, Brown & Co., 1899), p. 438.

31. "Consultation on 'The Church's Struggle,' " p. 123.

32. Nikos Nissiotis, "The Witness and the Service of Eastern Orthodoxy to the One Undivided Church," in *The Orthodox in the Ecumenical Movement*, ed. Constantine G. Patelos (Geneva: World Council of Churches, 1978), p. 233.

33. Ibid., p. 232.

34. Ibid., p. 233.

35. Ibid., p. 232.

36. Ibid., p. 233.

6. ORTHODOXY AND THE AMERICAN ORDER

1. See Martin Marty, *The Public Church* (New York: Crossroad Publishing Co., 1981), and Richard John Neuhaus, *The Naked Public Square: Religion and Democracy in America* (Grand Rapids, Mich.: Wm. B. Eerdmans Publishing Co., 1984).

2. Neuhaus, *Public Square*, p. 263. Neuhaus at least mentions Orthodoxy. In the vast majority of books and articles written on this and related subjects Orthodoxy simply receives no attention.

3. Stanley S. Harakas, "Orthodox Church-State Theory and American Democracy," *Greek Orthodox Theological Review* 21 (1976): 399–421, and "The Church and the Secular World," *Greek Orthodox Theological Review* 17 (1972): 167–99. Alexander F. C. Webster has written a highly instructive review and analysis of contemporary Orthodox social ethics which includes an evaluation of Harakas's work. "Antinomical Typologies for an Orthodox Christian Social Ethic for the World, State, and Nation," *Greek Orthodox Theological Review* 29, no. 1 (Spring 1984): 221–54.

4. Harakas, "Orthodox Church-State," pp. 400–1.

5. Ibid., pp. 406–7.

6. Ibid., p. 407.

7. Ibid., pp. 413–14.

8. Ibid., p. 418.

9. Ibid., p. 421.

10. Ibid., p. 414.

11. Ibid.

12. See Alexander Schmemann, *The Historical Road of Orthodoxy* (Crestwood, N.Y.: St. Vladimir's Seminary Press, 1977), pp. 66–70, 151–53.

13. H. Richard Niebuhr, *The Kingdom of God in America* (New York: Harper & Row, Publishers, 1937), p. 194.

14. Robert T. Handy, *A Christian America: Protestant Hopes and Historical Realities* (New York: Oxford University Press, 1971), pp. 110–11.

15. This was precisely the sort of reasoning used by the Supreme Court in two separate recent decisions. In *Grand Rapids School District* v. *Ball* (1985) and *Aguilar* v. *Felton* (1985) the Court struck down long-standing cooperative educational programs in which public employees and/or tax monies were utilized to assist parochial and private schools in remedial and enhancement programs for disadvantaged children. See *Supreme Court Reporter*, vol. 105, no. 18 (July 15, 1985).

16. Will Herberg, *Protestant — Catholic — Jew* (Garden City, N.Y.: Anchor Books, Doubleday and Co., 1960), p. 270.

17. Harvey Cox, *Religion in the Secular City* (New York: Simon & Schuster, 1984), esp. pp. 11–26.

18. For an interesting critique of both Neuhaus and Cox on this score from which I have drawn some instruction, see George Hunsinger, "Barth, Barmen and the Confessing Church Today," *Katallegette* (Summer 1985): 14–27.

19. Alexander Schmemann, *Church, World, Mission* (Crestwood, N.Y.: St. Vladimir's Seminary Press, 1979), p. 84.

20. John Courtney Murray, *We Hold These Truths* (New York: Sheed & Ward 1960), esp. chap. 2.

21. Ibid., p. 66.

22. Ibid., p. 214.

23. Aside from how one judges finally the positive or negative attributes of the "old" American order, Murray's proposition, while obtaining some plausibility twenty-five years ago, looks increasingly impossible today. My own experience of teaching *We Hold These Truths* in the classroom of the 1980s, even at a Roman Catholic institution, is that the students generally do not think the American order Murray describes, one yet rooted in republican virtues and biblical truths, is their world. Students point to Murray's own chastened expectations that America would make the necessary adjustments mid-century and steer back on the sure path of a civic consensus consciously informed by natural law and biblical truths. In his chastened prognosis students detect rightly that Murray also entertained the possibility that America might take a decidedly secularist and utilitarian course. Murray escapes student criticism with only the judgment that some of his worst expectations are coming true. Neuhaus, however, writing in 1985, is guilty of serious cultural miscalculation.

24. Franklin Littell, "The Basis of Religious Liberty in Christian Belief," *Journal of Church and State* 6, no. 2 (Spring 1964): 137–38.

25. The discussion which begins here on the relation between church and world follows closely George Khodre, "The Church and the World," *St. Vladimir's Theological Quarterly* 13 nos. 1-2 (1969), esp. pp. 36–42.

26. Irenaeus *Adv. Haeres.* 4. 18. 5, quoted by Khodre, "Church and World," p. 40.

27. John Howard Yoder, *The Priestly Kingdom* (Notre Dame, Ind.: Unversity of Notre Dame Press, 1984), p. 174.

28. See David Little, "The Origins of Perplexity: Civil Religion and Moral Belief in the Thought of Thomas Jefferson," in *American Civil Religion*, ed. Russell E. Richey and Donald G. Jones (New York: Harper & Row, 1974), pp. 185–210.

29. Yoder, *Priestly Kingdom*, p. 174.

30. Herberg, *Protestant*, p. 85.

31. H. Richard Niebuhr, *The Social Sources of Denominationalism* (Cleveland, Oh.: Meridian Books, World Publishing Co., 1957), p. 21.

32. Ibid., pp. 281–84.

33. Stanley Hauerwas, *A Community of Character* (Notre Dame, Ind.: University of Notre Dame Press, 1981), p. 110.

7. THE AMERICANIZATION OF ORTHODOXY

1. Alexander Schmemann, *Church, World, Mission* (Crestwood, N.Y.: St. Vladimir's Seminary Press, 1979), p. 8.

2. The *millet* system was established at the beginning of the Ottoman Empire as a means of organizing and separating subject peoples as semi-autonomous religious entities. Each *millet* was headed by the patriarch or religious hierarchy. In the case of Ottoman Armenians, the Armenian Patriarch of Constantinople was made responsible for the good behavior of the *millet* and was granted substantial control over the religious, cultural, and educational life of Armenians in the empire.

3. The effects of this new immigration have not been tranquil or entirely positive. The new immigration has disturbed the evolution of the Armenian Church in America from an immigrant to an "American" church. This is reflected in a divisive, sometimes acrimonious, struggle between the descendants of the old (Turkish) immigration and members of the new (Arabic and Iranian) immigration over the direction the Armenian Church will take for the next generation. Such a phenomenon is not new in the history of American religion and immigration. The most noteworthy example is the history of Jewish immigration (e.g., conflicts between German and Russian Jewish immigrants). But many Orthodox national churches have experienced similar inner-ethnic conflicts.

4. John Meyendorff, *Living Tradition* (Crestwood, N.Y.: St. Vladimir's Seminary Press, 1978), p. 87.

5. These observations regarding Herberg's thesis and his assessment of the status of Orthodoxy in America are based on conversations with him at Drew University during the early and mid-1970s.

6. Will Herberg, *Protestant—Catholic—Jew* (Garden City, N.Y.: Anchor Books, Doubleday & Co., 1960), p. 268.

7. Schmemann, "Problems of Orthodoxy in America 3, The Spiritual Problem," *St. Vladimir's Seminary Quarterly Review* 9, no. 4 (1965): 171–93.

8. Ibid., p. 180.

Index